Christ the King

Christ the King

The Messiah in the Jewish Festivals

SHIRLEY LUCASS

Foreword by Bethany Finch

RESOURCE *Publications* · Eugene, Oregon

CHRIST THE KING
The Messiah in the Jewish Festivals

Resource Publications
An Imprint of Wipf and Stock Publishers
199 W. 8th Ave., Suite 3
Eugene, OR 97401

www.wipfandstock.com

PAPERBACK ISBN: 978-1-5326-3226-6
HARDCOVER ISBN: 978-1-5326-3228-0
EBOOK ISBN: 978-1-5326-3227-3

Manufactured in the U.S.A.   02/18/19

To Neill

Our Champion
Without you we may never have known the King
Look after the horses till we get there

THE BIBLE IS A story of new beginnings, of new creation, of new songs. It begins with creation and ends with new creation, which is itself a new beginning and there are other new beginnings, new creations on the way and throughout them all, God is reigning and the people are singing a new song. It begins with a song and ends with a new song. It begins with a temple and ends with a temple. It begins with the sea being overcome and ends with the sea overcome for good. God rests at the beginning and at the new beginning God rests with us once again. We lost our intimacy with God when we listened to the wrong voice and the wrong song, when we rebelled and he had to "cover" our sin. His desire is that we co-labor with him in our journey back to Eden, to our new relationship with him, as new creations, covered, not with the skins of sacrificed animals but with the blood of his own sacrifice. So we don't get lost on the way, he gives us signs "I make known the end from the beginning, from ancient times, what is still to come," so that if we know the beginning, we will know the end when we see it. And each time we've strayed off the path, he's given us a new beginning, framed in such a way that we recognize the new in the old. And for the journey he has given us a song. He is the song. "Let those who have ears hear."

The lord is my strength and my song
he has become my salvation

Contents

FOREWORD

IT'S GOOD TO LIKE a book, but it's even better to be a friend of a great author. Thankfully I'm honored enough to have been raised by this author and to see the joy (and of course sometimes the frustrations) that came with her studying theology. While you read this book and get pulled into her eureka moments—I like to call them revelation moments, you won't get to see the joy as I did when mum either literally danced or you could see the fire in her eyes through tears as she discovered a hidden truth.

What made her so joyful in these moments? Firstly she got to know a whole new aspect of her creator God. Also, she got to share some of those moments and teach me the goodness and depths of the Father's heart. Now I don't want to speak on behalf of an entire generation, but I think younger Christians, like me, can admit we might have abandoned theology a little. We grew a passion and focus for living out our faith, and rightly so. However, this has meant that we deemed practice and encounter, at times, more important than true study of the word. If I'm honest, this was our reaction to seeing a generation before us, who we felt had their priorities the other way round. Therefore, we focused on encounter and neglected the word. It's good to know the author but if you truly love them, you want to read their book. By reading the Book you get to know The Great Author too. We encounter the Word through his words. Studying God's word and reading books like this, actually help us to encounter the Author in a new way.

That's exactly what this book does. Shirley draws us into the mysteries of God but adds a whole new depth for our generation to grasp in a way we can digest. This book will truly help us understand hidden depths of the Jesus we love. She draws us into those revelation moments by unpacking years of studying into digestible sections for us, the generation that expects instant answers. She managed to get someone like me, someone who gets frustrated by study, a Martha always struggling with her inner Mary, to sit at his feet and listen and in so doing to grasp enough of these revelations to want to go deeper and study more.

So I'm beyond thankful for this incredible author but even more for the Greatest Author who she is about to introduce to us all in a new way.

Bethany Finch
Kingdom Church Runcorn

PREFACE

HAVE YOU EVER WATCHED Season 2 of a series without first watching Season 1? You have that nagging suspicion that you are missing something, that there is part of the plot that you don't understand. Something happens, or a character acts in a certain way and it's not properly explained in the episode that you are currently watching. You feel that there is a piece of the story missing. I am in that position now, but the series is so good that I don't want to stop watching; I just wish I could access Season 1. There are numerous flashbacks to earlier parts of the characters' lives, which begin to fill in some of the gaps, but there is still so much missing. I have a sneaking suspicion though, that even if I could watch the first season, I would not have the patience, simply because I already know how some of the story pans out.

This is the type of scenario that I feel a great many people experience with the story of Jesus. We all know Season 2[1] very well since we have probably "watched" it countless times, but there are still parts that we don't understand because we haven't watched Season 1.[2] Numerous flashbacks[3] tells us something about the plot and how it is unfolding and something about the characters too, but unless we have watched Season 1 we are not going to get to grips with it properly. If, however, we *were* familiar with Season 1, then we would know that its conclusion left us with a real cliffhanger. In the final episode of the book of Malachi we are

1. The New Testament.

2. The Old Testament (I know it's obvious - but just in case . . .)

3. Sometimes these are obvious and begin with "This was in order to fulfill the prophecy . . . ," other times they might just be a line out of a Psalm or a prophecy or even Deuteronomy (!) with a footnote reference —if you happen to have a translation that does that. Often though, these are just allusions that if you're not familiar with the Old Testament (Season 1) you won't pick up on, such as the "*Ecce Homo*" of Pilate ("Behold the Man") John 19:5 that we'll look at in chapter 3.

told that the main character actually intends to show up in town.[4] There will be a little warning, but when he does arrive he will shake things up to such an extent that nothing will ever be the same again.[5] However, because we have missed Season 1, some of the impact is lost in episode one of the second season. When the Gospel of Matthew opens with what appears to be the credits, immediately we are confused. What has this to do with anything? Who is David, who is Abraham and what on earth is a messiah? It is only later in the episode that we begin to detect that it might actually be the denouement of the cliffhanger —that this might *be* the LORD coming to his Temple.[6]

Throughout this first episode,[7] perhaps more than any of the others, we are given lots of flashbacks trying to explain how the plot is unfolding, just as it was promised in Season 1. It is only in episode four,[8] however, that this becomes clear. Here, rather than relying on the characters to clarify the situation, a narrator is employed to endorse the fact that the main character has, as we expected, arrived in town:

In the beginning was the Word and the Word was with God, and the Word was God. He was with God in the beginning. Through him all things were made . . . The Word became flesh and made his dwelling among us.[9]

The first four episodes,[10] of course, are really just the same story, seen from the perspective of four different characters and therefore, although the plot remains the same, we see it and its main character from a different angle. The opening of Matthew's Gospel, which contains the genealogy of its main character, is hugely important, since it's the endorsement of his credentials. When we watch the rest of the story, therefore,

4. "I will send my messenger, who will prepare the way before me. Then suddenly the Lord you are seeking will come to his temple; the messenger of the covenant whom you desire, will come,' says the LORD Almighty." Mal 3:1.

5. "See, I will send the prophet Elijah to you before that great and dreadful day of the LORD comes." Mal4:5.

6. John the Baptist is acknowledged as the Messenger preparing the way of the Lord prophesied in Mal3:1 and specifically identified with Elijah, who Malachi (Mal4:5) said it would be. This also, therefore, by implication ratifies Jesus as the LORD, that is Yahweh.

7. Matthew's gospel has more direct quotations from, and allusions to, the Old Testament than any of the other Gospels.

8. John's gospel.

9. John1:1–2, 14a.

10. That is the Gospels.

we are left in no doubt that he is who he claims to be —that this is the main character come to town as we were promised. The Director makes it clear, because we need to know, who this Joseph guy is, that his lineage can be traced back to that of King David and indeed, even further back to Abraham. In fact, in anther episode[11] we find that the link goes as far back as Adam. Why is this important? Because, as we progress through the series we discover that the main character, claims to be the Messiah and for this claim to be true, then he must first be a King; not by declaration,[12] but by descent. At the execution, Pilate had a sign attached to the cross with the words "King of the Jews" written in the three languages that were in use at the time. When Pilate is asked to change the wording to read "This man *claims* to be the King of the Jews" he refused point blank. This is an important scene. If the main character *wasn't* found to be King of the Jews, then the whole plot would have collapsed. Why Pilate refused we're not told, but we do know that he spent time alone questioning Jesus and seemed really reluctant to have him crucified.

Once all four of the first episodes of Season 2 have been watched, you might be of the opinion that the story climaxed too soon. The main character dies and most of his friends don't seem to have understood the "back-story" either,[13] that is, why he, as the main character had to bow out so early, but as episode two states in its opening scene, it is "The *beginning* of the good news about Jesus the Messiah."[14] It's only after episode four that the story really begins to unfold. The good news is that we are not just spectators but are able to play an actual part in one of the episodes. What we don't know yet is, how it will all end. However, what we do have is a trailer for Season 3 entitled "Revelation," that is, when the Director is ready, the concluding season will be shown. Some people are under the impression that this final season is a record of what happened in the decades following the main character's resurrection and it was certainly written during that time and the characters that it mentions were present in Season 2. However, later scenes are apocalyptic, which literally means "veiled." The director is holding back on full disclosure. He does,

11. Luke 3:23–38.

12. Like a Jedi, declared by the Council.

13. Luke 24:17–27. Ironically in v.17 the disciples ask Jesus (without recognizing who he was at the time) if *he* didn't know what had happened in the last few days in Jerusalem, because although they knew the facts, they themselves hadn't understood the significance of it.

14. Mark 1:1.

however, give us an idea and a decent outline of the plot—the bad guy is defeated, the good guys win and ride off[15] into the sunset or in this case, into the city of golden streets and jeweled gates with living water and no more pain or death. It is the ultimate love story, although there is plenty of action along the way. The story opens with the main character and his friends living together in harmony and then the bad guy shows up. There is a fall (out) and lots of twists and turns and then, as we always hope, they get back together again; there's a bride and her groom and the closing scenes are of a wedding feast.

This is intended to be a kind of companion to the series, attempting to fill in the gaps, to provide clarity on the previous story, to explain some of the main character's titles. Since there's so much to cover it concentrates on just three of the sub-plots[16] which, once we become familiar with them, help us to understand the main character even more, so that when an allusion is made in Season 2 or in the musical[17] it becomes all the more understandable, and all the more enjoyable. It might be too, that once we understand the story and the other characters we will feel more equipped to play our part, whether that is in a starring role or simply as an extra.

---

15. "I saw heaven standing open and there before me was a white horse whose rider is called Faithful and True. . .the armies of heaven were following him, riding on white horses and dressed in fine linen, white and clean." Rev 19:11,14.

16. That is three of the major festivals, *Sukkoth, Yom Kippur* and *Pesach,* Feast of Tabernacles, Day of Atonement and Passover.

17. That is in church or whenever or wherever we worship.

ACKNOWLEDGEMENTS

I AM GRATEFUL TO all those who have contributed in some way to this work, in particular my two daughters, Beth and Heather whom I love with all my heart.

Thanks also to all my great friends, who have encouraged me, put up with my absence and made me coffee.Thanks in particular to Virginia who was the first person I entrusted it with and who attempted to make sense of my algebraic sentences. Thanks also to Ray who has been a great sounding board and inspiration and whose eyes actually light up rather than glaze over at the mention of theology (although he has since moved abroad!) Thanks also to Matthew Wimer who has been very patient and finally to Oscar who has been my constant companion through it all.

LIST OF ABBREVIATIONS

Mishnah:

Mishnah, tractate Aboth	m.Aboth
Mishnah, tractate Pesahim	m.Pesahim
Mishnah, tractate Sanhedrin	m.Sanhedrin
Mishnah, tractate Sotah	m.Sotah
Mishnah, tractate Sukkah	m.Sukkah
Mishnah, tractate Ta'anith	m.Ta'anith

Midrashim:

Bemidbar Rabbah	Bemid.Rab
Ecclesiastes Rabbah	Eccles. Rab.
Genesis Rabbah	Gen.Rab.

Josephus:

War	Jos. War
Antiquities	Jos. Ant.

Dead Sea Scrolls:

11Q Melchizedek Scroll	11QMelch

Introduction

I was meant to go to the Notre Dame chapel, even though I wasn't catholic, for the pre-graduation service to pick up a prize I had won. However, I wanted to attend the Anglican service, it wasn't a denominational thing, just that my friend I had studied with was doing one of the readings. It was during this service that the Dean of the Cathedral, who was delivering the sermon, suddenly stopped and said "I hadn't intended saying this, but I really feel the Lord wants to say to you, who are graduating today, that he wants you to "sing a new song." It was one of those moments when you knew something special had been said—that it was the Holy Spirit speaking.

The following autumn, for the first time since enrolling on the Masters Course in Jewish Studies, I walked into the huge library at Manchester University, onto the Religious Studies section and was overwhelmed by the number of books. I remember thinking, 'How on earth would anyone ever know that they had chosen the right books to study?" I wandered along rows of shelves, packed with whole volumes written in Hebrew, which I was never fully to master, and my attention was caught by a book on one of the top shelves entitled "Sermons from the Synagogue." I was intrigued, because in my ignorance, I thought sermons were only inflicted on Christian congregations. Being vertically challenged, I used the kick stool to reach it. I opened it at random and the first words I read were "The Lord wants you to sing a new song." The first words in the first book, the first time I had entered that library answered two questions—firstly I now knew how I would know which books to study—the Holy Spirit would guide me and secondly I now knew that this was the right place. Following, three months of torturous debate with myself, and anyone who would listen—I knew I had made the right choice. What I didn't realize at that point, was that I would go on to do a PhD about the concept of Messiah—investigating whether Jesus could in fact be considered to be the Messiah, even from a Jewish point of view and that "new song" is the phrase within the Psalms which is associated with the Messiah and what he will do.[1]

I assumed that proving that Jesus could have been the Messiah, even from a Jewish perspective (against the majority of Jewish[2] *and* Christian scholarship) was the "new song," as I discovered that, although believing he was the Messiah remains a matter of faith, denying that he *could have been*, was no longer viable. That is, I found that the type of Messiahship portrayed by Jesus in the New Testament *is* fully consonant with first century Jewish messianic expectations. However, although that is a "new song" in it own right, in that I believe I demonstrated that this formerly "closed question" was now open again for debate— it wasn't the only thing I had discovered.

Unearthing a new understanding of the concept of the Messiah also meant that I gained a new understanding of who Jesus is, and what he came to do. This isn't new in the sense that it counters our current understanding of him, but new in the sense that it brought a new awakening of the depth and breadth of what he came to achieve and who he is and how that has been woven throughout the Old Testament and the Jewish festivals in a way that connects not just the "Old" and the "New" Testaments as Christians like to call them, but connects creation and salvation, the Temple and the cosmos, baptism and Chaos waters, harvest and, first-fruits, the Passover lamb and the unbroken legs, the Hosanna of *Sukkoth* (the Feast of Tabernacles) and the triumphal entry; the torn veil of the temple and the broken body on the cross.

I am indebted to one writer in particular, Margaret Barker, whose phenomenal work on the first Temple and related topics has been instrumental in opening up how Jesus was perceived by the early church and what the roots of that are. There have been other writers who have also influenced my thinking, but none, like Margaret, who have made me want to dance in the library. Whilst dancing is also to be desired as a

---

1. Pss 33, 40, 96, 98, 149, Isa 42:10, Rev 5:9, 14:3.

2. Although Boyarin comes as close as he dare as an observant Jewish writer, to saying the same in his work *The Jewish Gospels.*

response to the LORD,[3] I believe that he wants us all to sing a new song—wherein he is no longer the gloomy recompense for our sins—but the LORD come to his Temple, the firstfruits of a new creation, the Lion of Judah and the Lamb of God.[4] These titles and symbols are not unfamiliar to us, but what we have not had is the framework into which *all* of these and *all* of his other titles fit.

When we understand the underlying ideology of sacral kingship, we understand what the Messiah was meant to do, and who he really is as well as what he came to achieve. This is the airy Christ,[5] not airy in the sense of vacuous, having no substance. How could it be? This is the God who got his hands dirty,[6] the one who challenged the authorities, overturned tables in the Temple, had his flesh torn to shreds—but airy in the sense of lofty, spacious; the "breath of life" airy, the one who breathed life[7] into his disciples. Airy in the sense of walking on water, entering as High Priest into the heavenly Holy of Holies and emerging not on clouds of incense, but on clouds of glory, riding as triumphal King into Jerusalem on the day the Passover lambs were chosen, dying on the same day they were slaughtered, rising on the festival of *Habikkurim*;[8] the firstfruits of the new creation. This is not Plan B, because Plan A took a wrong turn around Genesis 3. This is the Lamb who was slain from the foundation of the earth,[9] the one through whom "in the beginning"[10] all things were created and the one who holds all things together.[11] His life and story was not rewritten by the disciples once his Messiahship had "gone wrong," but was a fulfillment of all the same prophecies that are still considered to foretell the Messiah by the form of Judaism that didn't become Christianity.[12] The fulfillment of all the foreshadowing, written

3. As David demonstrated. 2 Sam 6:14.

4. I recognize that the cross is central to Jesus' role and that it is only through that we have salvation but I think sometimes it can overshadow the joy that it is meant to bring, the "life in all its fullness."

5 As in Stevie Smith's poem *Airy Christ*, New Selected Poems, New Directions.

6. Greig, *Dirty Glory*, 4.

7. *Ruach*, the Hebrew used of the Spirit in the Old Testament also means wind or breath.

8. The Festival of Firstfruits.

9. Rev 13:8.

10. Gen 1:1–31/John 1:1.

11. Col 1:17.

12. These can be found in the Jewish *Targumim*, but are in an accessible form in

into, and, practiced in the Jewish festivals—the King of Israel, the Messiah, Christ the King.

Why do we need to know this? We could argue we need to know because the secularist and humanist agenda is trying not just to silence us, or marginalize us, but to make Christians an irrelevance and in some ways I think we are aiding and abetting them. We're made to feel that it's intellectually untenable to be a Christian even though it was the Christians that insisted on the rationality of God and, Christians that lie behind the push for scientific investigation. We do need to know who is opposing us but more importantly we need to know who it is that is "for" us.[13] David "little more than a boy" went to face the enemy, while all the armies of Israel were too scared. David could face the enemy because he knew the source of his power. He said to Goliath "you come against me with sword and, spear and, javelin, but I come against you in the name of the LORD Almighty, the God of the armies of Israel, whom you have defied."[14] Most importantly we need to know because it transforms our thinking. It connects us back to creation and the seasons and to the myth that is "true myth" as Lewis was to say.[15]

David was confident he would win the fight because he knew who he was fighting for, he had also been Anointed to be King and, as a consequence filled with the Spirit of the LORD. He is the one from whose lineage Jesus would come, though not just King of Israel (and Judah) as David, but King of Kings, the name that's so important it's tattooed on his thigh. We need to know that too. We need to understand that as followers of the Messiah we are all anointed and are all, not just Kings who will reign at the end with him[16] but a royal priesthood, seated in the heavenly realms right now.[17] We are new creations because he is the King who died and, rose again the firstfruits of the new creation, that's why his final cry was "*tetelestai*" and why Mary thought he was the gardener. *We* are now the Temple, the place where God's name dwells, where he is now present in the world. All power in heaven and, on earth are given to him and he sends us out in his name, in that power. As sons and daughters of

Levey, The *Messiah: An Aramaic Interpretation.*

    13. "If God is for us, who can be against us?" Rom 8:31b.

    14. 1 Sam 17:47.

    15. That is C S Lewis. I give the full quotation below.

    16. Rev 5:10.

    17. Eph 2:6.

the King we have his authority. "For our struggle is not against flesh and blood, but against the rulers, against the authorities, against the powers of this dark world, and against the spiritual forces of evil in the heavenly realms."[18]

There's a critical moment in the middle of Mark's gospel—positioned there deliberately —where Jesus asks his disciples "Who do people say I am?" and they give him a variety of answers, obviously the things that they have heard people saying about him. He then asks the million dollar question: "Who do *you* say I am?" To which Peter answers, "You are the Messiah."[19]

Jesus *is* the Messiah, but he is also the King of Israel, the Son of Man, the LORD, the Servant, "by whose stripes we are healed," the Good Shepherd, the Lamb whose blood protects, the High Priest (in the order of Melchizedek) carrying out the final atonement and declaring the year of Jubilee; the "I am," the living water, the Rock, the bread from heaven, the living bread born in Bethlehem, the house of bread. He is the new Moses, leading a new Exodus, providing new manna and new living water, giving new laws on the mountain, setting up a new people of God at Pentecost, leading his people into a Sabbath rest. He is the Messiah that was foreshadowed and foretold in the Old Testament—as he told the disciples before their last journey into Jerusalem[20] and when they tried to fight off those who had come to arrest him[21] and on the road to Emmaus after his resurrection.[22] We need to know this, but these only scratch the surface. When we fully understand just how intricately entwined into the Old Testament and, prefigured in the Jewish festivals the Messiah is and how that plays out in the New Testament and informs our understanding of our continuation of that role, I believe we will not only be dancing like David but we will be singing a new song.

Before we sing the song though, we need to learn the words. In chapter 1, therefore, we will look further into why I think it's necessary to understand the importance of Jesus' title and role of King and how

18. Eph 6:12.

19. Mark 8:29.

20. Luke 18:32.

21 "Put your sword back in its place," Jesus said to him, 'for all who draw the sword will die by the sword. Do you think I cannot call on my Father, and he will at once put at my disposal more than twelve legions of angels? [I love that!] But how then would the Scriptures be fulfilled that say it must happen in this way?'" Matt 26:52–54.

22. Luke 24:25–27.

that impacts on our role in his Kingdom as I believe there is a lack of understanding of it amongst Christians. In chapter 2, we will consider sacral kingship in the surrounding cultures and how this illuminates our understanding of the person and role of the King in the Old Testament as well as in the New. In chapter 3 we will look at the Festival of *Sukkoth* (Feast of Tabernacles) and, consider the role of the King there and how that prefigures the role of the Messiah and then consider how that compares to the New Testament portrayal of Jesus as Messiah. In order to do this we will look at the stipulations for the festival in the Bible and then how the festival was celebrated during the Second Temple period. We will look briefly also at how it is celebrated today. We will also examine the links between the festival and the original Enthronement Festival to determine whether sacral kingship does underlie each of the festivals. We will follow this same format in chapters 4 and 5 where we will look at the festivals of *Yom Kippur* (Day of Atonement) and, *Pesach* (Passover).[23] Additional festivals will also be considered that fall within the cycle of the main festivals that we are looking at. Chapter 6 will then look at the related topics of our festivals, coronation and, Kingdom. Finally, chapter 7 will summarize the themes which have emerged from the festivals, which are: Temple, Sabbath, Jubilee and, New Creation and how they impact on the understanding of our role in the kingdom. Hopefully then we will have gained a deeper understanding of who Jesus is, what he came to do and our role in his kingdom.

23. In the following chapters we will refer to the festivals interchangeably with their Hebrew and English names dependent upon what is being discussed as, for example, it is easier to understand the connection between the Passover lamb and the Feast of Passover, rather than using the Hebrew name of *Pesach*. Similarly, referring to *Yom Kippur* as the Day of Atonement draws out the connection between atonement and the festival.

Chapter 1

UNDERSTANDING JESUS AS KING

Problem No. 1—Who is he?

JESUS IS ANNOUNCED AS King at his birth and proclaimed (at least in writing) as King at his death and yet in-between those two events, apart from his triumphal entry into Jerusalem, there appears to be very little that associates him with kingship. Despite the fact that there is actually a Sunday dedicated to Christ the King and more generalized use of kingship motifs in songs and the liturgy—Jesus as King doesn't seem to take up a lot of space in most Christians heads—particularly if those heads only made their first appearance post-millennium. The idea of Jesus as Messiah doesn't appear to figure massively in most Christians' thinking either and if it does, it also has the unfortunate tendency to make us feel uncomfortable, because as "well-informed Christians" we're aware that this is a Jewish term and despite the fact that we know that Jesus was Jewish, (although I've met a surprising number of exceptions to this), we also know that the Jewish people (Messianic Jews excepted) don't believe that Jesus is the Messiah. For most Christians then, Jesus is Son of God, or Jesus Christ—the Christ almost serving as a surname (as in the expletive "Jesus H Christ"). However, in reality, Christ is his title, and of course, the source of our own title 'Christian.' It simply means "Anointed"—the Greek form of the Hebrew *Mashiah* which we translate as Messiah. Although there were a number of people who were anointed

1

prior to Jesus—most usually Priests and Prophets, there was only ever one person who was called "*the* Anointed" (*ha-Mashiah*) and that was either the King or post-Exile the High Priest.[1] Nonetheless this connection between kingship and Messianism receives very little air time.

Of course, it could be argued, that the lack of knowledge may not be representative of the majority of Christians and certainly isn't the case when it comes to clergy. However, as part of my own search into where God was calling me, I was invited along to a number of training evenings by one of the ordinands from my Church. During the break, the lecturer, who also happened to lead the ordinand training program, was mentioning that she had a sermon to deliver on Sunday and as it was "Christ the King" week she was struggling to find anything in the New Testament to do with kingship. I suggested that it all depended on whether you knew what you were looking for. Rather than inquiring what I meant, she proceeded to hold forth on totally unrelated areas of kingship and with a metaphorical wave of the hand, the whole wealth of symbolism, the whole framework on which Messianism depends, the whole set of interconnections were dismissed, sadly not just from her conceptual framework, but also from that of the whole cohort of ordinands, that year and perhaps for years to come.

So straight away we have a problem—kingship—that is sacral kingship—the very concept upon which the whole Bible, Old and New Testaments stands, is either marginalized or misunderstood. One example of this misunderstanding is evident in the work of N T Wright, who whilst acknowledging the centrality of kingship, fails to trace it back to its roots at the very beginning of the whole story, back to Genesis 1, and also fails to acknowledge its reliance on sacral kingship. He states:

> You see, the reason Jesus wasn't the sort of King people had wanted in his own day is—to anticipate our conclusion—that he was the true King, but they had become used to the ordinary, shabby, second-rate sort. They were looking for a builder to construct the home they thought they wanted, but he was the architect, coming with a new plan that would give them everything they needed, but within a quite new framework. They were looking for a singer to sing the song they had been humming for a long time, but he was the composer, bringing them a new song to which the old songs they knew would form, at best,

---

1. That is the second exile, when those who had been taken into captivity in Babylon returned to Jerusalem c.538 BC.

the background music. He was the King, all right but he had come to redefine kingship itself around his own work, his own mission, his own fate.[2]

In some respects Wright is right (pardon the pun), but he makes the same mistake that even Mowinckel, the great Norwegian scholar made in his appraisal of Jesus' role in *Hans Son Kommer* (*He who Comes*), in suggesting that Jesus redefined the role he had come to play, only in Mowinckel's case he is talking about Jesus' role as Servant which we will see below is in fact a "type" of the King, that is a literary "replacement" for the King in the period of the Exile when there was no monarchy.

Jesus didn't redefine the role, he fulfilled it and this is what we will see when we consider just how he was prefigured in the Jewish festivals and how his death and resurrection were the second Exodus that fulfilled the first, just as the Rabbis had predicted, "as the first Redeemer, so shall the second redeemer be," that is Jesus was a "second Moses" just as Matthew is at pains to point out. This is not a redefinition, this is fulfillment. Jesus *was* singing a new song, but it was the song that had been written into Jewish tradition, written into the very songs that spoke of the Messiah,[3] from the very beginning, into the cosmos itself—not a reworking of it. The reworking, as Margaret Barker has suggested, took place at the time of the "reforms" of Josiah.[4] It is not just the New Testament that the lack of kingship is applied to, Fletcher-Louis also states: "The Pentateuch is almost devoid of royalty"[5] Again, on the face of it, this could be considered to be true, but I believe that it will become clear, that sacral kingship runs throughout the Bible. All the more reason therefore to understand what sacral kingship is so that we can see for ourselves just how it underpins the Old and the New Testaments.

The question we hope to answer here then and in particular for this new generation, is "Who do you say I am?" This is the question Jesus poses for every generation and it has been answered in numerous ways, some of them helpful, some of them less so. The other "gods" have their witnesses "who have eyes but are blind, who have ears but are deaf."[6]

---

2. Wright, *Simply Jesus*, 7.

3. Pss 33, 96, 98.

4. Barker, *What Did King Josiah Reform*.

5. Fletcher-Louis, *Jesus and, the High Priest*, 15.

6. Isa 43:8.

Secularism and humanism are on the rise and have very vocal advocates in increasingly influential places—but the LORD says to his people, to us:

> You are my witnesses and my servant whom I have chosen, so that you may know and believe me and understand, that I am he. Before me no god was formed nor will there be one after me. I, even I, am the LORD and apart from me there is no savior. I have revealed and saved and proclaimed—I and not some foreign god among you. You are my witnesses declares the LORD—that I am God. Yes, and from ancient days I am he.[7]

He is the God from ancient days but in so many ways now, the LORD is being defiled inside and outside the Church and if we are to be his witnesses, we need to know who he is in order to proclaim him. The problem then is how can we proclaim him King and pray for his kingdom to come if we don't understand kingship. If we did, we would understand that it underpins the biblical narrative and provides the framework into which all the different titles of Jesus and different paradigms of his death (Passover lamb, Servant and, High Priest) fit. This lack of understanding therefore leads us to overlook the multiple layers of symbolism that would further enhance and enrich our understanding of Jesus and the kingdom.

It is my belief that if we did understand this, and all that it entails, we would not only sing a new song, but all of the songs that we currently sing, would come alive to us. We would realize that when we sing about God as King, it's not just a title that speaks about majesty and rule, but one that is woven throughout the Old Testament, the Jewish festivals, the New Testament, the liturgy and, our festivals. It is no coincidence, that in the established Church, the week that culminates the liturgical year and precedes Advent, the beginning of the new liturgical cycle, is entitled Christ the King, because this is the lens through which the whole cycle of the year and the festivals should be viewed. It is the church's new year when we acknowledge Jesus as King. Therefore it shouldn't be a struggle to talk about Jesus as King in a sermon, it should be at the centre of *every* sermon. Just as the symbolism that represents this should be part of our intellectual furniture, but again often, this is not the case. Let me illustrate.

In a recent service I attended, the sermon started off really well; although it was part of the main service, it was predominantly intended

---

7. Isa 43:10–13.

for the ears of the baptismal party. The preacher made the connection between birth and new-birth, about being born in the flesh and in the spirit, but then went on about the need for Jesus to die, about God's punishment and, about sin and death; equating sin with smoking and drinking and, by the end of it, even I didn't want to be a Christian! It was part of that Church's tradition to preach the Gospel at a baptism service, in the belief that for the majority of the party, even those taking the vows, it may be one of the few times they would hear the Gospel. I very much doubt however that having heard this version of the "good news," the individuals in this party would be asking Jesus into their lives anytime soon.

I also wondered if the alienation of the baptismal party, was further exacerbated by the background displayed on the overhead screen to the song during communion—namely that of a trussed up lamb. I discussed this with one of the long-standing members of the congregation, wondering whether the baptismal party would understand the symbolism of it, to which the lady in question replied: "Well I don't understand it either." Whilst she may not be representative of the majority of the church, there does appear to be an increasing ignorance amongst Christians regarding the roots of our theology. The more I probe into these matters amongst Christians, the more it becomes apparent that so much of our symbolism is lost, washing over our heads. We sing about the Lamb; John 1:29 forms part of the lectionary readings; we speak of "Christ our Passover sacrifice"; we quite eagerly set up and attend Passover Seders, specially adapted for Christians[8]—and yet still we fail to perceive just how much Jesus is pre-figured in the Old Testament and in particular, in the Jewish festivals. Whilst this may be obvious to those fortunate enough to have been able to study the theology behind it, and one would hope that would include the clergy, (although the above example may suggest otherwise), what this may indicate, is that many contemporary Christians are no longer aware of the roots of their own theology and that the roots of that theology lie in sacral kingship.

The ignorance is even more surprising when viewed against the background of the numerous direct references or allusions to kingship that form part of the church's discourse. Anyone who doubts the claim or the centrality of kingship language within the church need only take a cursory glance at any of the material that the church uses in its worship. Setting aside for the moment the question of the New Testament

8. Ironically, not even at these are all the symbolism and intricate connections really understood and drawn out.

itself, if we consider the church calendar for example, the main festivals all contain themes of kingship, which, nonetheless, I would argue are no longer at the forefront of our consciousness. We have the Annunciation which is replete with kingship themes;[9] Christmas, when the Messianic prophecies are read, all of which speak of a coming King.[10] We then have Epiphany when the three Kings come to worship "the King of the Jews" who they have been told will be born in Bethlehem, David's city in accordance with the prophecy by Micah,[11] that is King David, from whose line the King Messiah is expected to come.[12] In the first week in January, we celebrate Jesus' baptism at the beginning of his ministry when he hears the words from heaven, echoing the words spoken to the King when he is enthroned as part of the autumnal festival.[13] We have Palm Sunday when Jesus rides into Jerusalem as King and Good Friday when he is crucified as "King of the Jews," followed by Easter Sunday when he rises on the festival of *Habikkurim*, the firstfruits festival celebrating the Exodus which we shall see is also connected with Kingship. We then have Ascension, where Jesus is enthroned at the right hand side of God (just as was said of the King in Ps110:1); Pentecost, when believers were anointed with the Holy Spirit, just as the King had been anointed and the Holy Spirit came upon him. Finally, Christ the King festival (N. *Jesu Christi Universorum Regis,* Our Lord Jesus Christ King of the universe in the Catholic tradition), the last Sunday in the liturgical year, before a new year begins. Just as the King had been enthroned in ancient Israel, to inaugurate the new year, Jesus is enthroned as King of the Universe to inaugurate the church's new year. All these connections are lost if we don't understand the significance of kingship.

It could be argued that we *are* aware of kingship as it features in so many of our songs, but I suspect that we only connect this with awe, with some vague idea of the kingdom and of god "reigning on high." The same could be said of the liturgy—do we grasp the significance of the allusion in the baptism service to the Exodus and the parting of the Red Sea and how that foreshadows Jesus' baptism and his death and resurrection? Do we understand why Jesus is referred to as High Priest in one part of the

9. Luke 1: 30–33.

10. Gen 49:10, Num 24:17, Isa 9:2–7, 11:1–9.

11. Mic 5:2–4.

12. Hence the genealogies in Matthew and Luke demonstrating Jesus' descent from David's line.

13. Ps 2:7.

liturgy and then as our Passover sacrifice in another? Why do we say in the creed that he is seated at the right hand side of the Father? These are not just random symbols plucked from the Old Testament, rather, as we shall demonstrate in the following chapters, all of these seemingly unconnected images, are, in fact, all directly connected with kingship. It is my belief that once we understand the centrality of kingship, its link with the Jewish festivals and the Temple, all the seemingly ill-fitting pieces of the jigsaw suddenly fall into place, and the picture not only makes sense, but is fuller and deeper with a richness and color that we've only caught a glimpse of before.

A similar argument is made about the lack of knowledge of the Temple, most notably by Margaret Barker, who has stated that there is a "black hole" in the centre of biblical studies, into which the Temple has disappeared.[14] This is hardly surprising as the two go hand-in-hand but again you could be forgiven for thinking that on the face of it, just as we could assert with kingship, although there are a number of references to it in the New Testament, the Temple doesn't appear to feature large in Jesus' consciousness. Apart from the cleansing of the Temple and the occasional reference to him going to the Temple, the major reference to it by Jesus himself, is the statement that it will be torn down and rebuilt in three days, by which John explains, Jesus was talking about his body. Whilst the Temple does still feature in Acts, with the believers continuing to visit there, apart from the reference to his mystical experience in the Temple, Paul's references to it all concern the transference of this image to the body of believers. This is something that we will also explore in the following chapters, because kingship and Temple are intimately connected, and both are central to our understanding of Jesus and therefore, our faith.

It may be relevant to ask at this point, why, if this is so important and, so obvious, is it only coming to light now? The answer would be that it isn't a recent phenomenon, rather different aspects of it have been the subject of research for many years. Although sacral kingship was researched mainly by Scandinavian scholars, a number of well respected British scholars also joined in this project. I believe, however, that the timing of this research (1950s onwards), left its message largely, if not unheard, at least not appropriated, as shortly after the main activity of these scholars there developed within New Testament studies a move

---

14. Barker, *Creation Theology*, 2.

towards demythologizing the Gospels and in some cases, Jesus himself.[15] Again this may be said to be the mirror image of what was happening on the Jewish side of scholarship with the movement which came to be known as the Jewish Reclamation of Jesus.[16] Both of these movements, I would suggest, were part of the post-Holocaust reaction to the recognition of the part that Christian theology and in particular the charge of deicide[17] and supersession[18] as well as the denigration and, mistreatment of the Jewish people on the part of the church, had played in laying the groundwork of anti-Judaism, which allowed the anti-Semitism of the late nineteenth century onwards to flourish.[19] The tendency therefore, within Christian New Testament scholarship was to move Jesus more toward the type of Messiah that Judaism claimed was expected, a purely human figure. I believe however, that once divorced from its mystical and mythical[20] elements, the church is in danger of diminishing its message or developing into something wholly other.

Furthermore, I believe it is these same elements of the faith that capture the imagination and hearts of the people. That's not to detract from the simple message of the Gospel. I believe the truth of the Gospels stands alone.[21] Nonetheless, having understood and begun to live by that simple truth, like any relationship, we want to find out more, to discover who this person is that we are in love with. When asked the greatest commandment, Jesus replied: "Love the Lord your God with all

15. Most notably Robinson's *The Myth of God Incarnate*.

16. See Hagner, *The Jewish Reclamation of Jesus*.

17. Deicide is the charge made by the church that it was "the Jews" that killed Jesus and, this has had a massively detrimental affect on Jewish-Christian relations.

18. Supersession is the doctrine that Christianity has superseded Judaism, which is now obsolete and, all the promises to Israel are now passed to Christians. This view has been widely challenged now and, I have discussed this in more depth in my other work.

19. In 1543 Luther published his pamphlet "*On Jews and their Lies*" and many of Hitler's earliest constraints on the Jewish people, including wearing the yellow star of David, were revivals of earlier Church practices decreed at the IV Lateran Church Council in 1215; the charge of Deicide was only rescinded by Pope Paul VI in Nostra Aetate, 28 October 1965.

20. I explain the usage of ` "myth" below.

21. I witnessed this quite recently when the first week after joining a Challenge group we had set up for people to explore Christianity and bring their questions and objections to God to be discussed, one of the group took away Mark's Gospel to read. The following week, he began to answer other people's questions. It was nothing that we, the group leaders had said, the Gospel spoke for itself.

your heart, with all your soul and with all your *mind.*" I believe that for so
long now, Jesus has been misrepresented and therefore, misunderstood.
He has been demythologized or radicalized. He has been divorced from
the natural world that he created; the vivid images of harvest: the plaited
bread in the shape of sheaves of corn, the vibrant colours of the fruit
and vegetables, that formed part of even my childhood in the industrial
North, have for the most part been replaced with envelopes for water-aid,
aiding the disjuncture of the church from her message of new creation.
His bride has been too busy trying to psycho-analyze herself, get the accounts in order, or wondering if she is offending anyone, that she has
taken her eyes off the groom and forgotten about the wedding feast she's
been called to, even denying at times that the groom exists.

I feel it is crucial, therefore, that we understand who he is in order to
be his witnesses, to capture the urgency of those words from Isaiah and
be filled with excitement about who he is, so full of enthusiasm (filled
with god—*en theos*) that it spills out of us. There are so many forces both
without and within that are working against that. Not just the threat of
persecution in the Middle East, nor the more insidious threat nearer to
home, nor the increasing secularist and humanist agendas but apathy
within some parts of the church itself; legalism, rather than love; the desire to uphold the institution rather than spreading the good news, right
through to the denial by some Dutch clergy of God's existence.[22] Nor
are they alone, according to a recent Yougov poll, 2 percent of Anglican
clergy don't believe in God either. The now retired, Rev. David Paterson
explains: "God is quite an important concept. But to talk about the "existence" of God is a nonsense. God "exists" only as a human idea."[23] In
addition, Jesus' divinity and his resurrection are rejected and doubts cast
on whether he existed at all.

I believe therefore that the resurgence in interest in the Temple,[24]
sacral kingship and the more mystical elements, not just of Christianity
but also of Judaism is not coincidental. I believe that rather than demythologizing Jesus or rationalizing God as the projection of our own hopes

22. A study by the Free University of Amsterdam found that one-in-six Dutch
clergy in the PKN and six other smaller denominations was either agnostic or atheist.
http://www.bbc.co.uk/news/world-europe-14417362

23. From an article in the *University Times* , Trinity College Dublin, 20.2.14 in an
interview with James Bennett editor.

24. As in the work of Crispin Fletcher-Louis, C R T Hayward and, the Temple
Studies Group, in particular Margaret Barker.

and longings, we need to do just the opposite—we need to re-engage with our own mythology. Unfortunately even part of the established church is also following this trend, making services "seeker-friendly," devoid of liturgy, ritual, lectionary readings and, joint prayer; with thematic "talks" that look at spiritual disciplines rather than the good news, and songs that contain no theology or symbolism. Rather than five minute baptisms, we need to understand what baptism is all about—that it isn't just a ritual that Jesus underwent as a prelude to his ministry, but rather a foreshadowing of his death and resurrection. When we look at this through the lens of sacral kingship we realize that Jesus is going under the waters of Chaos, dying to self and rising again to new life. We realize that the words that Jesus heard at his baptism were those spoken to the King at his enthronement. Only then will we understand the symbolism of our own baptism and recognize that this theme pervades the Old Testament and provides the background to the crossing of the Red Sea and that of the Jordan.

Baptism becomes then, not just a rite of passage, nor even a nod to folk religion,[25] but an active part of the renewal of the covenant, that we as individuals are taking part in. Then, when we join in the words of baptism, whether leading it or participating as part of the congregation, the images and themes, the symbolism and connections all build up this picture of just who it is we're worshipping; who it is we're serving. We recognize that we too have died to sin, risen again from the Chaos waters and are seated in the heavenlies; that we are a royal priesthood; we are the Temple, being rebuilt, with Jesus as the cornerstone and the apostles and prophets as the foundation. We may already be aware of this from scripture, but once we understand the background to all of these concepts I believe that the picture that emerges is so much richer and deeper than even we had realized. We need to recapture our vision of the Kingdom, which has almost become a jaded term. Although we shy away now, quite understandably, given our history, from anything which sounds militaristic, as the change in the baptism liturgy confirms,[26] recognizing sacral kingship as the backcloth, re-engages us with our role

---

25. Although I think we would do well to re-embrace these elements and, recognize the power they have over the popular mind. Something I will consider in the following chapters.

26. That is with the removal of "soldier" from the section which used to say "remain a faithful soldier and servant to the end of your days."

as sons and daughters of the King.[27] It captures our imagination as C S Lewis intended with the kingdom of Narnia,[28] even reconnecting the Church of England with its patron saint.[29] This is the power of symbolism especially when integrated into a myth, remembering that myth doesn't mean something that isn't true, but is a way of expressing a truth. This is something Lewis was most adamant about, that the Gospels were myth, but true myth, myth that had actually happened.

> The heart of Christianity is a myth which is also a fact. The old myth of the Dying God, without ceasing to be myth, comes down from the heaven of legend and imagination to the earth of history. It happens at a particular date, in a particular place, followed by definable historical consequences. We pass from a Balder or an Osiris, dying nobody knows when or where, to a historical Person crucified (it is all in order) under Pontius Pilate. By becoming fact it does not cease to be myth: that is the miracle.[30]

In the following chapter we will consider some of these myths as they form part of the ideology of sacral kingship in the cultures that surrounded and influenced Israel and will consider how these formed the background to Israel's understanding of kingship. As it says in Ecclesiastes,[31] God has set eternity in the hearts of all men and therefore

27. In one church I know the uniformed flags were recently hung in the roof space and, the man who did it said, it gave him goose pimples, because it looked like the King's hall. We speak of Jesus as the champion of our faith, we sing of the Lord 'marching out in splendor.' In Revelation, Jesus is the rider on a white horse and on his robe and on his thigh he has written "King of Kings and Lord of Lords"(Rev19:16). These are the images that evoke an emotional response that wants to go out and, defend the Kingdom, to enlarge it, bringing the lost and the broken into its safety, not I would suggest images of bar charts on Diocesan 'dashboards' looking for ways to increase Church numbers.

28. 'From a spiritual point of view, Lewis famously talked of the 'baptism of the imagination' which literature could provide; he envisaged the Narnian stories producing an effect which was only to be fully realized in later life, when the reader encountered an idea (or image or story) which they recognized as having met before. According to his biographer: His idea, as he once explained to me, was to make it easier for children to accept Christianity when they met it later in life. He hoped that they would be vaguely reminded of the somewhat similar stories that they had read and enjoyed years before. "I am aiming at a sort of pre-baptism of the child's imagination.' A Clerk of Oxford, *C S Lewis, The Medievalist,*

29. St George and the Dragon is another version of the Chaos myth.

30 Lewis, *God in the Dock*, 66–67.

31. Eccles 3:11.

the idea of sacral kingship appears in all the cultures surrounding Israel, but it was Israel who God chose to be a light to the nations, to spread the knowledge of the one true God, whose King would in fact, not just in title, but in reality, be Son of God. The King who, rather than undergoing mock rituals that mimicked the creation myth where the God fought with the forces of Chaos and overcame them as a prelude to creation would *actually* do battle with the forces of Chaos, once and for all. Israel expected an anointed King who really was the Son of God, who would defeat the forces of Chaos through his own death and resurrection and bring about re-creation, new life not just physically and annually but a spiritual and eternal new creation and new life. Israel expected and then witnessed the reality that lay behind the myth and ritual of the cultures that surrounded her.

God breathed life into Adam and Jesus breathed life into his disciples and the Church needs to be brought to life again, to have God's Spirit breathed into us bringing new creation, just as it did "in the beginning." Understanding sacral kingship turns what seems to be a negative—sin, death, punishment, all of the things in the sermon I mentioned earlier, into a positive—re-birth, new creation, joy; life in all its fullness. Sin is still part of the story, but we need to understand it in its wider context, we need to understand how it affects not just us, but the earth.

> The eternal covenant, also described as the covenant of peace or wholeness, underlies the biblical world view. The creation was established and secured by the bonds of this covenant, and these bonds could be broken by human sin. If one or two bonds were broken, the system could cope with the breach, but if too many were broken, then the whole system collapsed. This was "the wrath," the inevitable result of human sin, unless some priestly process intervened to protect the creation and human society. The bonds of the covenant embraced in one system heaven and earth, the visible and invisible creation, the natural world and human society.[32]

Only then do we want to dance in the library, to capture the excitement, that we are meant to be a part of mending the world, and this not just in a practical way, but as part of the Church, as we learn from temple theology, it was the liturgy of the Temple that maintained the cosmos. It has been said that the liturgy is the work of the people, but it doesn't have to be set formal liturgy, although I believe that has a place, it is about

---

32. Barker, *Creation Theology*, 4.

worshipping together, enjoying the festivals together, the appointed times with our God. Not admitting to our faith, apologetically, suggesting that we *may* have some good news, but in a "racing through the countryside, filled with the joy of celebration" kind of way.[33] In a way that says that Jesus came to renew creation, and as part of that creation, we are renewed in him.

Problem No. 2—What did he come to do?

The second problem that leads on from this is that if we fail to understand who Jesus is we're less likely to understand what he came to do. On one level, we all understand that he came to carry out a once and for all atonement for our sins (though there is much debate about what this means). This is nonetheless, what was expected of the Messiah in the 11QMelch scroll from amongst the Dead Sea Scrolls. It was expected that the Messiah would make the Great Atonement on the Tenth Jubilee—a date which, although disputed by some, has been aligned with the final years of Jesus. Although McKnight is at pains to point out, that the "Story of Jesus" is the completion of the "Story of Israel," he unfortunately labors the point without actually making the connection in any meaningful way.[34] However, that is exactly what needs to be done in order for us to understand just what Jesus' role was and in order to do that, just as with the question about who Jesus is, the answer lies in the role of the King, because the King's role, as we pointed out earlier, provided the basis of the concept of Messiah—he was the *hameshiah, hammelek,* the Anointed King. Thus by examining sacral kingship and how it runs throughout the Old Testament and into the New, and in particular how it is evidenced in the Jewish festivals, we will come to a much deeper understanding of what the Messiah was expected to do and in fact what Jesus, the Messiah did.

How does that tie in with our theology of the cross, because whichever way you look at it the cross is central to Christianity? I believe that it does and that it explains what the cross was doing, what Jesus came to do, not in a mutually exclusive way to the other models traditionally used to explain it, but in a way that fully integrates it with the *heilsgeschichte*

33. Rend Collective 'Joy of Celebration' video.
34. McKnight, *The King Jesus Gospel.*

(salvation story) of the Old Testament. This is therefore the second problem that I believe sacral kingship helps to address.

When I first became a Christian in my early thirties, I was always
slightly uneasy about the cross—it was explained to me, quite clearly, in
a number of ways, and on some levels I understood it, but none of the
answers really satisfied me. I couldn't see why it was necessary, nor, when
I became more familiar with the Scriptures, where it had actually come
from, apart from perhaps some connection with the animal sacrifices in
the Old Testament, but even then, I didn't understand why it had to be
done that way. I realized it was quite literally the crux of the Christian
faith and I understood all the models used to explain it, ransom, substitution, etc, but I still felt like there was something missing, that I had
somehow missed the point. Unfortunately, when you start to voice this
kind of doubt, the automatic response is to regurgitate exactly those sorts
of models again, in the belief that I hadn't properly understood them,
that "the scales had not yet dropped from my eyes." I had no problem
believing that Jesus was God, that he had been incarnate, and that he had
died for our sins and rose again, I just didn't understand why—why the
cross and why the blood and the resurrection reconciled us back to God.

Several years later, I was helping out on a local Alpha course when
the vicar was attempting to answer the same question "Why did Jesus
die?" Although she followed the explanation in the Alpha booklet, she
nonetheless felt the need to add "Yes I know it's a bit odd." She then went
on to say that she had never really understood it herself and even when
she had asked the Oxford-educated vicar down the road, who lectured in
New Testament theology—he couldn't explain it in a way that satisfied
her either. Even more recently, and perhaps more surprisingly, during
the Boxing Day 2014 Desert Island Disc program, Justin Welby, the present Archbishop of Canterbury, principal leader of the Church of England
and head of the worldwide Anglican Communion answered the question
of how he had become a Christian by describing how a fellow student
explained to him "the simple thing that on the cross Jesus died so that
in some extraordinary way, I could know God and it just made sense."[35]
Perhaps not as surprising as we may have initially thought, given the fact
that the Doctrine Commission of the Church of England also appears
to be at a loss to explain it. In fact the BBC website on religion states:
"There is no single doctrine of the atonement in the New Testament.

35. https://www.bbc.co.uk/programmes/b04vd69f. This is not a criticism of Justin
Welby, just an illustration of the church's seeming inability to explain the doctrine.

Perhaps, even more surprisingly, there is no official church definition either."[36] Although on one level it wasn't a problem, it didn't hamper my relationship with Jesus or my growing in faith, on another, I think it held me back from evangelism. When trying to explain to someone who had never heard about it, you did feel, like the vicar I mentioned above, that somehow you had to qualify it. Despite the good news that this was the means by which we are set free, what lay behind it seemed so negative and so disconnected.

When I came to study theology for myself, despite the benefit of numerous modules on New Testament theology and on the "New Theologians" I found nothing that explained it any clearer to me. I understood the four models of atonement proposed by McGrath,[37] but didn't see how that all fitted into the bigger picture of an expected Messiah, with the Old Testament as its backdrop. Nonetheless these models continue to be taught in Biblical seminaries and in New Testament studies; so why then do we need to know about kingship? I believe we need to know, because it explains, in a way that none of the other models do, why Jesus came, died and rose again, as well as unearthing the intricate links that exist between not only the texts but also the themes, motifs and expectations of the Old and New Testaments. That is to pick up our analogy from the preface, Season 2 flows smoothly out of Season 1. There's no change in the plot or the main character, the story continues as the Director intended.

Similarly, when I came to study them, I couldn't understand the controversy surrounding Jesus' titles, in particular, that of the Son of Man, considered by some scholars, not to be a title at all, but rather a circumlocution.[38] This is Jesus' preferred self-designation. It didn't make sense to me that Jesus would refer to himself so frequently in this way if it didn't constitute a title and didn't convey something specific, particularly in light of Mark 8:30–where, once he has been identified as the Messiah by Peter, Jesus immediately refers to himself as Son of Man and identifies this role with that of his death and resurrection. Nonetheless whole volumes have been devoted to trying to unravel this "problem." Nor is this the only title to court controversy and christological speculation, others include Son of God, High Priest, Lamb of God, Messiah and Servant, not to mention King! We will look at each one of these in the following

36. http://www.bbc.co.uk/religion/religions/Christianity/beliefs/whydidjesusdie

37. That is the cross as sacrifice ;the cross as a victory; the cross as forgiveness; the cross as a moral example. McGrath, *Christian Theology*, chapter 12.

38. That is an aramaic way of saying 'I'.

chapters where it will become clear that, rather than having to treat each title as a completely separate entity, searching for convoluted meanings, each of them is in fact, directly connected with Jesus' role as King and in turn, intimately connected with the Jewish festivals. Similarly we will consider the three major paradigms that are used in the New Testament to describe Jesus' role, and in particular his death and resurrection and which, on the face of it, also seem to be unrelated, these are: Passover Lamb, High Priest and Servant. However, once we understand the relationship of each of these to the Jewish festivals and to the concept of sacral kingship, we will see that these too, conform to a coherent pattern.

In the following chapters therefore, we will consider the evidence for sacral kingship and how the discrete Jewish festivals were all originally derived from, or shared their rationale with the original autumnal New Year Festival at which the enthronement of Yahweh was celebrated and creation renewed. We will consider the King's role in this ceremony and the understanding that he was the human manifestation of the LORD at this point and how his dying, rising and enthronement are to be found in each of these festivals as is the desired outcome of them—*mishpat*—justice in its widest sense of salvation, re-creation, renewal and social justice. We will see that he is the new Moses, leading his people into Sabbath rest, the Passover lamb, whose blood atones and protects, the High Priest in the order of Melchizedek, announcing the year of Jubilee; the Servant by whose stripes we are healed and that each of these are linked to the role of the Messianic King. Then, rather than being limited to models, such as those proposed by McGrath, (none of which see the cross as the fulfillment of what had gone before in the Old Testament), we will recognize it as the means by which Jesus fulfilled his role as King, and understand that this is not a marginal concept in the New Testament, but the *central* concept, which incorporates all his other roles as High Priest, Passover Lamb and Servant.

Acknowledging that the concept of the Anointed has undergone development and transition within the Hebrew Scriptures/Old Testament and Judaism itself and that each of Jesus' titles can be traced as part of that development, also clears away many of the scholarly contentions: was the Servant an individual, or Israel? Had Jesus taken this Old Testament concept and made it uniquely his own? Was the designation of Jesus as High Priest in the order of Melchizedek, an attempt to align him with the priesthood, even though he wasn't descended from the line of Aaron? How could he be both the Passover Lamb and the scapegoat of the Day of Atonement? Furthermore how could a Jewish Messiah be understood as Son of God and worshipped as LORD? Finally how could he even be said to be Messiah when, almost every Jewish writer, past and present says that he doesn't fit into first century Jewish messianic categories. All of these apparent anomalies disappear when we realize that each of these titles and each of these roles derive from the title and role which in itself was seen to be problematic—that of King and that they all, including the title and role of King itself make up the concept of Messiah. Nonetheless it's not just on the basis of the type of Messiah, i.e divine, nor his role as a suffering Messiah that died for our sins, that Jewish writers reject Jesus as Messiah, but on the outcome of that role. The Messiah was expected to bring about certain messianic conditions—the restoration of the Temple, the restoration of Israel as a sovereign nation, the restoration of the Davidic monarchy, the ingathering of the exiles and an era of peace and goodwill. According to the Jewish writers, Jesus didn't fulfill any of these conditions, therefore he didn't bring about the Messianic Age, consequently he can't have been the Messiah. We will look at each of these conditions in the following chapters and in particular chapter 7 and see that in fact Jesus did fulfill each of them, even though at the time of his death, the Temple was still standing. We will also see that we have a part too in bringing about the messianic conditions and this leads us into the next problem.

Problem No. 3—What is our role?

The third and final problem is, having understood who Jesus is and what he came to do, what impact does that have on our role? Surely that's stated in the Great Commission?[39] We are to be his witnesses. Like courtroom witnesses however, it appears that many of us have been silenced by the opposition:

> With atheists becoming more strategic in championing their godless worldview, the increasing reticence of Christians to engage in faith-oriented conversations assumes heightened significance. Why would a Christian be reticent about living and sharing his faith in Jesus Christ? Could it be because neither the Word nor the LORD is real to them? And could that be

39. Matt 28:18–20.

because the doctrine presented to most Christians is illogical, self-contradictory, confusing, bland or unmotivating?[40]

What if instead we were to understand that as King, Jesus came to cleanse the cosmos, renew creation, to set the captives free and to bring life in all its fullness?

Once we understand more fully who Jesus is[41] and what he came to do, then surely we will be in a better position to know what we're supposed to be doing, to be able to sing a new song, to dance alongside the Lord of the Dance as he builds his kingdom. To follow the rider on the white horse with the tattoo on his thigh, to take part in the adventure, where the King riding on a white horse comes to save us from the Dragon and take us to his home where the streets are golden and the gates are jeweled, to be his bride and enjoy the wedding feast he has prepared.

We are sons and daughters of the King. He's paid with his life to keep us safe from the Dragon and from ourselves, he's set his blood as a cover over us to protect us. He's given us every fruit from every tree for our delight, even access to the Tree of Life. He's given each of us our own quest and his Spirit to guide us and comfort us and help us to grow our own fruit. He's showered us with spiritual gifts and placed his armor at our disposal so that we are fully equipped to carry out our quest, our assignment. He has a plan and purpose for each one of us.[42] Whatever our individual quest, he wants us to expand his kingdom, to set the oppressed free, to feed the poor and house the homeless so that justice, *mishpat* is established; to bring his healing and wholeness, his Sabbath rest for all his creation, including the earth itself. He wants us to sow seeds for his harvest, to make his living water available to all, to be renewed and be renewers. He wants us to guard the shore, to keep the Chaos waters at bay, to maintain order and most of all to love him, be loved by him and show his love to others.

---

40. Sweet, *The 10 Biggest Issues.*

41. I don't even begin to imagine that this is a full portrayal of who Jesus is; this can only begin to scratch the surface. It may just be one line in a new song, but it's a start.

42. "'For I know the plans I have for you' declares the LORD, 'plans to prosper you and not to harm you, plans to give you hope and a future.'" Jer 29:11.

Chapter 2

SACRAL KINGSHIP

Introduction

IN THIS CHAPTER WE are hoping to discern what it means when we talk about Jesus as King. If, as I've said in the last chapter, kingship is so integral to our understanding of Jesus and something that will deepen our relationship with him then we need to understand it. However, one of the reasons the lecturer I mentioned in chapter one could say that she was struggling to find anything to say about Jesus as King is because, like her, most people don't understand what kingship looked like in ancient Israel. At the time of Jesus there hadn't been an Anointed King for over 500 years; what there had been, was a High Priest who in place of the King had now become *the* Anointed. Whilst we could just look at the High Priest's role as *the* Anointed in the Day of Atonement since this was the major cultic role of the King,[1] we still wouldn't have a full picture of what it meant for Jesus to be, "King of the Jews," as other elements of this role are to be found in the other two festivals that we will also consider, *Sukkoth* and Passover

We need, therefore, to look at kingship in ancient Israel, which despite some arguments to the contrary, a number of scholars agree, was

---

1. We will be looking at that in chapter 4 as High Priest is also one of Jesus' major titles and the Day of Atonement one of the paradigms that explain his role as the Anointed.

sacral. When writers talk about Jesus' kingship it's said that it wasn't political and that's true, Jesus makes that clear at his trial "my Kingdom is
not of this world."[2] However it doesn't mean it was a purely "spiritual"
kingship, this was instead sacral kingship, the type of kingship that featured within all the cultures that Israel was associated with, the kind of
kingship that Frankfort describes:

> If we refer to kingship as a political institution, we assume a
> point of view which would have been incomprehensible to the
> ancients. We imply that the human polity can be considered by
> itself. The ancients however experienced human life as a widely
> spreading network of connections which reached beyond the
> local and national communities into the hidden depths of na-
> ture and the powers that rule nature . . . whatever was significant
> was imbedded in the life of the cosmos and, it was precisely the
> King's function to maintain the harmony of that integration.
> This doctrine is valid for the whole of the ancient near east and,
> for many other regions.[3]

Sacral kingship therefore encompassed both roles—political and,
cultic, because as Frankfort says, in the ancient near east there was no
distinction, both are intertwined. So how does that look? To get a better grasp of it we need to look at the cultures that surrounded Israel
because Israel didn't exist in a vacuum. There's ample evidence, even in
the Old Testament itself,[4] that Israel was influenced by the cultures that
surrounded her particularly Babylon (Mesopotamia/Assyria), Canaan
and Egypt as these were the cultures that Israel had been most involved
with—taken into Exile in 722 BC by Assyria, and, then in 586 BC cap-
tured and taken into Babylon - the Babylonian influence is still evident
in the Hebrew names for the months as these were taken over from there
as well as the calendar change following the return from exile in 536BC
when the new Temple was built (or the old rebuilt). Much earlier than
that, Israel had been in Egypt for 400 years, when Joseph had brought

2. A further problem that this causes is that mainly Jewish writers (but also a
number of Christian writers) suggest that Jesus messiahship failed, that is it was intended to be political but when he was tried and crucified, a different type of messianic
ideal had to be concocted, hence the 'suffering and dying' messiah that many claim
was contrary to what Judaism at that time expected. This was the focus of my first book
where I examined this claim and dismissed it.

3. Frankfort, *Kingship and the Gods*, 3.

4. Even as late as Nehemiah/Ezra the Israelites were told to get rid of their foreign
wives so they wouldn't be influenced by them and turn to their gods.

his father and brothers there to avoid the famine in Israel where they eventually became slaves of the Egyptian empire and the Pharaoh until the Exodus, the foundational salvation event when Moses led the people out of slavery to the Promised Land. The Promised Land being Canaan and evidence of this culture's influence on Israel is apparent throughout the prophets—who are constantly telling the people to do away with their *Baal*'s and *Asherah* idols representing the gods of Canaan.

Therefore, with this in mind, it's clear that in order to understand how sacral kingship functioned in Israel it is necessary to look at sacral kingship in the cultures that surrounded Israel and, undoubtedly influenced its idea of kingship. As it says in 1 Sam 8:5 they ask for a King "like all the nations" the Hebrew *ke* indicating of the same type, not just similar. This is because, not only is there some ambiguity about kingship expressed in the Old Testament but also because on the surface kingship does not play a major part in Old Testament theology. There are a number of possible explanations offered for this ambivalence. Some scholars suggest that the Old Testament underwent redaction at the hands of the Deuteronomists who instigated a move away from sacral kingship as the focus of Israel's religion onto the keeping of Torah and the rise in the influence of the Mosaic tradition. It is also suggested that Josiah's reform, was in fact a purge of the older religion rather than of pagan practices.[5] In order to understand the concept of kingship in Israel therefore we need to supplement our knowledge from the ideology of kingship in the countries which are held to have influenced her.

> There is very little direct evidence about the religious function of the King, but there are many hints that the King was very important and, some historical reconstructions make him central . . . Much is said about the Kings and their activities, but the impression left from clues in the text is that some important data have been suppressed at a time when the monarchy was no longer a reality.[6]

---

5. "We can never know for certain what it was that Josiah purged or why he did it . . . A thousand years after the event themselves, even mainstream Jewish texts remembered that the Temple had been drastically changed, that large numbers of people had left the land, and that the true Temple would only be restored in the time of the Messiah." Barker, "What Did Josiah Reform?"

6. Grabbe, *Priests, Prophets,* 20.

What follows is only the briefest outline of each of the areas as we are only interested in establishing whether a pattern can be discerned whereby we can ascertain if sacral kingship did exist in ancient Israel and is observable in the Old Testament and whether that can then be traced through to the New Testament. Most of the evidence for the latter two will be presented in the following chapters when we examine the three Jewish festivals and how they relate to our understanding of Jesus and his role. The section on the surrounding cultures offers only a generic view of sacral kingship based on those features which the cultures shared in common. To have presented all the evidence for sacral kingship in the surrounding cultures would not only have taken up so much space, it would also have proved tedious.[7] The main evidence for the surrounding cultures has been presented in my previous work. There are also numerous volumes on each ancient culture as well as on sacral kingship. The fact that in recent years there has been a move towards a greater understanding and acceptance of the existence and the important role that sacral kingship played in Israel and the fact that Israel was influenced by the cultures surrounding her, stands as further proof of this.[8] Our main concern is to draw out the salient features of sacral kingship so that we can identify them both in the Old Testament portrayal of the King and, that of the New Testament portrayal, thereby providing a framework for our understanding of Jesus' role as King. For ease of comparison I've presented the information under the headings of "The King," "Creation," "The New Year Festival," and, "The Temple" and looked at each of the areas under these headings. However, although our main concern in this chapter is to establish what sacral kingship looked like and whether it is evident in the Old and New Testaments, there are certain elements of kingship that are unique to the Old and New Testaments and are therefore not found in the surrounding cultures. Accordingly, we will also consider these briefly as we go along.

The important point to remember is that this doesn't change any part of the story or the belief system. What it does do, I believe, is

---

7. In effect it would have taken a whole book. This formed the bulk of my previous book which took sacral Kingship as the basis of proving that Jesus did fit into Jewish messianic categories, i.e demonstrating that he could have been the Messiah, even from a Jewish point of view, which as far as I am aware had not previously been demonstrated.

8. Idel, *Messianic Mystics*; Collins and Collins, *King and Messiah;* Eaton, *The Psalms.*

enhance our understanding; draws us into the mythology and allows us to become immersed in the imagery, to recognize the symbolism and to be touched in a more profound way by just who this Jesus is, so that when we acknowledge him in liturgy or song or when we read passages that declare that he is King of Kings, we actually understand what that means in all its fullness. It is similar to those well known optical illusions, when you look one way you see an old woman and, when you look the other way it's a beautiful girl. No trickery, no need even to turn it different ways. It's just a matter of training your eye to see it one particular way or another. One doesn't detract from the other and they both co-exist. This is how it is when we understand what we are looking for. It's not a case of twisting anything or adding or detracting from the New Testament, but just a matter of perception.

The King in the Surrounding Cultures

The cultures surrounding ancient Israel were not monotheistic; there was a high god and, his consort goddess and, their son, usually functioning as fertility god and a number of other gods with particular functions. In each culture the King either represented or was understood to be the earthly manifestation of the high god but also at times represented the fertility god, his son. In some cultures the King was divine at birth, in others this was the result of his function in the cultic ritual of the festivals, whereby he "became" divine as he was anointed and enthroned:

> The King stood at the apex of society, on the borderline of the divine dimension. His involvement in the royal *cultus* took him across this divide, so that he became divine in order to represent his people and, to acquire benefits on their behalf most effectively. He became a man again to bring these benefits down to earth. This capacity for transformation was probably understood to be instituted by the rite of unction [anointing] which took place only once, at or in relation to his installation.[9]

The King was also given the titles Shepherd or Good Shepherd, Chosen, Servant and, Son of God. In his identification with the god the King was "the breath of life" to his people and associated with the tree of life and life-giving water. In Egypt the King's *Ka* or life force was personified and worshipped as a god in its own right. The King also fulfilled the

9. Wyatt, *There's such Divinity*, 202

role of High Priest, particularly at the most important festival—the New Year Festival, a form of which took place in each of the cultures we are considering.

The King in the Old Testament

Here there is a Most High God (*El Elyon*) and his son Yahweh, the God of Israel. Creation, fertility[10] and, the giving or withholding of rain is associated with Yahweh, therefore suggesting he is in effect the fertility god.[11] Whilst there's nothing in the Old Testament to suggest that Yahweh had a consort goddess as in the surrounding cultures, Yahweh and, *Asherah*[12] have been linked in a recent archaeological find.[13] Nonetheless throughout the Old Testament there are images of God "marrying/being wedded to/being betrayed" but, this is always with his people Israel. Also mentioned are sons of God and angels whose names end in "*el*" the Hebrew word for God. Whilst the sons of God have been equated with angels, Heisler makes a case for them as distinct beings, as the different names for them suggest.[14] This is evident in Deut 32:8 where in the council of the gods, *El Elyon* allots the countries of the world to the sons of god, but Jacob (Israel) is allotted to Yahweh.[15] This is also evident in the book of Daniel. However throughout the scriptures, particularly in the Psalms,[16] whilst at times *El Elyon* and Yahweh appear independently,

---

10. Deut 11:13–15

11. Ps 65:9–13

12. Yahweh has also been linked with *Anat* (another name for *Asherah*) in a fifth-century BCE Jewish Aramaic papyri from Elephantine in Egypt. Day, *Yahweh and the Gods,* 144.

13. On an eighth century BC piece of pottery found in the Sinai desert at Kuntillet Ajrud there is an inscription asking for a blessing from Yahweh and his *Asherah*. The *Asherah* that the prophets denounce were in fact representations of a Canaanite goddess.

14. Sons of God are *benei elohim,* whereas angels are *malakhim* (literally messengers). This does not detract from Jesus' unique status as the only begotten Son and Heisler explains this. Heisler, *The Unseen Realm.*

15 This assembly of gods or sons of god is also evident in Job 1:6–12 and in Psalm 82.

16. Pss 7:17, 9:1–2, 21:7, 77:10–11, 83:18, 92:1–4. 2 Sam 7:8-17 is the promise that forms the basis of messianism.

at others they are spoken of in parallel[17] suggesting identification,[18] in other words there existed within Israel, the idea of a Father God and his Son, who were in some way *ehad* (one). The Rabbis were well aware of this seeming ambiguity that flew in the face of the strict monotheism that became the hallmark of Judaism (and Christianity—although Christianity's version of Father and Son plus the Holy Spirit is not accepted as monotheism within Judaism).[19] Nonetheless in the commentary on Genesis, *Genesis Rabbah*, the rabbis attempt to explain the different names of God as different functions and, what is particularly interesting from our perspective is that *El Elyon*, God Most High is equated with God's aspect of justice and, Yahweh with his aspect of mercy.[20]

The King is the LORD's[21] that is Yahweh's Anointed,[22] and, at his anointing and enthronement was understood to be the earthly manifestation of Yahweh. Anointing was understood to change the one anointed. It is linked with the endowment of Yahweh's Spirit and, apotheosis, that is becoming divine. Following his anointing Saul was 'turned into a different person' and, when David was anointed as King 'the spirit of Yahweh came mightily upon [him]'.[23] In Psalm 2, at his enthronement the King becomes God's son[24] and the father-son relationship between Yahweh and the King is evident elsewhere.[25] A close association between the King

17. Parallelism in the Old Testament is a device used to associate two ideas or persons together.

18. It's also widely acknowledged that Yahweh eventually took over the attributes of El the Canaanite God. Emerton, *Studies in the Pentateuch,* 99–100.

19. The Jewish prayer the *Shema* said thrice daily by Jewish men begins with the words *Shema Yisrael, adonai eloheinu adonai ehad*. 'Hear O Israel, the Lord our God, the Lord is one' *ehad*, the word quoted as the proof text against the Christian doctrine of the Trinity, is in fact the word used about the union of Adam and Eve, that is, as the Spice Girls so neatly put it "when two become one."

20. This is interesting because we will see in later chapters that Jesus is in fact Yahweh, the God of Israel, come to his Temple as Malachi prophesied (Mal 3:1).

21. LORD in the Old Testament translates the Hebrew Yahweh, the name of Israel's God.

22. Pss 2:2, 18:50, 20:6, 28:8, 89:38, 51 and 132:10.

23. 1 Sam 16:13.

24. Ps 2:6–7 Collins concludes that the Israelite enthronement ceremony was influenced by Egyptian sacral Kingship and concedes 'At least as a matter of court rhetoric, the King was declared to be the son of God, and could be called an *elohim*, a god. Collins, *King and Messiah*, 15. We will look at enthronement Psalms in the next section.

25. Pss 89:26–27; 110:1.

and God, which has been understood to hint at the divinity of the King is also evident in 1 Chron 28:5 which states that Solomon (David's son) has been chosen "to sit upon the throne of the kingdom of the LORD over Israel" and that Yahweh will be his father and Solomon his son and following his enthronement the whole assembly "bowed their head and prostrated themselves before the LORD and the King" 1 Chron 29:20. This is also evident in Psalms such as Ps 68:24–25. In the prophets we encounter a Servant figure who we will argue is a type of the King. As well as being designated Servant, like the King he is also God's Chosen One on whom his Spirit rests.[26] Elsewhere in the prophets we encounter "one like a Son of Man" who again functions in the role of the King, being given an everlasting Kingdom and dominion.[27]

Yahweh is the source of life giving water and the breath of life to his people and, because of his association with Yahweh the King is understood to be the one through whom all blessings flow from Yahweh to the people. The King is also entitled Shepherd,[28] Servant,[29] Chosen One[30]and, High Priest in the order of Melchizedek (Ps 110:4). Although in the Old Testament the Spirit is the breath of life,[31] there is no indication that the Spirit is worshipped, as was the case with the Pharaoh's *Ka* in Egypt, nonetheless there is evidence, right from the beginning in Genesis, of the Spirit[32] functioning in his own right.

As stated above, as well as having things in common with the surrounding cultures there are some features of the King unique to the Old Testament. For example, King David is the King par excellence and, it is from his line that the idealized anointed King, that is the Messiah is promised.[33] There are therefore a number of prophecies about a Davidic King: he will be born in Bethlehem, David's city (Mic 5:2,4), he will be from the stock of Jesse (that is David's father) and, the Spirit of the LORD will rest on him (Isa 11:1–2). He will be born of a virgin and he will be God manifest, that is *Immanuel* (God with us) Isa 7:14. His divinity is also

26. Isa 42:1.

27. Dan 7:14.

28. Ps 78:71.

29. Pss 89:20, 132;10. David is designated the LORD's servant 28 times in the Old Testament.

30. Ps 89:3.

31. Gen 2:7.

32. "and the Spirit of God was hovering over the waters." Gen 1:2.

33. Pss 89:24, 132:11.

expressed in another prophecy: "He will be called Wonderful counselor, Mighty God, Everlasting Father, Prince of Peace" and, he will reign on David's throne establishing justice and righteousness (Isa 9:6–7).[34]

The King in the New Testament

In the New Testament we also encounter a High God, *El Elyon* (the Most High God) and his son Yahweh. Jesus is not only identified with Yahweh[35] but also expressly identified as son of the Most High God (*El Elyon*).[36] Jesus in his identification with Yahweh is also therefore associated with creation, fertility and, rain but also here in the New Testament he is the author of the new creation (2 Cor 5:17) and the source of life giving water (John 7:37). There is a complete identification between Jesus (Son of God) and the Father as there was in the Old Testament.[37] Whilst there is no suggestion in the New Testament that Jesus had a consort, he is however the bridegroom[38] and the church is his bride.[39] Although angels feature in the New Testament, the term "sons of God" is applied to the followers of Jesus.[40] In the Old Testament we saw that Yahweh was the God of Israel and in John 1:11 it says that Jesus "came to what was his own and his own people did not accept him." He also said that he had come only "to the lost sheep of Israel" (Matt 15:24). Nonetheless, Jesus was also "a light for revelation to the Gentiles" (Luke 2:32); Israel was his first priority and it was Israel that was expecting the Messiah, the "Good Shepherd" but he had come that all men might be saved.

As in the Surrounding cultures and the Old Testament, the New Testament King (Jesus) is also the earthly manifestation of Yahweh, the God of Israel and, Son of the Most High God (*El Elyon*). He is also *the* Anointed (Christ) and at his baptism was anointed with the Holy Spirit

34. Each of these prophecies is understood to relate to the Messiah and can be found in the *Targumim*.

35. There are a number of instances of a Yahweh/Jesus identification which we will look at this more closely in the next chapter. See also the note on *kyrie* below.

36. Mark 5:7, Luke 1:32.

37. 'Whoever has seen me has seen the Father.' John 14:9. "Believe me that I am in the Father and the Father is in me." John 14:11.

38. Matt 9:14–15, Mark 2:18–20, Luke 5:33–35, John 3:29.

39. 2 Cor 11:2, Rev 22:17.

40. Luke 6:35, 20:36; John 1:12; Rom 8:14, 16; 9:26, Gal 3:26, 4:6, 2 Cor 6:18, 1 John 3:1, 2.

where he was proclaimed by God as his Son, just as the Kings in ancient Israel were anointed at their enthronement and proclaimed by God to be his Son (Ps 2:7). In 1 Chron 29:20 we saw that the whole assembly bowed before the LORD and, the King. In the New Testament it says that "every knee shall bow, in heaven and on earth and under the earth" before Jesus, the Lord[41] and King. Jesus' titles include Good Shepherd, Servant, Chosen One, High Priest in the order of Melchizedek and, Son of Man. He is the source of living water and the breath of life.[42] He is also the one through whom all blessings flow to the people (Eph 1:3) and here, as in the Old Testament the Spirit is spoken of as a separate person and functions in his own right (John 14:26).

We saw specific prophecies of the Messianic King in the Old Testament and each of these are fulfilled by Jesus in the New Testament, further strengthening his identification as King. When the Magi are searching for the King of the Jews, they are told that he will be born in "Bethlehem in Judea" and that this is in accordance with the Micah5:2, 4 Scripture. This is just after we have been told that Jesus was born "in Bethlehem in Judea" (Matt 2:1), that is David's city. Joseph is also told by an angel of the Lord, that Jesus' birth would fulfill the Isa 7:14 prophecy of a child being born of a virgin who will be Immanuel "God with us." In Luke 1:26–33 we are told Mary is a virgin who will give birth to Jesus, the Son of the Most High, that is God. Joseph is from the line of David as is Mary thus fulfilling the Isa 11:1–2 prophecy that the King will be "from the stock of Jesse." In the New Testament therefore Jesus is presented as the Messianic King which is further endorsed in the title of Christ attributed to him throughout, that is Anointed.

We have established, therefore, a very brief outline of what the person of the King looked like in the surrounding cultures and, found that those features were also to be found in the Old Testament and in the New Testament. In this next section we will look at the *role* of the King, in the surrounding cultures, in the Old Testament and in the New Testament. However in order to do that we need to first familiarize ourselves with the creation narratives of each of them in order to understand, what the function of the King was, because as stated earlier, one of the main functions of the King was his role as High Priest in the cult, at the New Year

---

41. In the New Testament 'Lord' is the translation of the Greek word *kyrie*, which in the Septuagint (the Greek translation of the Old Testament) translates Yahweh.

42. John1:4, 20:22.

Enthronement festival which was understood to recapitulate the conditions of creation and, thereby bring them about once again.

Creation in the Surrounding Cultures

The importance of the New Year festival lies in its connection with the
creation myth of the culture. The creation stories vary, but there are identifiable common features, these are:

- The chief god battling with the forces of Chaos
- the forces of Chaos depicted as either the cosmic sea, a dragon or
  huge sea monster
- these are often identified with the physical enemies of the culture.
- the earth being created following the god overcoming the forces of
  Chaos
- creation taking place on the primeval hill where a Temple is built
- humanity being created
- the god resting in the Temple.

All of these are visible in the *Enuma Elish*, the Babylonian creation
narrative, written in 11th century BC which will serve as an example.
This details the cosmic conflict which takes place between the gods Tia-
mat personified as the primeval ocean and *Kingu Marduk*, a younger god
kills them both and creates the universe by splitting Tiamat's body in two.
Marduk then becomes the chief deity 'Lord' and 'King' and, sits on his
throne. The Temple-city of Babylon is created and, a great feast is held at
Esagil in order to dedicate the new Temple in which Marduk then rests.
Humanity is created from the blood vessels of *Kingu* to serve the Gods.
The *Enuma Elish* was recited at the New Year festival, confirming the link
between the New Year festival and the original creation myth.

Creation in the Old Testament

The creation story in Genesis begins with the earth being covered with
water (the deep/*tehom*).[43] God separates the waters as a prelude to the

43. Gen1:2 the etymological similarity has been noted between *Tehom* and *Tiamat*
the Babylonian Goddess whose body was split and used to create the cosmos.

rest of creation.[44] However the idea that the waters had to be subdued before creation began is more clearly evident in Job[45] and in a number of Psalms such as Ps 74:12–17.[46]

> Yet God my King is from of old,
>
> working salvation in the earth
>
> You divided the sea by your might;
>
> you broke the heads of the dragons in the waters.
>
> You crushed the heads of Leviathan . . .
>
> You established the sun and moon.
>
> It was you who set all the boundaries of the earth;
>
> you made both summer and winter.

Here God in his role as Creator is expressly identified as King and, as a prelude to his act of creation he defeats the Chaos waters which are identified with Leviathan/the dragons in the waters.[47] The Chaos waters are also identified as *Rahab* and associated with the Pharaoh and Egypt.[48] The Exodus is therefore understood as a recapitulation of the original creation story as is the story of the Flood. The word used to describe the water that overcomes the Egyptian chariots and the waters of the flood *Tehom*, is also the word used to describe the waters in Gen 1:1, suggesting that they all represent the same phenomenon, that is the Chaos waters and evil. In later Rabbinic literature Moses is cast in the role of King and, in the Book of Jubilees, Noah functions as priest with both stories exhibiting the link between creation and salvation that we will explore further in the following chapters. It also demonstrates that the *chaoskampf* (struggle with the Chaos waters) is the major theme that runs throughout the Old Testament. Leviathan is also associated with the Serpent. "In that day the LORD will punish with his sword, his fierce, great and, powerful sword Leviathan the gliding serpent, Leviathan the twisting serpent, and he will

---

44. Gen 1:6.

45. Here Yahweh describes his acts of creation and asks Job: 'Who shut up the sea behind doors when it burst forth from the womb and when I said 'This far you may come and no farther; here is where your proud waves halt. Job 38:8–11. See also Job 26:12.

46. See also Pss 89:9–12, 93:1–4,104:5–7,10–30.

47. These are many headed, like the beasts from the sea in Daniel 7:6 (and also Revelation 13:1). A Babylonian myth has the chaos dragon as 7 headed.

48. See also Job 26.12, Ps 89:10.

slay the dragon that is in the sea."[49] There is therefore an eschatological element to the creation story, God defeated the chaos waters/serpent/dragon that is the forces of evil at creation and he will defeat them again "on that day," a term which is used to describe the Day of the Lord when he will come to finally defeat Chaos/evil once and for all.

Whereas in the surrounding cultures human beings were created for the sole purpose of working for the gods, here humanity is the pinnacle of creation, created in the image of God (*betselem*). "In biblical texts *tselem* is usually a cult statue, an idol of a god."[50] So that "humanity is created to function as the creator god's statue, his living, breathing idol."[51] Therefore accordingly Gen 1:26–27 can be rendered "Let us make man in the place of our image . . . And created the Adam in the place of his statue, instead of God's idol he created him . . . '[52] Fletcher-Louis comments: "Again, according to Genesis 1, false idolatry is a tragedy—it entails a denial of humanity's vocation and privilege to be and act on behalf of God himself."[53] Nonetheless, Adam *is* given work to do (he is directed to look after the garden) however the Hebrew verbs used here, when they are used elsewhere in the Old Testament are associated with the priesthood.[54] God's command to Adam has also been identified as a royal fiat so that Adam in effect is set on earth in a royal priestly role.

Having overcome the waters of Chaos, following his act of creation, God rests in his Temple (the cosmos) on the seventh day. However, that's not the end of the story. The forces of Chaos, in the form of the Serpent rise up again and "defeat" Adam. As a consequence fertility is compromised—childbirth will be painful, the earth which was pronounced "good" as a consequence of God overcoming the forces of Chaos is now cursed, producing thorns and thistles. Adam is barred from the fertile

49. Isa 27:1. Further allusions to Leviathan/sea monster/dragon are found in. Job 3:8, 7:12, 41:1–34.

50. He gives the following examples, Num 33:52; 1 Sam 6:5; 2 Kgs 11:18; Ezek 7:20; 16:17; Amos 5:26; Dan 2:31, 32, 34. Fletcher-Louis, *Further Reflections*. 3.

51. Fletcher-Louis, *Further Reflections*, 3.

52. Fletcher-Louis, *Further Reflections*, 4

53. Fletcher-Louis, *Further Reflections*, 4.

54. 'Adam had been the original anointed high priest in the Temple of creation. He had been set in the garden to *till it and keep it* (Gen 2.15), and the tree of life had been intended as his food. 'Till it and keep it' are Temple words. 'Till' translates the word used for Temple liturgy, and 'keep' means 'guard' in the sense of preserving. Adam the high priest was set to serve and preserve the creation'. Barker, *Adam the High Priest*.

Garden of Eden and God tells Adam that food can now only be obtained "by the sweat of your face."[55] In the Old Testament therefore we have:

- The chief God battling with the forces of Chaos
- the forces of Chaos depicted as either the cosmic sea or a dragon or huge sea monster
- the earth being created following the God overcoming the forces of Chaos
- creation taking place on the primeval hill where a Temple was built
- humanity being created
- the God resting in the Temple.
- the forces of Chaos threatening to take over again.

Creation in the New Testament

The creation story of the New Testament is that of the old; the account in Genesis is implicitly accepted. Jesus himself refers to it[56] as does Paul.[57] Nonetheless here we learn that Jesus also participated in creation. John's gospel begins with the words "*en arche,*" "in the beginning," the same words that open Gen 1:1 in the Septuagint, the Greek translation of the Old Testament. In Genesis we learned that God spoke the world into being and here in the New Testament we learn that Jesus is the Word and that everything was made through Him. "In the beginning was the Word and the Word was with God and the Word was God. He was with God in the beginning. Through him all things were made; without him nothing was made that has been made."[58] The idea that everything was created through Jesus is also reiterated in John 1:10 and, in Col 1:15 Jesus is called "the firstborn over all creation. For in him all things were created . . . all things have been created through him and for him." Whether this means all things were made through him (as in from him) as with *Tiamat* in the *Enuma Elish* is uncertain, however Rev 13:8 could be read in that way.

---

55. Gen 3:19.

56. Matt 19:4–5

57. Rom 5:15–18

58. Jesus is also called 'the author of life' (Acts 3:15).

In the New Testament the King is not just associated with the creator God, but he is the earthly incarnation of the creator God. "The Word became flesh and made his dwelling among us," that is "God with us" further confirmation that he has fulfilled the Immanuel prophecy of Is7:14 concerning the King. In this expanded creation account in John 1, Jesus is called "the light of the people," fulfilling another of the Isaiah prophecies about the coming King: "The people walking in darkness have seen a great light on those living in the land of deep darkness a light has dawned."[59] In the Genesis creation account God said "let there be light" and he separated the dark from the light and that was Day One. This is before the creation of the heavenly lights, the sun, moon and, stars and, therefore, it has been suggested, must represent something else.[60] We also encounter the idea that we saw in the surrounding cultures that as King/God he is the apex of the cosmos "He is before all things and in him all things hold together."[61]

In the creation myth of the surrounding cultures and the Old Testament God overcame the forces of Chaos, which was re-enacted with the King "as" God in the New Year Festival. In the New Testament the King who is also God/Son of God not only demonstrates his mastery over the waters by walking on them and stilling them, the waters are also identified with the forces of evil.[62] Jesus is anointed at his baptism with the Holy Spirit and it's from this point that he takes up his role as Anointed King, that is Messiah, with the words from Psalm 2, used at the New Year festival and spoken to the King, here spoken directly to Jesus, the King by God: "Just as Jesus was coming up out of the water, he saw heaven being torn open and the Spirit descending on him like a dove. And a voice

---

59. Isa 9:2.

60. This has been amply illustrated by Margaret Barker: " . . . Day One is the state of unity concealed at the heart of the Temple, concealed within the creation. It was known as "eternity," which in Hebrew is the same as 'the hidden place.' The Holy of Holies represented this state, concealed from most human eyes by the great veil of the Temple which symbolized matter." Barker, *Creation Theology*, 3.

61. According to Rashi, an important Jewish commentator the word spoken at creation was in fact the Tetragrammaton, that is Yahweh and we saw above that Jesus is equated with Yahweh and Jesus is the Word (John1:1).

62. In Mark4:39, Jesus uses a word from the same root *phimos* (to muzzle) to quieten the storm as he used in Mark1:25 to quiet the evil spirit possessing the man in the Synagogue further strengthening the idea that the waters he controls are the chaos waters/forces of evil which also confirms the Jesus/Yahweh/David connection. David has mastery over the waters in Ps89:25.

came from heaven: 'You are my Son, whom I love; with you I am well pleased."[63] His baptism, when he became *the* Anointed foreshadowing his final battle with the forces of Chaos at the New Year festival,[64] before his act of creation.[65]

We saw in the surrounding cultures that the Chaos waters as the adversary of the King/god were also associated with a dragon and in the Old Testament with Leviathan and a serpent. In Gen 3:15 God tells the serpent that Eve's seed/offspring will crush his head. The serpent here traditionally is associated with Satan and this passage known as the *protoevangelium*, that is the first gospel, because the "seed" is understood to be Jesus. Satan is also identified as a "great dragon, that ancient Serpent" in Rev 12.9 and identified as Jesus' adversary in Luke 4:1–2.

In the Old Testament we saw that Chaos/evil was also associated with physical enemies (Egypt/Pharaoh) and both Jesus[66] and John the Baptist link the scribes and Pharisees, who oppose Jesus with serpents.[67] Jesus also expressly links them with the devil in John 8:44.[68] Although it was the Romans who actually crucified Jesus, it was the chief priests and "the teachers of the law," that is the scribes and Pharisees that called for Jesus' death. Jesus is the "last Adam" who reverses the effects of the fall of the first Adam, and just as Adam was made in the image of God, the new creation bears the image of Jesus (2 Cor 3:18). Also in his act of reversal the thorns that grew up as a result of Adam's fall are worn as the crown of the King by the Second Adam.

---

63. In Ps 2:7 the "One who is enthroned in heaven' says of his Anointed 'I have installed my King on Zion, my holy mountain' and he says to him: 'You are my son, today I have become your father.'"

64. Passover takes place in the Spring in the first month of the year, Nissan.

65. 2 Cor 5:17.

66. "You brood of vipers. How can you who are evil say anything good?" (Matt 12:34) and again in Matt 23:33 "You snakes! You brood of vipers!'"

67. You brood of vipers! Who warned you to flee from the coming wrath?' (Matt 3:7).

68. We need to be careful here though that this is not understood as Christian supersessionism, Jesus is not speaking against his own faith (this is clear in Matt 23:1–3). He is speaking against the hypocrisy, which is clear from the rest of the passage Matt 23:4–39.

New Year Festival in the Surrounding Cultures

The New Year festivals would occur either annually or twice a year in the spring and the autumn, the times of possible agricultural crisis when current crops were harvested, new seeds sown and, the rains were depended upon. The times when it was believed that the forces of Chaos threatened to overwhelm the earth again and undo creation. The coronation of new Kings always took place at the New Year festival. The fact that the creation narrative of the cultures were read out as a feature of the New Year festivals indicates the connection between the two—that is, the New Year Festival was a "reenactment" of the original act of creation. It was however much more than this—it was understood that through the myth and ritual of the festival, the same conditions as that of the original creation would be brought about again.

Although the New Year festivals differed across the cultures there were several shared main features, these included the King "as" the God: being anointed, suffering humiliation, undergoing a 'mock battle' with the forces of Chaos,[69] "dying," being raised up again, being enthroned and in some cultures this also involved a sacred marriage[70] between the King/ Queen (that is the god/goddess).The King not only represented the god, but also corporately represented the people and as such the humiliation and/or "death" of the King was understood to atone for the land and the people.[71] There were other elements which featured in some of the cultures, in Mesopotamia for example, the King's humiliation involved the removal of his crown and insignia, following which he would be slapped across the face. This was understood to constitute a liminal period in which the natural order of things was reversed, that is the King temporarily lost his power and status and Chaos threatened.[72] The festival often involved crossing over water, representing the cosmic/Chaos waters. As a result of these rituals including his anointing and enthronement, the King's enemies were said to be 'under his feet," the rains and harvest would be "guaranteed," the earth would be created anew—re-created,

---

69. Depicted as the waters of Chaos/a dragon/ a sea monster as well as the country's physical enemies.

70. In some of the cultures the goddess was also prominent, as in the case of the Hittite sun goddess *Arinna*, also entitled Queen of Heaven and Earth.

71. Mowinckel, *He that Cometh*, 38–39.

72. Representing a space in time where heaven and earth are close together for a short period, much in the same way that a "thin" place does in celtic thinking.

order (*ma'at*) was restored, the people's physical needs were met and prisoners were released. As a hymn for Egypt illustrates: "They that hungered
are satisfied and happy, they that thirsted are drunken, they that were
naked are clad in fine linen, they that were in prison are set free and he
that is in bonds is filled with joy." [73]

Ma'at, right order however, encompassed more than physical elements, the moral, spiritual and physical were all bound together. "The
purely secular—in so far as it could be granted to exist at all—was the
purely trivial." [74] *Hammurapi*, the Mesopotamian King at his enthronement in the New Year Festival is entreated by the Gods *Anu* and *Enlil*
to "cause justice to shine in the land, to destroy the wicked and the evil,
that the strong oppress not the weak, to conduct the people, make the
land enjoy righteousness, rightly to conduct orphan and widow, rightly
to conduct the oppressed." [75]

The King therefore was understood to be the god manifest on earth,
but at times represented the son of the god. He was anointed and through
the rituals of the New Year festival he atoned for the sins of the people.
Through his humiliation, death, raising up, enthronement and sacred
marriage, he recapitulated annually what the god had done at creation,
overcoming the forces of Chaos and ensuring that right order was restored and as result the life-giving rains would come and the harvest
would be ensured, the earth re-created including the regeneration of
morality and social justice. Thus in Egypt: "The King is himself *ma'at, he
is* the cosmic law . . . " [76]

New Year Festival in the Old Testament

Although the major New Year Enthronement festival in Israel was in the
autumn, and formed part of the celebrations, elements of this festival are
to be found in two of the other major festivals which came to prominence
post-exile, that is Day of Atonement and Passover. We will look at these
as well as *Sukkoth* in much closer detail in the following chapters and
how they impact on our understanding of the role of the Messiah in the

---

73. Engnell, *Studies in Divine Kingship*,14.

74. Frankfort, *Kingship,* 3.

75. Engnell, *Studies*, 41

76. Mowinckel, *He that Cometh*, 93. *Ma'at is* the also personified as the goddess
of justice.

New Testament. However here we will simply look briefly at whether a New Year Enthronement festival similar to that in the surrounding cultures can be identified from the evidence in the Old Testament. What we are considering here therefore is the pre-exilic New Year Enthronement festival which took place in the autumn. Let's just remind ourselves why we need to prove this—if we find that sacral kingship did exist in Israel and that there was an enthronement festival, it will, as stated earlier, provide us with a framework which will enable us to understand Kingship in the New Testament and be able to form a better picture of who Jesus is and what he came to achieve.

We have already noted that opinion is still divided on the existence of an autumnal enthronement festival in Israel, but more recent scholarship is leaning towards this being a reality, as Brunson states: "In this regard it would do well to recognize that lack of imagination in historical research may distort results no less than unrestrained speculation does." His conclusion therefore is: "It is probable that the autumn festival included a central role for the King in the cult, and was characterized by a celebration of kingship, both that of Yahweh and his vice-regent, the Davidic King. It is not implausible that the festival included an enthronement ceremony for the King. Even though speculative, it is possible that the King participated in a ritual battle, humiliation and reconsecration."[77] Whilst this may be said through gritted teeth (it has not been popular in academic circles to admit this), the evidence I believe is overwhelming and this is for the most part found in the Psalms, the cultic setting for which has long been acknowledged: "The Psalms are littered with cultic allusions, which only make sense if they were used in public worship in the Temple in Jerusalem."[78] This is corroborated by later Jewish tradition. The enthronement festival was also understood to be a covenant renewal festival.

A number of Psalms are considered to be enthronement Psalms used at this ceremony, specifically Pss 47, 93–100, 145, although there are many more. In these we see the King (who is also High Priest)[79] undergo various forms of suffering[80] or humiliation,[81] being overcome by the

---

77. Brunson, *Psalm 118 in the Gospel of John,* 33–34.

78. Day, *Psalms,* 15.

79. Ps 110:4.

80. Pss 86:7; 102.2.

81. Ps 69:7.

Chaos waters,[82] in others he is mocked by his enemies[83] or pursued by them.[84] Often these are spoken of in parallel suggesting their association. In Psalm 69 for example the King cries out:

> Let me be delivered from my enemies
>
> and from the deep waters
>
> Do not let the flood sweep over me
>
> Or the deep swallow me up
>
> Or the pit close its mouth over me[85]

In some he talks of his life coming to an end,[86] following which he is raised up[87] and enthroned,[88] with his enemies under his feet.[89]

It is interesting that prior to the new wave of scholars who accept sacral kingship, it had often proved difficult to determine a historical setting for these Psalms as Longman illustrates: 'We are somewhat at a loss to understand exactly what kind of historical background generated such a thought.'[90] Indeed. What seems much more likely, is that they do in fact represent the same phenomenon as in the surrounding cultures—that they form part of the autumnal New Year Enthronement festival.[91] As in the surrounding cultures the ritual is linked to the original creation story and the battle with the Chaos waters:

> O LORD God of hosts,
>
> who is as mighty as you, O LORD?
>
> You rule the raging of the sea;
>
> when its waves rise you still them.
>
> You crushed *Rahab* like a carcass;
>
> you scattered your enemies with your mighty arm.
>
> The heavens are yours, the earth also is yours;

82. Pss 18:4–6; 69:1–2.

83. Pss 22:7–8; 69:7,19; 89:51.

84. Pss 3:1; 7:1–2: 17:8–12; 56:1; 59:1; 64:1;are just a few.

85. Ps69:14–15.

86. Pss 30:3; 88:3–5.

87. Pss 18:16–17; 30:1–3; 40:2; 144:7.

88. Pss 2:6; 110:1.

89. Pss 47:3; 110:1.

90. Longman II, "The Messiah," 18.

91 See Eaton, *The Psalms*, 65 and Collins and Collins, *King and Messiah*, 12 who also identify this.

the world and all that is in it—you have founded them.[92]

The Psalms were used in the Temple and therefore, as in the surrounding cultures the creation narrative is spoken at the new near festivals. At *Sukkoth* and Passover, the *Hallel* are recited, a block of Psalms comprising Pss113–118 that also contain a number of these themes. Parallels between the King and Yahweh also suggest that following his enthronement the King 'is' Yahweh manifest.[93] As we saw with the person of the King, there are also elements within the King's role that are found in the Psalms that are specific to Israel but which we will see are also found in the role of the King in the New Testament:

- he is protected by God[94]
- he is betrayed by his friend "[95]
- he is silent during his suffering[96]
- he is mocked by his enemies[97]
- his hands and feet are pierced[98]
- he is given vinegar to drink
- he is abandoned by God[99]
- none of his bones are broken[100]

Although the element of atonement is not a major feature of the Psalms, it is evident in Psalm 65. It is however more prominent in the prophets. In the following chapter we will look at the Servant figure in Second Isaiah, who is a "type" of the King and whose suffering, death and exaltation very closely resemble that of the King. In chapter 4 we will also

92. Ps 89:8–11

93. See for example Ps 98:6 "with trumpets and the sound of the horn make a joyful noise before the King, the LORD."

94. "For he will give his angels charge over you, to guard you in all your ways. On their hands they will bear you up, lest you dash your foot against a stone." Ps 91:11–12.

95. "Even my bosom friend in whom I trusted, who ate of my bread, has lifted the heel against me" Ps 41:9.

96. Pss 39:2, 9.

97. "Commit your cause to the LORD; let him deliver - let him rescue the one in whom he delights." Ps 22:8.

98. Ps22:16.

99. "My God, my God, why have you abandoned me." (Ps 22:1). See also Ps 43:2.

100. Ps34:20.

consider the Son of Man figure, particularly found in the book of Daniel and how the role of this figure also resembles the role of the King.

There is no hard evidence of a sacred marriage within the Psalms,[101] nonetheless, the building of a *sukkah* has been associated with the sacred grove of the surrounding cultures which is associated with the *hierogamy*[102] and it is interesting to speculate whether this motif lies behind the continuing practice of Jewish weddings being conducted under a *chuppah*.[103]

Although the building of a *sukkah* is naturally associated with the festival of *Sukkoth* which follows on from new year and Day of Atonement, doubt has been cast on the traditional reasons given for this, that it is to commemorate Israel living in "booths" i.e *Sukkoth* during the Exodus as in fact they would have lived in tents. The idea that this was a temporary dwelling of course could just be the intention. However, the fact that these are made of 4 specific species of vegetation, all of which are connected to water and fertility, might also suggest that this may have originally been associated with a sacred marriage. At *Yom Kippur*, part of the autumn festival, young girls went out into the fields so that they could be chosen as a bride.[104]

The outcome of the ritual was that the covenant had been renewed.[105] The people "sing a new song"[106] in thanksgiving for these new conditions. Rains[107] and harvest[108] are "guaranteed," the earth renewed, "re-created."

> By your strength you established the mountains. . .
> You silence the roaring of the seas,

101. Psalm 45 may prove an exception as the King is also called God and it is understood as a wedding psalm.

102. That is sacred marriage between the King/Queen representing the God/Goddess which is thought to ensure fertility of crops etc.

103. The *chuppah* is constructed by the groom and the groom is greeted with the words 'Blessed be he that comes in the name of the Lord" that is the traditional greeting given to the coming King. Throughout the ceremony the blessings recited celebrate the Kingship of God and his role as creator. The *ketubah*, that is the covenant between the couple is read out and the connection with the *sukkah*/Temple is made as the smashing of a glass commemorates the destruction of the Temple. The ensuing *yihud* of the couple ensures the continued fertility of Israel.

104. *m. Ta'anith* 4:8.

105. See Kraus, *Worship in Israel* and Weiser, *The Psalms*.

106. Pss 33:3; 40:3; 96:1; 98:1; 144:9; 149:1.

107. Pss 65:9–10; 68:7–9; 72:6; 107:35–36;147:8.

108. Pss 65:11–13; 67:6, 104:10–28, 144:12–15.

> the roaring of the waves. . .
> You visit the earth and water it
> you greatly enrich it. . ..
> you provide the people with grain. . .
> the pastures of the wilderness overflow. . .
> the meadows clothe themselves with flocks.
> the valleys deck themselves with grain"[109]

Judgement and justice are a further consequence: "Give the King your justice, O God."[110] The term used here *mishpat*[111] incorporates the idea that order has been restored and this includes physical needs being met: the blind are healed,[112] the poor are helped[113] orphans and widows looked after,[114] there is freedom from oppression[115] and prisoners set free.[116] It is the King who is the channel of these blessings from/'as' Yahweh.[117]

New Year Festival in the New Testament

Spring and autumn were both associated with the new year and in the New Testament the trial, death, raising up and enthronement of the King are associated not only with the spring festival of Passover but also with the autumnal festivals of Day of Atonement and *Sukkoth*. We will look at precisely what form this association takes in the following chapters which will each be dedicated to one of those festivals and how they relate to Jesus, but here we just want to outline how Jesus' death and resurrection, as well as other points in his life and ministry also fitted into the same framework of sacral kingship, exactly like the King in the Old Testament. We have established earlier that in the New Testament Jesus is called "the Anointed" (Christ), he is announced at his birth as King and is tried

109. Ps 65:6–13.

110. Ps 72:1.

111. This occurs approximately 64 times in the Psalms, meaning justice, judgement and ordinance.

112. Ps 146:8.

113. Pss 74:21; 107:41; 109:31; 132:15; 140:12.

114. Pss 10:14; 146:9.

115. Ps 10:18.

116. Ps 146:7.

117. Ps 72:1.

and crucified as "King of the Jews." Jesus' death took place at Passover (although elements of *Sukkoth* are noted) both of which are New Year festivals associated with a particular harvest and the early and late rains.

At his temptation the devil quotes Ps 91:11–12 to Jesus, which we saw was quoted to the King. Prior to his death Jesus was betrayed by one of his disciples Judas, who had just shared bread with him (Mark 14:17–20). At his trial he remains silent (Mark 15:5). He was spit on, slapped and humiliated in the same manner as the Servant which we will see in the following chapter is a "type" of the King. He is mocked: "He trusts in God - let God deliver him now . . . "(Matt 27:43). Lots are cast for his clothing (Mark 15:24). He is given vinegar to drink (Mark15:23). At his crucifixion his hands and feet are pierced (Luke 23:33). He feels abandoned by God "My God my God why have you abandoned me" (Mt27:46). None of his bones are broken (John 19:33–37). Each of these was also said of the King in the Old Testament. Jesus' face is slapped and a "crown" and "royal clothing" are put on him and then removed (John 19:1–4; Matt 27:31) which is reminiscent of what happened in the Meso-potamian ceremony, and like that, constitutes a liminal period where the natural order is reversed—the King of Kings is subject to his creation, in a temporary "loss of power" when the forces of Chaos threatened to overcome him. Therefore like the King in the Psalms and the surround-ing cultures, Jesus is mocked and humiliated, dies, rises up again and following his ascension is enthroned at the right hand side of God with his enemies under his feet.

In the Old Testament creation narrative, Adam's disobedience breaks the covenant and causes the fall, as a result of which "creation was subjected to frustration"[118] and "the whole earth has been groaning as in the pains of childbirth."[119] In the New Testament it is Jesus' obedience (to death on the cross) that reverses the fall.[120] The thorns that spring up as the result of Adam's actions Gen 3:18 become the crown that Jesus wears as King in his act of reversal, before the new creation.

The result of his death was atonement (1John 2:2), the renewal of the covenant (Heb 9:15), new creation (2 Cor 5:17; Gal 6:15) life-giving water (John 4:10; John7:38), harvest (Matt 3:12), judgement (John 5:22) and justice (*mishpat*) in the form of healing (Matt 4:23), freedom from

118. Rom 8:20.

119. Rom 8:22.

120. Rom 5:12–17.

oppression, relief for the poor, widows and orphans helped and, prisoners set free. All of the conditions that Jesus said he had come to fulfill when he read out of the Isaiah scroll at the beginning of his ministry (Luke 4:16–21):"The Spirit of the Lord is upon me because he has anointed me to bring good news to the poor. He has sent me to proclaim release to the captives and recovery of sight to the blind, to set the oppressed free, to proclaim the year of the Lord's favor." As the Anointed King and High Priest Jesus was the channel of these blessings for his people and as a result they sang a new song.[121] As in the Old Testament, there is an eschatological element to the creation story in that there will be a new heaven and a new earth and a new Jerusalem and a final defeat of the forces of Chaos (Rev 20:10) "there will be no longer any sea" (Rev 21:1) and a final new song.[122] Similarly, as in the surrounding cultures and the Old Testament, there is a sacred marriage—the bridegroom[123] will return for his bride,[124] be united with her[125]and take her to the wedding feast.[126]

The Temple in the Surrounding Cultures

A feature of both the creation narrative and the New Year Festival was the building of a Temple. Following the act of creation the god built a Temple to rest in. At the New Year Festival either a reed hut was constructed or a Temple which had already been built would be dedicated. Therefore the King as "god" re-enacts what took place at creation and thereby replicates it. The Temple (or reed hut) in turn represented the cosmos, and the god[127] resting in his Temple following his act of creation was the god resting in his creation.

"In the ancient world the rest of gods was always in a Temple; in fact, Temples were built with the purpose of deity resting in them. This rest of the gods often involved their taking control of the cosmos. A god could rest because order had been achieved and everything was ready to run smoothly. Deities ran the cosmos from their Temple. When stability

121. Phil 2:6–11.
122. Rev 14:3.
123. John 3:29.
124. Eph 5:27; Rev 21:9; Rev 22:17.
125. 2 Cor 11:2; Rev 19:7
126. Matt 22:2; Rev19:9
127. Often this took the form of an idol that represented the God.

had been assured, the regular daily business could be carried out without interruption."[128]

The Temple in the Old Testament

In the Old Testament creation story, like those of the surrounding cultures, God creates, following his subduing of the Chaos waters, and rests in his Temple. In the original creation story this is the cosmos,[129] in the Exodus story, which in itself is a new creation story, it is the Tabernacle where God rested which is also modeled on creation as we'll see below. Later it was the Temple in Jerusalem, built on the primeval hill[130] which is also understood to be the place where creation took place,[131] where God rested. "The Temple was a model of the creation, and the liturgy of the Temple preserved the creation. Genesis 1 was not an account of the historical process of creation, but a record of the great vision granted to Moses and others of how the world is made. In the six days when Moses was on Sinai, before the LORD called to him (Exod 24:16), he saw the six days of creation, and was then told to replicate these when he built the tabernacle."[132]

In Temple symbolism then the Holy of Holies was Day One, the source of light of Gen 1:3–5. Each of the ensuing days represent a part of the Temple. The veil representing Day Two, that is the vault that separated the heavens from the earth and the "the table with bread, wine and incense was the third day, when the plants were created. The seven branched lamp represented the lights of heaven created on the fourth day, the altar of sacrifice represented the non human creatures, and the High Priest was the human, male and female as the image of God."[133]

128 Walton, *Creation in Genesis 1:1–2:3*, 60–61.

129. There is a complete correspondence between the cosmos, the Tabernacle and the Temple which we will consider below.

130. There is some speculation about whether the Temple is built on Mt Moriah or Mt Zion but topologically now, both form part of the mountain ridge on which Jerusalem is built.

131. The same idea prevails in Israel as in the surrounding cultures, that the land of the nation in question was understood to be the centre of the earth both physically and metaphorically. The *even shetiyah* (foundation stone) lies underneath the altar in the original Temple and as its name implies was understood to be the foundation stone of the world. We will look at this further below and also in the next chapter.

132. Barker, *Creation Theology*, 2.

133. Barker, *Creation Theology*, 3.

The correspondence between the Temple and creation is also suggested in the fact that Eden is aligned with the Holy of Holies where God dwells, with the Garden of Eden attached to it as was the case in the ancient Near Eastern palaces.[134] The Garden therefore corresponds to the Holy place in the Temple where the Menorah stands, which has also been associated with the Tree of Life and the Bread of the Presence associated with Adam's food in the garden.[135] This is interesting as the Bread of the Presence was the food of the priests and Adam was understood as we saw above as High Priest. Furthermore Eden, the dwelling place of God is the source of the river flowing into the Garden, just as in Ezek 47:1 water was expected to flow from under the Holy of Holies, the dwelling place of God in the future eschatological Temple and in Rev 22:1–2 the river of the water of life flows from the throne of God and of the Lamb.[136] God walks back and forth (using a form of *hlk*) in Eden, which is also how God's presence is described in the tabernacle in Leviticus 26:12 and Deuteronomy 23:14.[137]

"From the idea that the Temple was considered a mini cosmos it is easy to move to the idea that the cosmos could be viewed as a Temple."[138] Therefore when we read that God rested from his work of creation, he is in fact resting in his Temple, that is the earth, as was the case in the ancient near east. The association of rest and Temple is also evident in God's choice of Solomon as the one to build the Temple. God says to David: "But you will have a son who will be a man of peace and rest, and I will give him rest from all his enemies on every side. His name will be Solomon and I will grant Israel peace and quiet during his reign."[139]

The Temple in effect represented the world and this idea is evident in other Jewish sources[140] Josephus, writing in the first century CE de-

---

134. In the Book of Jubilees 8:19 it says that Noah knew that the Garden of Eden was the Holy of Holies.

135. Garden symbolism is evident in the decorations of the Temple. 1 Kgs 6:18, 29, 32, 35 and 1 Kgs 7:18–20.

136. Beale, *Temple and the Church's Mission*, 74–75.

137 Morrow, *Creation as Temple-Building*, 10.

138. Walton, *The Lost World*, 7.

139. 1Chron 22:9. Solomon sounds like and may be derived from Hebrew word for peace, *shalom*.

140. Josephus describes the Temple in three different sections, two corresponding to the land and the sea and the third section corresponding to heaven. Josephus, *Ant*.3.7.7.

scribes the different parts of the Temple as "representing" the different parts of the earth. It is in this context that the liturgy of the Temple was understood to maintain the cosmos. We will look at this in much more detail in chapter 4 when we consider the Day of Atonement, but it is important to understand that the Temple and the cosmos were closely associated, that Adam was King and High Priest and that the High Priest "represented" the Lord. The rituals of the Temple were integral to the well-being of the cosmos; in effect the LORD, the creator through the rituals in the Temple, was renewing his creation. The tabernacle was to be set up "on the first day of the first month,"[141] that is the Tabernacle was to be set up at the new year, which we have seen is associated with creation. We will see in the following chapter that *Rosh Hashanah* the New Year festival celebrates Creation[142] and later the Temple was dedicated at *Sukkoth,* which forms part of the New Year festival.

In the surrounding cultures we saw that the creation narrative formed part of the New Year Enthronement festival and it has been suggested that this is also the case with Genesis: "Genesis 1–3 in its account of creation, presents the cosmos as one large Temple, the Garden of Eden as the Holy of Holies and the human person as made for worship. The very content and structure of Genesis 1–3 is in a very real sense liturgical."[143] Having overcome the waters of Chaos, following his act of creation, God rests in his Temple (the cosmos) on the seventh day. Seven is a symbolic number in the Old Testament and plays a significant part in the way that Genesis 1–3 is structured,[144] enhancing the suggestion that in fact it is liturgical and meant to be read as part of the New Year ritual, just as the *Enuma Elish* was in Babylon.

The Temple in the New Testament

The Temple in the New Testament is the Second Temple rebuilt following the exile. There were those, such as the community at Qumran that thought the Temple in Jerusalem was corrupt and saw themselves as the Temple. Nonetheless the Temple in Jerusalem was where God could be encountered and was where the three pilgrim festivals of *Sukkoth, Pesach*

141. Exod 40:1–2.

142. See chapter on *Rosh Hashannah.*

143. Morrow, *Creation as Temple-Building,* 1.

144. Morrow, *Creation as Temple-Building,* 1–3.

and *Shavuot* were held as well as the daily Temple service. Although God was "present" in his Temple, it was only the High Priest that could enter the Holy of Holies to encounter God and that was only on the Day of Atonement. In Mal 3:1 it was prophesied that the LORD would come to his Temple and we saw above that Jesus is Yahweh. He is God incarnate and therefore in his incarnation, the "place" where God could be encountered. Following his cleansing of the Temple as a foreshadowing of his cleansing of the cosmos, the people asked for a sign of his authority to do this, to which Jesus replied: "Destroy this Temple and I will raise it again in three days."[145] John makes it clear that he is talking about his body and his resurrection after 3 days. At the moment of his death, the curtain in the Temple tore in two, revealing the Holy of Holies and signifying that God's presence was now available to all who sought him.[146] In the New Testament the Temple is also associated with new creation: Jesus is the cornerstone of the new Temple with the apostles as its foundation and those that follow Jesus, the new creation[147] are the living stones of the Temple where God is present.[148] They are also a Royal Priesthood, restoring the role that Adam forfeited[149] and enjoying Sabbath rest.[150]

Conclusion

Even in such a brief outline a number of identifiable features are evident that span all three areas—the surrounding cultures, the Old Testament and the New Testament. The King representing God (in the New Testament—God himself) recapitulated the original act of creation at the New Year festival, thereby bringing about the conditions that prevailed at the original creation. This involved him undergoing a form of trial and in some cases humiliation, his "dying" (again in the New Testament the King/God actually dies) and being raised up and enthroned at the right hand side of God (in the New Testament - the right hand side of God the Father). The result of which was justice (*ma'at*/*mishpat*) incorporating judgement, healing, freedom from oppression, the poor and the hungry

145. John 2:19.

146. Matt 27:51.

147. 2 Cor 5:17.

148. Eph 2:20–22; 2 Cor 6:16.

149. 1 Pet 2:9.

150. Heb 4:9–11.

being satisfied, widows and orphans being looked after and prisoners being set free. There was also life giving water and a new creation. In the
Old and New Testament this also renewed the covenant.

Chapter 3

SUKKOTH

Introduction

SO FAR THEN WE have discovered that in the cultures that surrounded Israel sacral kingship looked like this: the King, whose titles included Good Shepherd, Servant and Chosen One was understood to be the physical manifestation of the high god of the culture but was also associated with the young fertility god. As well as his political function he had a major role as High Priest, particularly evident at the New Year festival. Here the King following his anointing underwent some sort of trial—understood as the cosmic battle between the god and the forces of Chaos. As part of the ritual, the myth (that is the creation narrative) was read out. The humiliation and "death" that the King undergoes in this ritual was understood to atone for the sins of the people. His subsequent enthronement once again produced all the same benefits that were part of the original creation—the forces of Chaos were defeated (also representing the nation's physical enemies) and therefore order was restored. As a result fertility was guaranteed, life-giving water, harvests—new creation. This also applied to humans, not just physically procreating, but also involved a spiritual and moral regeneration of the people.

What makes this kind of thinking difficult for us to understand is our detachment from the reality of how dependent we are on the seasons, on the sun and rain, and on crops being harvested. We might catch a glimpse of this when we see people displaced or starving on our TV's because of lack of rain or too much rain, but how often do we associate what ends up on our plate with the sun rising every day, the rains coming at the right time and the seasons recurring when they should? In the Old Testament the giving or withholding of rain is understood as a blessing or punishment from God, because it is in fact, a matter of life or death. Rain—life-giving water is salvation, the earth re-creating. Salvation *is* re-creation, the earth renewing itself after the death of winter—new creation. Jesus doesn't just pluck these images out of thin air; his parables are not just agriculturally based because he was talking to peasant farmers, he used these metaphors because they had a real basis in life. Salvation and creation are linked throughout the Old Testament and the New Testament and they were linked in the ancient cultures.

Although the enthronement festival at which atonement was made and the covenant renewed took place during the autumnal New Year festivals of *Yom Teruah* and harvest festival of *Sukkoth*, this was pre-exile. Following the return from exile in Babylon, the monarchy no longer functioned and the Day of Atonement became, as the name suggests, the major atonement festival in Israel, with the central role still being performed by the Anointed, only now this was the High Priest. This is the festival we will be considering in the next chapter. However, in this chapter, having looked at how the Enthronement Festival was carried out pre-exile, we will consider how *Sukkoth* and *Rosh Hashanah* (as *Yom Teruah* came to be known) were celebrated *post-exile*. In these chapters therefore we are looking for two things—firstly whether the evidence from the festivals also confirm that sacral kingship lies behind them and secondly, as sacral kingship is the basis for messianism, whether there is evidence that Messiah was prefigured in them, and if so, is there evidence that Jesus' life and ministry fulfilled what had occurred in the festivals.

Yom Teruah/Rosh Hashanah

At the pre-exilic New Year festival the King's entrance and enthronement were signaled by the blowing of trumpets (*shofarim*) as we see from the following enthronement psalm:

> God ascended amid shouts of joy,
> the LORD amid the sound of trumpets.
> Sing praises to God, sing praises,

sing praises to our King, sing praise
For god is the King of all the earth;
sing to him a psalm of praise.[1]

Yom Teruah, is the New Year's day which precedes the harvest festival of *Sukkoth* (Feast of Tabernacles). The instructions given for the festival are: "On the first day of the seventh month[2] you are to have a day of sabbath rest, a sacred assembly commemorated with trumpet blasts."[3] The fact that the festival falls on the seventh new moon of the year, makes it also a 'Sabbath' month. There's little further information in the Torah about this festival but in the *Mishnah* it is called *Rosh Hashanah*, "Head of the year" and as the name suggests it is the New Year festival. It is also associated with the creation of the world. We saw in the previous chapter, following his act of creation, God rested on the seventh day, the Sabbath, in his Temple (that is the cosmos) and the instructions for the festival call for the people to not just cease from work, but to have "a sabbath rest." However if *Rosh Hashanah* celebrates creation, we might expect that the command to rest would come on the seventh day. In fact, the actual anniversary of the creation of the earth occurs on twenty-fifth Elul, that is towards the end of the previous month. Therefore, *Rosh Hashanah* (*Yom Teruah* in the Torah) actually coincides with the Sabbath day of creation. This is also known as a day of remembrance the day that God is crowned as King of the earth and celebrates the creation of Adam and Eve. It is said that only then, when he had created people to acknowledge it, could he be enthroned as King. In fact, there is a *Midrash* that says that Adam's first words were "The Lord is King for ever and ever."

Present Day Festival

The kingship of God is also evident in the present day celebrations of *Rosh Hashanah*, which take place over two days. A loaf is baked in the shape of a crown to celebrate God's kingship and in the synagogue the prayer "*Avinu malkenu*" is said during this period. This prayer is 52 lines long, with each line beginning with "*avinu malkenu*"—"Our Father, our King." It also contains the line "Our Father, our King, let salvation (*Yeshua*) soon

1. Ps 47:5–7.

2. There are two calendars within Judaism, a cultic and a civic one, hence although this is the 7th month, it is the New Year festival.

3. Lev 23:23–24.

flourish for us." Therefore, right at the heart of the synagogue New Year service when God is crowned as King, there is a prayer that *Yeshua*,[4] will flourish. The contemporary understanding of *Rosh Hashanah* is that in essence, it is about crowning God as King. Prior to the *Rosh Hashanah* service, in the final days of *Elul*, *selichot*, that is extra prayers of penitence are added to the synagogue service because *Rosh Hashanah* is understood as a judgement day, associated with its original name of *Yom Teruah* (as the *shofar* is associated with judgement). On this day the righteous are sealed in the Book of Life and the wicked in the Book of Death. Those who meet neither category, have until *Yom Kippur* to repent and make amends; firstly with people and then with God, before the books are closed, symbolized by the closing of the door of the ark where the Torah scrolls are kept.

Another feature of the festival, which also has Enthronement Festival connotations is *Taschlich*. This takes place on the first afternoon of *Rosh Hashanah*.[5] It involves going to a body of water—either the sea or river or even a pond.[6] Here each person's sins are ceremonially cast into the water accompanied by a special prayer which contains the line "sing to the Lord a new song," which is a feature of a number of the Enthronement Psalms and which also has messianic connotations. One explanation for this practice is that it is in response to the scripture that God will cast our sins into the sea (Mic 7:19). Other reasons given are that Jewish Kings were anointed next to rivers and, therefore, it is appropriate to crown God as King during *Rosh Hashanah* next to a river. Another is that it is in order to contemplate God's mercy in preventing the waters from flooding the dry land, which sounds very much like celebrating God's victory over the Chaos waters which seems also to be in the background of yet another reason given, which is that Satan tried to stop Abraham from fulfilling God's command to carry out the sacrifice of Isaac and so he had a river appear before him. Nonetheless Abraham waded into it whereupon God dried it up. In other words we have the same phenomenon here at the New Year Festival that we found in the pre-exilic New Year Festival, that water is associated with the forces of Chaos, that is evil

4. This is Jesus' name in Hebrew.

5. Unless it is a Sabbath.

6. There is a stipulation that it should contain fish. There's no particularly convincing argument why this should be but it could be suggested that the water has to be "living water," and therefore rather than representing the Chaos waters, they instead represent the "Living Water" that absorbs the sins.

which God conquers by "drying them up" as he did at the Red Sea, which we will see in chapter 5 is itself a recapitulation of the creation story. The idea of sins/evil being cast into the water is also evident in the New Testament story of the Gadarene swine where the demonic spirits are cast into the herd of pigs who then run headlong into the lake, that is back into the water from which they originated. One of the obligations of *Yom Teruah*, is hearing the *shofar* being blown. "The *shofar* was used regularly in the Temple service and Jewish tradition holds that the sounds of the *shofar* will announce the arrival of the Messiah, just as they greeted the ancient Kings of Israel." As it says in 1 Kgs 1:39 "Zadok the priest took the horn of oil from the sacred tent and anointed Solomon. Then they sounded the trumpet (*shofar*) and all the people shouted 'Long live King Solomon.'" Although *Yom Teruah* is known as the feast of Trumpets and *teruah* is the word used for the sound of the trumpet blast, it can also mean loud shouts.

1 Thess 4:13–18 talks about Jesus' second coming "the day of the Lord" and says that this will be announced "with a loud shout, with the voice of the archangel and with the trumpet call of God." A similar picture is given in 1 Cor 15:51–54 which actually calls this event "the last trumpet." This is what we read in Joel 2:1 "Blow a *shofar* in Zion, and sound an alarm on my holy mountain! Let all the inhabitants of the land tremble, for the day of the Lord is coming; surely it is near." The Day of the Lord used throughout the Old Testament has several time frames. It can refer to a time in the near future, a day of judgement when the LORD will bring about his justice, but more often than not, has an eschatological intent, referring to a final day of judgement and the LORD's appearance. Therefore the trumpet/*shofar* sounding is associated with the arrival of the King and Messiah as well as with the final judgement, and in the New Testament we find exactly the same, that the trumpet heralds Jesus' second coming as King and this will begin the final judgement:

> And I saw a great white throne and the one sitting on it. The earth and sky fled from his presence, but they found no place to hide. I saw the dead, both great and small, standing before God's throne. And the books were opened, including the Book of Life. And the dead were judged according to what they had done, as recorded in the books.[7]

---

7. Rev 20:11–13.

Genesis 22, the binding of Isaac or *Akedah* as it is known within Judaism, is the reading for the second day of *Rosh Hashanah* and is also linked to the *shofar* and therefore the original name of the festival *Yom Teruah*. The importance of this passage for Judaism can be gauged by the prominence it is given in the synagogue—not only is it read at *Rosh Hashanah* as well as once in the Torah cycle of readings,[8] but it is read at every morning service. It is one of the foundational texts for Judaism as it is understood that through Isaac's merit, resurrection is made possible. We will see that this is also a prefiguring of Jesus.

The Akedah

In the story, God tells Abraham: "Take your son, your only son, whom you love—Isaac—and go to the region of Moriah. Sacrifice him there as a burnt offering on a mountain I will show you."[9] Isaac is the son that has been miraculously conceived by Sarah who was "very old and past the age of childbearing."[10] "On the third day,"[11] Isaac ascends Mt Moriah, carrying the wood for his own sacrifice. When he asks where the lamb for the burnt offering is, Abraham answers "God himself will provide the lamb."[12] Just at the point of sacrifice, an angel of the LORD stops Abraham and he finds a ram whose head is stuck in a thicket, that is a bush of thorns, and the ram is then sacrificed in place of Isaac. According to Rabbinic tradition the ram that God provided was created before the beginning of the world.[13] In effect, therefore Isaac is "resurrected" on the third day, as Abraham prophesied "we will come back to you."[14] This is also the interpretation in the New Testament:"Abraham reasoned that God could even raise the dead, and so in a manner of speaking he did receive Isaac back from death."[15] As a result of his obedience Abra-

---

8. The entire Torah is read throughout the course of the year, in the synagogue services alongside portions from the prophets - the *haftarah*.

9. Gen 22:2.

10. Gen 18:10.

11. Gen 22:4.

12. Gen 22:8.

13. *m.Avot 5:6.*

14. He said this to the two servants that accompanied them up to that point. Just Isaac and Abraham went on from there and so the fact that Abraham says "*we* will return" suggests he expected Isaac to return with him. Gen 22: 4–5.

15. Heb 11:19.

ham, "Father of many,"[16] is told that through his offspring (or seed) all nations on earth will be blessed.[17] What is interesting however, is that in the Jewish *Midrash*[18] on this story in *Genesis Rabbah*[19] Isaac is 30 years old and goes willingly to be sacrificed. In this account too, Isaac carries the wood for his own sacrifice but here it is compared to a cross.[20] Even more intriguingly, in the *Midrash*, Isaac actually dies and comes back to life. Therefore, as this all takes place "on the third day" Isaac in effect dies and rises again on the third day.

This is understood within Christianity as a foreshadowing of Jesus' sacrifice. Jesus, the only Son of God, also miraculously conceived, the One whom the Father loves, also carried the means of his own sacrifice, the wooden cross, to the place of crucifixion. Mt Moriah[21] which was to become the site of the Temple,[22] where the festivals and sacrifices took place that also foreshadowed his final sacrifice. Jesus is the substitutionary Lamb that makes atonement and redeems the world,[23] "the lamb that was slain from before the foundation of the earth."[24] Jesus is the lamb whose head was crowned with thorns. As both the Father and Jesus prophesied, he died and rose again "on the third day"[25] and through his death all nations on earth are blessed.

Jesus' genealogy is traced back to Abraham[26] and the promise to Abraham specifically states that "Kings will come from you." That this isn't just meant physically but spiritually is explained by Paul in Rom

16. The patriarch, formerly known as *Abram* "exalted Father."

17. Gen 22:18—the change of name in Gen 17:5 reflecting the promise that Abraham will be the father of many nations.

18. *Midrash*, plural *Midrashim*, can simply mean a Rabbinic method of interpreting Scriptures but it also refers to particular works written on particular biblical books as in this case with *Genesis Rabbah* (*Rabbah* just means "great." *Midrashim* often take seeming anomalies such as "Let us make man in our image" in Gen 1:26, which appear to fly in the face of the strict monotheism of Judaism and weave explanations around them.

19. The *midrash* on Genesis.

20. *Genesis Rabbah* 56.3. Cf also *Pesikta Rabbati* ch. 31, 143b. This is a medieval *Midrash* on the festivals.

21. Jesus' crucifixion also took place on the slopes of Mt Moriah.

22. 2 Chron 3:1.

23. "The Lamb of God that takes away the sin of the world" John 1:29.

24. Rev 13:8.

25. Matt 16:21.

26. Matt 1:2

4:11–17. 'Now the promises were made to Abraham and to his seed. It does not say: "And to his seeds" referring to many, but referring to one, "And to your seed," who is Christ' (Gal 3:16). Gen 22:13, has caused problems for translators as the Hebrew word *achar* which occurs here, does so in an awkward sequence. It is generally translated as "behind" but can also mean "afterwards" or "later" and has led to several interpretations, one of which suggests that when Abraham looked up and saw the ram, it wasn't that he saw the lamb "behind him" or "later" or even "afterwards" but what he was seeing was "the later days," *achareit yomim*, that is the last days and a future sacrifice. In John's gospel, Jesus in fact says: "Your father Abraham rejoiced to see my day: and he saw it, and was glad."[27] The promise to Abraham was that all nations would be blessed through him and that's what Paul makes clear: "Understand then, that those who have faith are children of Abraham. Scripture foresaw that God would justify the Gentiles by faith, and announced the gospel in advance to Abraham: 'All nations will be blessed through you.'"[28]

The *Akedah* also forms part of the messianic expectation within Judaism, directly linked with the Messiah *ben* Joseph, that is the Messiah, (son of Joseph) who dies in battle as a prelude to the Messiah *ben* David (son of David) coming as the triumphant Messiah. The *Akedah* is also understood as a means of redemption for others,[29] and associated with atonement.[30] It is said that the *shofar* made of the left horn of the ram, is for judgement and was also blown at Sinai at the giving of the Torah. As mentioned above, hearing the *shofar* is one of the stipulations for *Rosh Hashanah*, and is the reason the *Akedah* is linked to this festival. The right horn of the ram is said to be the one which will be used to announce the coming of the Messiah.[31] We saw above that the expectation within Christianity is that when the Messiah returns, "The Day of the Lord," will be a time of judgement which will be announced by the blowing

27. John 8:5–6.

28. Gal 3:8.

29. *b. Yerushalmi, Ta'anit* 2:4, 65d . That is, in the Talmud. This contains the Mishnah and the Gemara and contains *halakhah* and commentary on the Mishnah. There are two Talmuds, the Palestinian Talmud (*Yerushalmi*) written c. 390 AD and the Babylonian Talmud (*Bavli*) written c. 500 AD, which is considered the more authoritative.

30. "When your children shall become entangled in sins, what are they to do? They are to take the ram's horn and blow into it and I will remember the *Akedah* of Isaac and pardon their sins." *Pesikta Rabbati*, 40.

31. *Tz'enah Ur'enah*. This is a 16th century commentary on Torah including *midrashic* insights and ethical teachings by Rabbi Yaakov Ashkenazi.

of the *shofar*. This will announce the return of Jesus, son of Joseph who died and was resurrected, the triumphant Son of David who will sit on the throne of his father forever. A further *Midrash* on the *Akedah* also sees Isaac's soul flying from his body as the sword touched his throat, but returning when the voice "between the cherubim" said "Lay not thy hand upon the lad." It continues: "And Isaac rose, knowing that in this way the dead would come back to life in the future."[32] It is interesting that this *Midrash* suggests a Temple setting,[33] as the binding of Isaac, takes place on Mt Moriah, which we said above, is the site of the Temple. In Judaism, therefore, the *Akedah* is also associated with resurrection, and it is through Isaac's merit that the dead will be resurrected, which provides a further parallel with Jesus who said: "I am the resurrection and the life. The one who believes in me will live, even though they die; and whoever lives by believing in me will never die."[34]

Therefore themes from the Enthronement Festival are visible at *Rosh Hashanah*. This is a New Year Festival, celebrating the original act of creation and God's enthronement as King as well as a sabbath rest for the people. The readings for the festival also contains themes of kingship, sacrifice, atonement and with the ritual of *Tashlich*, the casting away of sins to their place of origin, the Chaos waters. The use of the *shofar*, not only connects this with the story of Isaac, which in Jewish tradition is understood as Messianic but also announces the coming of the King and judgement. These themes all resonate with Christianity. The period we are in now, the Messianic era, the time between the Messiah's first coming and his coming again, is a time of repentance; it's a time when we are called upon to carry out the great commission of "making disciples of all nations"[35] in fulfillment of God's word to Abraham. The binding of Isaac foreshadows Jesus' sacrifice, as the substitutional lamb (not just for Israel, but for the world). For those who know Jesus, their names are already written in the Lamb's book of life.[36] When Jesus comes back, the *shofar* will sound both to signify he is King and Messiah, but also to signify

---

32. *Pirkei Rabbi Eliazar,* thought to be composed in the first half of the 8th century it is a *midrash* with a continuous narrative, using lots of different sources, not just Torah.

33. The LORD was understood to be seated between the Cherubim in the Holy of Holies.

34. John 11:25–26.

35. Matt 28:16–20.

36. Rev 21:27.

judgement.[37] Jesus' followers are new creations[38] experiencing their sabbath rest in him[39] until he returns when there will be a new creation; a
new heaven and a new earth.[40] All sin and evil will be no more as there
will be no more sea,[41] therefore the Chaos waters are defeated for good
and there will be no need for *Tashlich*.

As well as considering how kingship would help us to deepen our
understanding of Jesus, we said we would look at the different titles that
are used for him in the New Testament because these are not just random
epithets chosen to describe him, these are all integral to his role as King/
Anointed. This flies in the face of some scholarship that either denies that
these are in fact titles, particularly in the case of the Son of Man[42] or, as is
the case with the title Servant, assert that Jesus, by applying it to himself,
was the first to associate it with the Messiah.[43] Since Servant is one of the
most frequently used titles, it is worth considering it now as it is most
closely associated with *Sukkoth*. As we will see, the Servant figure is, in
fact, a "type" of the King and as we discovered in chapter 2, Servant is one
of the titles of the King in the ancient near east.

The Servant

We have already noted that the monarchy effectively came to an end
following the destruction of the Temple in Jerusalem and the exile into
Babylon and it is during this period that the Servant figure emerges in
the writings of Isaiah. Isaiah is traditionally held to be made up of three
parts First Isaiah chapters 1–39 representing pre-exilic writing, that is
before 586BC, Second (or Deutero-Isaiah) chapters 40–55 and written
during the exile (586–538) and Third (Trito) Isaiah, chapters 56–66 written following the return from exile. The Servant figure is found mainly in
Second Isaiah, that is, that part which was written during the exile when
there was no monarchy[44] and therefore no hope of a Messianic King. The

37. 1 Thess 4:13–18.

38. 2 Cor 5:17.

39. Heb 4:9–11.

40. Rev 21:1.

41. Rev 21:1.

42. See for example Maccoby, *The Mythmaker,* 43.

43. Mowinckel, *He That Cometh,* 257

44. Zerubbabel, a descendant of David led the rebuilding of the Temple but did

Servant figure therefore, represents the King, or rather a "type" of the King.[45] Typology forms an important aspect of the theology of the Bible and is used extensively not only to demonstrate the continuity of themes but also imbuing something or someone with a whole range of symbolism and images that would otherwise be difficult to convey. Although the main sections for the Servant are chapters 40—55, there are passages within these chapters that have been identified specifically as "Servant Songs."[46] Nonetheless, Servant motifs and passages appear elsewhere. It is worth noting that Isaiah, along with Zechariah, contain numerous Messianic allusions and prophecies and therefore unsurprisingly are quoted extensively within the New Testament.

We saw mainly from the Psalms, that the King is called Servant (Ps 89:20) he is chosen (Ps 89:3) anointed (Ps 2:2 18:50) and has Yahweh's Spirit upon him (Ps 51:11;1 Sam 16:13). He is betrayed by a friend he shared bread with (Ps 41:9). He undergoes a trial where he is despised and rejected (Ps 22:6–7; Ps 118:21–22). He is also abandoned by God (Ps 22:1). He is innocent (Ps 26:1–7) and unjustly accused (Ps 83:5). He is stripped of his royal insignia (Ps89:39,44); lots are cast for his clothes (Ps 22:18) and he is offered vinegar to drink (Ps 69:21). His hands and feet are pierced (Ps 22:16). Although oppressed and afflicted he is silent (Ps 62:5). He dies, is raised up and enthroned at the right hand side of God with his enemies under his feet (Ps 110:1). He will bring justice (Ps 72:1) and an everlasting covenant. (Ps 89:3–4). There will be fertility (Ps 72:2–6), miraculous water (Ps 107:35) and a new song (Ps 96:1).

When we look at the Servant Songs there are striking parallels: the Servant is the Chosen One (Isa 42:1) anointed[47] and has Yahweh's Spirit upon him (Isa 42:1). He is a light to the nations (Isa 42:6). He is despised

---

not reign as King.

45. Typology is when a person or figure takes on the attributes and role of a previous person, in this case the Servant takes on the role and attributes of the King.

46. These were originally identified by Duhm, who identified four 'Servant Songs'. The first: Isa 42:1–4, the second Isa 49:1–6, the third Isa 50:4–9, the fourth Isa 52:13–53.12. This idea was generally accepted although Servant motifs are found elsewhere in Isaiah.

47. This is usually rendered as "disfigured," but it has been argued that in fact the Hebrew can be read as "anointed" which as the Servant is a type of the king and understood messianically in both Judaism and Christianity, would seem the better option. This is based on the Isaiah scroll at Qumran which has an extra letter, an *aleph* which would then read "I have anointed" *masahti* or "my anointed one," *moshati*. Barker, *Text and Context*, 6.

and rejected (Isa 53:3), struck and humiliated (Isa 50:6), whipped (Isa 53:5) and spat upon (Isa 50:6). He is innocent (Isa 53:9) and unjustly accused (Isa 53:8) and takes on our pain and suffering (Isa 53:4). He is bruised and pierced for our transgressions (Isa 53:5), he was oppressed and afflicted but didn't open his mouth, he was silent "like a lamb led to the slaughter"(Isa 53:7). His life was an offering for sin (Isa 53:10) and it's through his death that atonement is made (Isa 53:5). He is given as a covenant (Isa 42:6). He died and was assigned a grave with the wicked and with the rich (Isa 53:9). He will be raised up and exalted (Isa 52:13). As a result he will bring justice to the nations (Isa 42:1, 4), there will be fertility (Isa 54:1–2) and living water (Isa 55:1) and an everlasting covenant (Isa 55:3). There will be a new song (Isa 42:10).

When we look at the New Testament we find that Jesus who is also King and whose death and resurrection are spoken of in terms of that of the King in the Psalms, is also referred to[48] and refers to himself in terms of the Servant.[49] Once again we cannot fail to notice, not just the similarities, but the numerous parallels between what is said about the Servant and Jesus' suffering, death and resurrection:

Jesus is God's chosen (Luke 9:35; 23:35), the Anointed (Matt 1:1). The Spirit came upon him at his baptism (Mark 1:10). He is a light to the nations (Luke 2:32). Following his arrest he is struck on the cheek (John 18:22), whipped (Matt 27:26) and spit upon (Mark 14:65). He is mocked (Matt 27:31). He is falsely accused (Mark14:56; Luke 23:1–2) but remains silent (Mark 15:5). He is rejected by the people (John 19:15) and abandoned by God (Matt 27:46). Lots are cast for his clothes (John 19:24). His life was given as an atonement for sin (Rom 5:11) to renew the covenant (Heb 9:15). He died amongst the wicked (Mark15:27) and he was buried in the grave of the rich (Matt 27:57). He rose from the dead (Matt 28:6) and is exalted in heaven (Phil 2:9). He will bring justice to the nations. (Matt25:31–33). There will be a new creation (2 Cor 5:17) and a new song (Rev 5:9–13).

In Acts 8:26–39 we are told that a eunuch from Ethiopia was reading "from the prophet Isaiah." The portion he was reading was Isa 53:7–8, which begins with the lines "He was led like a lamb to the slaughter." This is a passage from the fourth Servant Song in Isaiah. When the eunuch

---

48. Matt 8:17; Luke 22:37; Acts 8:32–35; Rom 15:21.
49. Mark9:12, Rom 5:19; Phil 2:7,9;1 Pet 2:24–25.

asked Philip[50] who this was talking about, Philip "began with that very passage of Scripture and told him the good news about Jesus" (Acts 8:35), therefore directly identifying Jesus with the Servant in Isaiah, and in particular, the suffering Servant of the fourth Servant Song. In light of the scholarly speculation about the Servant figure, it is interesting therefore that Peter was specifically answering the Eunuch's question: "who is the prophet talking about, himself or someone else?"(Acts 8:34).[51]

Further allusions to Jesus as Servant are found in 1 Pet 2:22–25 "He committed no sin and no deceit was found in his mouth. When they hurled their insults at him he did not retaliate . . . he himself bore our sins . . . by his wounds you have been healed . . . for you were like sheep going astray." Also at the Last Supper Jesus says "It is written: 'And he was numbered with the transgressors'" a quote about the Servant in Isa 53:12 and says: "I tell you that this must be fulfilled in me. Yes, what is written about me is reaching its fulfillment."[52] Matthew indicates that the healings that Jesus performed were also in fulfillment of the Isaiah prophecy: "He took up our infirmities and bore our diseases."[53] The close parallels, therefore, between the figure of the King in the Psalms and the Servant in Isaiah confirm that the Servant was a continuation of the expectation of a King Messiah, even during the exile when the monarchy had ceased to function. The fact that Jesus' suffering, death and resurrection also match this point for point, further confirm that he fulfilled the roles of both the King and the Servant, that is he was the expected Messianic King whose suffering, death, resurrection and enthronement would bring about the Messianic conditions that the enthronement festival and the Servant's role prefigured.

Sukkoth and the Anointed King

Sukkoth is called "the season of our joy." God's instructions for the festival are: "Be joyful at your festival!" and not just for one day—for seven days—everyone—sons, daughters, foreigners, servants, fatherless and

50. Philip had been directed by the Holy Spirit to go to the Eunuch's chariot and stay near it (Acts 8:29).

51. The Servant figure has been identified as either an unknown figure, the people Israel, or even the prophet Second Isaiah. However I believe the evidence, presented here, speaks for itself; not to mention Philip's answer.

52. Luke 22:37.

53. Isa 53:4.

widows—even the priests.[54] It was the harvest of wheat and grapes and as the final harvest for the year, when all the other harvests had been safely gathered in, it was a time of real celebration. It was so important it became known simply as *haHag, the* festival. The festival was a reminder of how the Israelites lived in temporary dwellings (*Sukkoth*) in the desert wandering of the Exodus and one of the main features of the festival was the instruction to make a *sukkah* and dwell in it for the duration of the festival. This has been reduced in the present day festival to eating at least one meal each day in the *sukkah*. Further instructions on keeping the festival include how to make the *lulav* (Lev 23:40). This is made from the branches of three different types of tree, the myrtle, the willow and the palm tree. Although there are various Rabbinic explanations for the particular species involved, as we noted in chapter 2, they all have strong associations with fertility[55] and the waving of the *lulav* has also been interpreted as a fertility rite. The fourth element is the *etrog,* a citrus fruit which looks like a large lemon. It has also been suggested that the two items together, the *lulav* and the *etrog,* represent male and female which again has connotations of fertility.

The *lulav* was carried during the Temple service when the *Hallel,* Psalms 113—118 were said during the procession around the altar when people would cry "Hosanna," "save us."[56] This line is from Ps118, which not only contains the Messianic theme of the cornerstone that we will consider below, but is also an enthronement Psalm, which contains a line from the Song of the Sea,[57] which was sung following the parting of the Red Sea during the Exodus, which in itself is a recapitulation of the overcoming of the Chaos waters at creation. We will see below that the Exodus which provides the rationale for *Sukkoth,* contains the same themes as the Enthronement Festival, namely the overcoming of the forces of Chaos, resulting in fertility and new creation. This is made even clearer in the water libation ceremony, which reached its climax on the final day of the festival. This was, in effect, a rain-inducing ceremony. The priests

---

54. Deut 16:14.

55. The palm is associated with the tree of life, the willow symbolizes moisture, the myrtle is associated with the Egyptian goddess of fertility *Astarte* and the *etrog* is the "fruit of goodly trees."

56. Hosanna, more precisely *Hoshiana,* literally means "save us" but has come to be a declaration of praise.

57. "The Lord is my strength and my song, and he has become my salvation." Ps 118:14; Exod 15:2.

accompanied by a procession of the people chanting the *Hallel* went to the pool of Siloam to draw water from there in a golden jug. When they returned to the Temple, the water would be poured out on the altar to accompany the morning sacrifice. Wine and water were poured out together on the altar, although from different vessels, with different sized holes so that the liquids emptied at the same time.[58] Wine is symbolic of blood and this is understood as a foreshadowing of the blood and water that poured from Jesus' side at his sacrifice.[59] This happened each day. However, on the final day they circled the altar seven times repeating "Hosanna," "Save us!" Hence this day was known as *Hoshana Rabbah*.

John's Gospel tells us that at *Sukkoth*, Jesus went up to Jerusalem to the Temple and "On the last and greatest day of the Festival"—that is on *Hoshana Rabbah*—when the water pouring ceremony reached its climax—he "stood up and said in a loud voice 'Let anyone who is thirsty come to me and drink. Whoever believes in me, as Scripture has said, rivers of living water will flow from within them.'" Jesus, whose name means salvation, is therefore saying "the salvation you have been praying for is here, you've been praying for rain, but I bring living water." As John explains: "By this he meant the Spirit, whom those who believed in him were later to receive."[60] Jesus is therefore declaring that he is Yahweh come to his Temple as he had promised.[61] He is also declaring that the water (in the form of rain), that the people were asking God for throughout *Sukkoth* and in particular, on this last day, was a foreshadowing of the Spirit that would be poured out on those who believed in him, as Joel prophesied.[62]

We don't know which scripture Jesus was referring to, although the passage from Joel is a distinct possibility, there are a number of others which he may have had in mind, such as Zech 12:10.[63] Another possibil-

58. "They each had a hole like to a narrow snout, one wide and the other narrow, so that both bowls emptied themselves together' *m.Suk* 4:9. As the footnote explains this was because wine flows more slowly than water.

59. "Instead one of the soldiers pierced Jesus' side with a spear, bringing a sudden flow of blood and water." John 19:34.

60. John 7:37–39.

61. In Jer 2.13, and 17:13 Yahweh is the source of living water, further strengthening the Jesus/Yahweh identification.

62. Joel 2:28–32, which Peter was to quote when the Holy Spirit was poured out on the disciples in Jerusalem at Pentecost (Acts 2:17–21).

63. "And I will pour out on the house of David and the inhabitants of Jerusalem the Spirit of grace and supplication."

ity is Isa 12:3 "With joy you will draw from the wells of salvation," which
would seem particularly appropriate as it is linked with this ceremony
in the *Mishnah*. In addition, the Hebrew word for salvation, as we noted
above, is in fact Jesus' name *Yeshua*, so in effect, the scripture from Isa 12:3
reads: "With joy you will draw from the wells of *Yeshua*." Jesus had earlier
explained to the Samaritan woman who had offered him a drink at the
well: "Everyone who drinks this water will be thirsty again but those who
drink the water that I give them will never thirst. Indeed the water I give
them will become in them a spring of water welling up to eternal life."[64]
Also in the *Mishnah* it states "He that has never seen the Water Drawing - has never in his life seen joy."[65] Therefore at *Sukkoth*, the festival at
which God commands his people to be joyful, at the most joyful part of
the festival, the water libation, Jesus, the one at whose birth the angels
declared "We bring you good news of great joy"[66] declares that he is the
living water, *Yeshua*, the salvation that was promised from the beginning
and which the festival foreshadowed.

Although Jesus entered Jerusalem as King at Passover, it has long
been recognized that there are elements from *Sukkoth* in his triumphal
entry. The fact that palm branches[67] were waved at him,[68] the shouting
of "Blessed is he who comes in the name of the Lord" from Ps 118:26,[69]
which we have just seen, also forms part of the water drawing ceremony
at *Sukkoth*,[70] as well as the application of Zech 9:9, as Zechariah is particularly concerned with *Sukkoth*. This would also appear to confirm
my earlier suggestion that the original Enthronement Festival was frag-
mented and elements of it can be seen in the three festivals that we are
considering here. Just before his triumphal entry Jesus gave his disciples
the instructions: "Go to the village ahead of you, and at once you will find

---

64. John 4:13–14

65. *m.Suk.* 5:1.

66. Luke 2:10.

67. Although the name for the whole article made from the three species is *lulav*,
the word's literal meaning is palm frond, the plural being *lulavim*.

68. "A very large crowd spread their cloaks on on the road, while others cut
branches from the trees and spread them on the road." Matt 21:8, Mark 11:8. In John's
gospel, these are explicitly identified as palm leaves John 12:13.

69. This same Psalm continues: "the LORD is God, and he has made his light
shine on us. With boughs in hand join in the festal procession up to the horns of the
altar."

70. Pss 113–118. This is however also recited at Passover.

a donkey tied there, with her colt by her. Untie them and bring them to me."[71] This is understood as direct fulfillment of the Zechariah prophecy quoted by Matthew:

> Rejoice greatly, Daughter Zion!
> Shout, Daughter Jerusalem!
> See, your King comes to you,
> righteous and victorious,
> lowly and riding on a donkey,
> on a colt, the foal of a donkey.[72]

This is also understood as a Messianic prophecy in Judaism: "As the first Redeemer was, so shall the latter Redeemer be. What is stated of the former Redeemer? And Moses took his wife and his sons, and set them upon an ass (Exod 4:20). Similarly will it be with the latter Redeemer, as it is stated, Lowly and riding upon an ass"(Zech 9:9).[73] This detail about the Messiah is also seen in Gen 49:10–11 where Shiloh, that is the Messiah "binds his foal to the vine, his colt to the choice vine; he washes his garment in wine and his robe in the blood of grapes." The mention of wine and grapes here is also interesting as wine is symbolic of blood and grapes are associated with judgement, both of which are features of *Sukkoth*.

It becomes apparent that the coming King in Zech 9:9 is Yahweh who brings the promise of rain and fertility: "The LORD their God will save his people on that day as a shepherd saves his flock . . . Grain will make the young men thrive and new wine the young women. Ask the LORD for rain in the springtime. It is the LORD who sends the thunderstorms. He gives showers of rain to all people and plants of the field to everyone." [74] He is also the one who has been pierced: "they will look on me the one they have pierced' and they will mourn for him 'as one mourns for an only child, and grieve bitterly for him as one grieves for a firstborn son"(Zech:12:10b). This is followed by the promise of atonement: "On that day a fountain will be opened to the house of David and the inhabitants of Jerusalem to cleanse them from sin and impurity."[75]

---

71. Matt 21:1–3.

72. Quoted in Matt 21:5.

73. *Eccl. Rab.*1.28. The *Midrash* on Ecclesiastes or *Qoʾelet*.

74. Zech 9:16–10:1.

75. Zech 13:1.

Not only is the background to these verses *Sukkoth* but the parallels with Jesus are quite marked. Jesus, who is Yahweh rides into Jerusalem as King on a donkey and on a colt the foal of a donkey as Zechariah prophesied (Matt 21:1–3). Zech 9:16–10:1 ascribes the giving of fertility and rain to Yahweh, the coming King. Jesus stood up at *Sukkoth* in the Temple and said that he is the source of living water. The King who has ridden in to Jerusalem is pierced, and will be mourned as an only child, as a firstborn and a consequence of his piercing is atonement. Jesus is the firstborn and only child of *El Elyon,* the Most High and as a consequence of his piercing there is atonement. When Jesus' side is pierced with the sword at his crucifixion, Zech 12:10 is quoted and applied to Jesus "These things happened so that scripture would be fulfilled . . . They will look on the one they have pierced." [76] and Rev 1:7 states: "Look he is coming with the clouds and every eye will see him, even those who pierced him; and all the peoples of the earth will mourn because of him."

However, as well as water, light is also a feature of the *Sukkoth* festival, evident in the line from Ps118 quoted above: "The LORD is God and he has made his light shine on us, with boughs in hand join in the festal procession." In the Temple, on the first night of the festival, the people descended to the Court of Women where there were golden candlesticks approximately 25 meters high[77] "and there was not a courtyard in Jerusalem that did not reflect the light of the *Beth ha-She'ubah.*"[78] This again was a really joyful occasion: "Men of piety and good works used to dance before them with burning torches in their hands, singing songs and praises. And countless levites [played] on harps, lyres, cymbals and trumpet and instruments of music on the fifteen steps leading down from the Court of the Israelites to the Court of the Women, corresponding to the Fifteen Songs of Ascents in the Psalms."[79] The Songs of Ascent are Psalms 120–134. The Fifteen Songs were sung on the 15 steps and according to legend,[80] King David wrote the songs when the Chaos waters threatened to rise up and flood the earth. David threw a shard of pottery into the pool with the divine name written on it, which caused the waters to be subdued and go down again, but later realized they had gone too

---

76. John 19:37.

77. According to the Talmud they were 50 cubits high and one cubit is 0.5 meters.

78. *m.Suk* 5:1.

79. *m.Suk* 5:4.

80. Patai, *Man and Temple,* 56.

far and the earth wouldn't be watered. He therefore composed the Fifteen Songs of Ascent so that the waters would ascend nearer to the surface and water the earth, thus clearly linking the Temple, King David, the Divine Name and the Chaos waters with *Sukkoth*.[81] The Light ceremony was originally a sun worship ceremony which further links *Sukkoth* with themes of fertility.[82]

At the end of the festival Jesus "again spoke to the people and said 'I am the light of the world. Whoever follows me will never walk in darkness, but will have the light of life.'"[83] Therefore, immediately following the festival of *Sukkoth* and the Light ceremony that lit up all of Jerusalem, Jesus declares that he is "the light of the world." John had already told us that Jesus was the "light of all people;"[84] the "true light that gives light to everyone,"[85] the light that "shines in the darkness and the darkness has not overcome it."[86] In Matt 4:16 we are told that Jesus went to live in Capernaum, in "Galilee of the Gentiles" in fulfillment of the messianic prophecy from Isa 9:1–2 "The people walking in darkness have seen a great light; on those living in the land of deep darkness a light has dawned." Furthermore, at his dedication in the Temple, Jesus is identified by Simeon as "a light to lighten the gentiles."[87]

Hag ha-Asif

The fact that Jesus' parables are littered with allusions to agricultural themes, seeds, harvest, etc could be put down to the audience he was addressing, but, not all of his listeners were simple rural folk. He also spoke with the learned. What is more likely is that Jesus was using seed, water, harvest as ways to explain the kingdom, because in fact those were the metaphors and images that resonated with people. These were also images that were associated with all the major festivals, each of which,

81. *m.Suk* 5:4

82. "When they reached the gate that leads out to the east they turned their faces to the west and said 'Our fathers when they were in this place turned with their back toward the Temple of the Lord and their faces toward the east, and they worshipped the sun toward the east; but as for us our eyes are turned toward the Lord." *m.Suk* 5:4.

83. John 8:12.

84. John 1:4.

85. John 1:9.

86. John 1:5.

87. Luke 2:29–32.

originally at least, were connected to a particular harvest. The image of harvest is particularly relevant to the festival of *Sukkoth*, which is also known as *hag ha-Asif*, the festival of ingathering. It was the harvest of wheat and grapes. This is especially interesting as the "ingathering of the exiles" forms one of the messianic expectations of Rabbinic Judaism. We saw above that Zechariah relies heavily on themes from *Sukkoth* and in the final chapter *Sukkoth* is the festival that will be celebrated on the Day of the LORD, when all the nations will be gathered in. There is a tradition that Jesus will return at *Sukkoth* and gather in the exiles, to "the Holy City, the new Jerusalem"[88] which doesn't need the sun or the moon to shine on it because "the Lamb is its lamp"[89] and where he offers "water without cost from the spring of the water of life."[90] All of which are elements foreshadowed at *Sukkoth* and fulfilled in Jesus who declared himself at the festival to be the source of living water and the Light of the World.

Furthermore, the particular crops harvested at *Sukkoth*, those of grapes and wheat are also associated with judgement. Grapes are associated with God's wrath[91] and the wine they produce with his cup of wrath.[92] The sifting of wheat from chaff is also an image used in the Old Testament for judgement.[93] It is therefore no coincidence that the Temple, whose rituals sought to avert God's judgement and wrath was built on the threshing floor of *Araunah*.[94] Jesus is also associated with both images. At his death he "drank the cup of wrath"[95] and his return will set in motion the final judgement:

"I looked and there before me was a white cloud, and seated on the cloud was one like a son of man with a crown of gold on his head and a sharp sickle in his hand. Then another angel came out of the Temple and called in a loud voice to him who was sitting on the cloud. 'Take

88. Rev 21:2.

89. Rev 21:23.

90. Rev 21:6.

91. "I have trodden the winepress alone; from the nations no one was with me. I trampled them in my anger and trod them down in my wrath; their blood spattered my garments and I stained all my clothing." (Isa 63:3).

92. "Take from my hand this cup filled with the wine of my wrath and make all the nations to whom I send you drink it." Jer 25:15. See also Isa 51:17, 22.

93. Pss 1:4; 35:4–6; Job 21:17–18; Isa 17:13; 29:5; 41:2; Jer 13:24.

94. 2 Chron 3:1.

95. This is the cup of which he spoke at Gethsemane which we will look at further in chapter 5.

your sickle and reap, because the time to reap has come, for the harvest of the earth is ripe.' So he who was seated on the cloud swung his sickle over the earth and the earth was harvested. Another angel came out of the Temple in heaven, and he too had a sharp sickle. Still another angel, who had charge of the fire, came from the altar and called in a loud voice to him who had the sharp sickle, 'Take your sharp sickle and gather the clusters of grapes from the earth's vine, because its grapes are ripe.' The angel swung his sickle on the earth, gathered its grapes and threw them into the great winepress of God's wrath."[96]

Therefore, Jesus, Son of Man and King will take part in the judgement and the harvest of the earth, a harvest associated with grapes and the wrath of God. He will have a sharp sickle in his hand to carry out the harvest. This is the same image that John the Baptist applied to Jesus at his baptism "His winnowing fork is in his hand and he will clear his threshing floor, gathering his wheat into the barn and burning up the chaff with unquenchable fire."[97] Therefore, not only are all these images from *Sukkoth* connected with God's plan of redemption but they are also associated with Jesus, as the festivals, as Paul said, are a shadow of things to come.[98]

The Temple

As mentioned earlier, Zechariah is full of messianic references that are also linked to *Sukkoth*.[99] However, if Christianity was the only form of Judaism that saw these prophecies as messianic, it could be laid open to the charge that it read its own "particular" version of messianism back into the Old Testament texts. Indeed, that is exactly what the majority of Jewish writers claim. What the Jewish writers fail to acknowledge however, is that the most of these prophecies are also understood as messianic within the form of Judaism of which they are heirs.[100] Therefore, the fact that in the New Testament so many of these prophecies can be applied

96. Rev 14:14–19.

97. Matt 3:12.

98. Col 2:17.

99. There are too many to allude to here so we will just look at those that are directly linked with *Sukkoth*.

100. There are in fact approximately 71 direct quotes or allusions to Zechariah in the New Testament. Kaiser, *The Messiah*, 211.

to the biographical details of Jesus' life adds further weight to the New Testament claim that Jesus is the Messiah, as the claim is substantiated by prophecies that are accepted as Messianic by both of the major forms of Judaism to emerge from the first century, that is both Christianity and Rabbinic Judaism.

In Zechariah there are two main figures who are called "olive trees"—Zerubbabel the "King"[101] and Joshua the High Priest. The olive, as the source of the anointing oil signifies that they are Anointed. However, neither of these figures are understood as *the* Messiah, but are simply "symbolic of things to come."[102] Nonetheless, Zechariah is told by the LORD to place the crown on the head of Joshua the High Priest rather than Zerubabbel the King.[103] This not only demonstrates the link between the offices of King and High Priest in Messianic thought but also demonstrates, that in fact the High Priest was to take over the role of the King as *the* Anointed. These two stand by the Menorah,[104] which represents the Glory of the LORD, that is his presence. This is exactly what the pillar of fire did in the Exodus and the *ner tamid* does in the present day synagogue. We noted above that Jesus (and the Servant whose role he fulfilled) was the "light to the Gentiles" and "the true light that gives light to everyone" and the one who glorified God,[105] that is made him manifest.

A further designation of Messiah is attested here, that of the "Branch." This is mentioned in Zech 3:8 and Zech 6:12–13, and in this instance is linked with the building of the Temple: "Behold the man, whose name is the Branch, and he will branch out from his place and build the Temple of the LORD. It is he who will build the Temple of the LORD, and he will be clothed with majesty and will sit and rule on his throne. And he will be a priest on his throne. And there will be harmony between the two."

Following his arrest, Pilate presents Jesus to the people saying: "Behold the man"[106] the words John records,[107] taking us by allusion to

---

101. He was of the line of David and would have been King but with the demise of the monarchy he was governor of Judah.

102. Zech 3:8.

103. Zech 6:11.

104. Zech 4:2–3.

105. John 13:31.

106. These words are perhaps best known in their Latin version '*Ecce homo*' from the Vulgate translation of the Old Testament and now often associated with paintings of Jesus' trial.

107. John19:5.

Zechariah and demonstrating that this is *the man,* Jesus, the Branch,[108] that is the Anointed, who will build the Temple of the LORD and will be clothed in majesty and will rule on his throne. In him, the role of High Priest and King will finally be harmonized.[109] Jesus himself quotes Zech 13:7 to prophesy that his disciples will desert him. "I will strike the shepherd and the sheep will be scattered" (Mark 14.27). The Shepherd as we saw in chapter 2 is a title of the King. In addition, in Zech 11:12–13 we find a foreshadowing of what will happen to Judas having betrayed the Messiah: "They took the thirty pieces of silver the price set on him by the people of Israel, and they used them to buy the potter's field, as the Lord commanded me."[110] There are further passages in Zechariah that also link Jesus with the building of the Temple. In Zech 4:7 the "capstone" which is interpreted as referring to the Messiah[111] is associated with Zerubbabel. As Jesus is from the line of Judah[112] his lineage also includes the Kings David, Solomon and Zerubbabel.[113] A later *midrash* on the building of the Temple also expects a descendant of Zerubbabel to be the King Messiah who will build the Temple: "from the tribe of Judah were descended Solomon, who built the first Temple, and Zerubbabel who built the second Temple; and from him will be descended the King Messiah who will rebuild the Temple."[114] The capstone was the final stone which had a vital role to play in the stability of the Temple. The Messiah, then is the one who will not only rebuild the Temple but who is also the capstone of the Temple.

Psalm 118:22 the last part of the *Hallel* recited at the water pouring ceremony also talks about a stone: "The stone the builders rejected has become the cornerstone." This is the cornerstone of Isa 28:16: "See I lay a stone in Zion, a tested stone, a precious cornerstone for a sure

108. Other passages in the Old Testament also identify the Branch as the Messiah Isa 4:2, 11:1 Jer 23:5–6, 33:15.

109. This will become evident in chapter 4 when we consider the Day of Atonement.

110. Matthew records Judas' change of heart, having betrayed Jesus for 30 pieces of silver, he throws the coins in the Temple and hangs himself. The chief priests decide to buy the potters field with the money as a burial ground for foreigners. Matt 27:1–10. Matthew says it is to fulfill the prophecy in Jeremiah (19:1–13; 32:6–9) but it also fulfills the Zechariah prophecy, which most bibles also reference.

111. *The Messiah,* Levey, 98.

112. He is the Lion of Judah (Rev 5:5).

113. Matt 1:1–6, Luke 3:31–34.

114. Levey, *The Messiah,* 99.

foundation."[115] In the ancient near east the cornerstone of a Temple held special significance; it was the foundation stone, once it was in place, the rest of the building was built round it and confirmed to its angles. Jesus himself quotes Ps 118:22 after teaching the parable of the tenants, indicating that he was in fact the son in the parable who is killed by the tenants and the cornerstone, that was rejected in the prophecy.[116] This is reinforced by the fact that he does this in the last few days before his rejection and crucifixion, immediately following his triumphal entry as King into Jerusalem where he was greeted with words from the same Psalm, "Blessed is he who comes in the name of the Lord,"[117] further confirming that this is what he meant—he was the messianic King who they were about to reject and kill. This provoked the reaction in the chief priests and the teachers of the law to search for a way to arrest him "because they knew he had spoken this parable against them." That is, they were the ones who would reject the King's son, the cornerstone.

Following Pentecost, Peter also quoted this passage to condemn the Jewish leaders[118] and quotes both passages (Isa 28:16 and Ps 118:22) indicating that the stone that was rejected, that is Jesus, has become the cornerstone of the new Temple which is made up of the "living stones" of his followers.[119] Jesus is the capstone and the cornerstone, but he is also the "stone that causes people to stumble and a rock that make them fall."[120] As Peter explains: "They stumble because they disobey the message."[121] For those who believe he is the Messiah, Jesus is the cornerstone and the capstone of the new Temple but for those who don't he is the stone that causes people to stumble; as Jesus says "Blessed is anyone who does not stumble on account of me." This is just after he has identified himself as the Messiah to John's disciples.[122] The idea of Jesus as the

115. Although Zion is actually a hill which forms part of the Temple mount, it also has a metaphorical usage in the Bible whereby it means God's dwelling place, which also links it with the Temple.

116. Matt 21:42, Mark 12:10, Luke 20:17.

117. Ps 118:26.

118. Acts 4:11.

119. 1 Pet 2:4–7.

120. This is also said of Yahweh in Isa 8.14 again confirming the Jesus/Yahweh identification.

121. 1 Pet 2:8.

122. Matt 11:6.

cornerstone of the new Temple is also taken up by Paul.[123] Yet a further stone is mentioned in Zechariah: "the LORD says 'See I have set a stone in front of Joshua! There are seven eyes on that stone and I will engrave an inscription on it . . . and I will remove the sin of this land in a single day.'"[124] It has been suggested that this could be the signet with the Name that the High Priest wore on his forehead when he bore the sin of the people[125] and therefore when he emerged from the Holy of Holies, he was "coming in the name of the Lord," as the people were to proclaim of Jesus on his triumphal entry with the words from Ps118:26.[126] Although not directly connected to these stones, at his entry into Jerusalem, Jesus is told by the Pharisees in the crowd to stop his disciples from proclaiming him as King to which Jesus replies: "I tell you if they keep quiet, the stones will cry out."[127] The whole of creation knew who he was, all things were created through him. The Word, the breath of God of which the very atoms which formed the stones were made, wanting to burst into praise and proclaim that their Creator had come.

Rebuilding the Temple is one of the Messianic expectations within Judaism. However, at the time of Jesus the Temple was still standing, therefore when Jesus says that the Temple will be destroyed and rebuilt in three days, as John explains, he is referring to his body. This is not just in some metaphorical sense. The Temple was the place where God was present amongst his people, as the Tabernacle had been before it. In John's Gospel it is said that the Word, that is Jesus, was made flesh and tabernacled (*skeine*) amongst his people. Another reason given for the temporary dwellings, the *sukkah* which feature at *Sukkoth*, the Feast of Tabernacles is that they serve as a reminder that the life we have here is temporary and that we are dependent upon God for our existence as the Israelites did. A reminder that God provided sustenance in the desert wanderings of Israel and will continue to provide, but also a reminder that our tabernacle, our flesh is temporary, just as Jesus tabernacled in the flesh with us on earth for a short time so that we could be enthroned with

123. Eph 2:19–20.

124. Zech 3:9. In Revelation the Lamb has seven eyes (which are linked to the seven spirits (Rev5:6). There are various interpretations of what this symbolizes including the possibility that it refers to the seven spirits mentioned in Isa 11:2 or it could also refer to the Holy Spirit, as 7 is the number of perfection.

125. Exod 28:38.

126. Barker, *Great High Priest,* 220.

127. Luke 19:39.

him for eternity. It is also interesting to speculate whether the *sukkah* also represents the Temple, which in turn represents the cosmos, much as the reed huts, which were constructed during the New Year Enthronement Ceremony represented the Temple in the cultures surrounding Israel, particularly as *Sukkoth* in the Old Testament is the festival at which the Temple was dedicated.

Matthew is the only one to record that Jesus is hailed as Son of David on his entry into Jerusalem, and the only one who records the healing of the blind and lame in the Temple suggesting a link between the two. This is interesting, as before David conquered Jerusalem he is taunted by the Jebusites,[128] who said "You will not get in here; even the blind and lame can ward you off,"[129] which is followed by the comment: "That is why they say 'The blind and the lame' will not enter the house."[130] In Lev 21:18 the blind and the lame are amongst the descendants of Aaron who were not allowed to be priests. Matthew is therefore highlighting the great act of reversal that Jesus is about to accomplish. He is the Messiah, entering Jerusalem from the East, from the Mount of Olives; hailed as the Son of David, healing the blind and the lame who, as part of the new creation would now not only be *allowed* in the Temple but would become *part* of the Temple. Living stones, no longer *barred from being priests* but *part* of the *Holy Priesthood*. In Matthew, Jesus' triumphal entry occurs immediately after the has healed two blind men as he was leaving Jericho who also hail him as Son of David.[131] Immediately they "received their sight," they follow Jesus, in contrast to the "blind" Pharisees who don't see who Jesus is. "Woe to you, teachers of the law and Pharisees, you hypocrites! You shut the door of the kingdom of heaven in people's faces. You yourselves do not enter, nor will you let those enter who are trying to."[132] Jesus is therefore demonstrating that it is not anything external that bars you from God's presence, that makes you unclean but the internal state of your heart; that ritual cleansing is no longer the means of entering God's presence, but rather being cleansed by his blood.

In the final chapter of Zechariah, there are several prophecies concerning the Day of the LORD, that is when the Messiah is expected that

128. The Jebusites were the original inhabitants of Jerusalem.

129. 2 Sam 5:6.

130. 2 Sam 5:8.

131. Matt 20:29–33.

132. In this passage (Matt 23:1–33) Jesus criticizes the hypocrisy of the Pharisees and calls them "blind guides," "blind fools," "blind men," "blind Pharisee."

are expressly identified with *Sukkoth*: "On that day his feet will stand on the Mount of Olives, east of Jerusalem . . . on that day there will be no sunlight . . . on that day living water will flow out from Jerusalem . . . the LORD will be King over the whole earth . . . on that day there will be one LORD, and his name the only name . . . on that day there will no longer be a trader in the house of the LORD Almighty."[133]

Jesus, Yahweh incarnated, enters Jerusalem, from the Mount of Olives in the East,[134] as LORD and King over the whole earth.[135] He enters the Temple and expels the traders from there. He is the source of living water which will flow from Jerusalem following his crucifixion[136] at which the sun is eclipsed.[137] As we saw in chapter 2 the Temple is a microcosm of the universe and therefore Jesus' act of cleansing the Temple was a foreshadowing of his cleansing the cosmos, just days later, through his atoning death on the cross.

Therefore Zechariah is not only full of messianic prophecies but is also closely associated with *Sukkoth*. Here, we have a King and a High Priest[138] who are both anointed and "symbols of things to come," a stone which is linked to the removal of sin by the LORD in one day. We have the Branch, a descendant of Zerubbabel who will build the Temple and a Messianic King riding into Jerusalem on a donkey and on a colt, the foal of donkey. This King will be pierced by the people who will then mourn for him as a firstborn son, as a consequence of which a fountain will be opened to cleanse the people from sin and there will be rain for the harvest and fertility. When the Lord comes and reigns, he will gather in the exiles[139] and all people will go up to Jerusalem to worship him as King and celebrate the festival of *Sukkoth*. Therefore *Sukkoth*, the festival of joy; the harvest festival and festival of ingathering celebrates the restored

---

133. Zech 14:4–9, 21.

134 Jesus enters Jerusalem from Bethphage and Bethany on the Mount of Olives and it's from there that he sends for the donkey and the colt, therefore he would actually have stood on the Mount of Olives (Matt 21:1–2.).

135. Rev 19:16.

136. The Holy Spirit, (the living water John 7:39) would be poured out onto the disciples in Jerusalem at Pentecost (Acts 2:1–4; Joel 2:28).

137. Matt 27:45.

138. The High Priest here is named Joshua, which is the English spelling of *Yeshua*, Jesus' Hebrew name. *Iesous* is the Greek transliteration of *Yeshua*, whose English spelling is Jesus. Therefore Joshua and Jesus are essentially the same name.

139. Zech 10:10.

relationship with God, the pouring out of water as God's blessing and the celebration of God's presence as a light amongst them.

In the New Testament Jesus, the Messiah, rides into Jerusalem as King (and High Priest) on a donkey and on a colt the foal of a donkey understood as direct fulfillment of the Zechariah prophecy. He says that the old Temple will be destroyed (as it is in 70 AD) and that he is the cornerstone of the new Temple, but also the stone that will cause people to stumble if they don't believe. He is pierced by the people, and his death and resurrection cleanse sin in a single day, and the fountain of living water, the Holy Spirit is poured out on those who believe in him. Although we don't know the day or the hour,[140] tradition has it that Jesus will also return at Sukkoth, when all people will worship him as King and there will be living water and the tree of life bearing 12 crops of fruit and leaves for the healing of the nations.

Jesus at Sukkoth

Given all the imagery and symbolism associated with *Sukkoth* which ties in directly with Jesus, it would make perfect sense to expect his return at *Sukkoth*. Perhaps even more so when we consider that there is also a school of thought that suggests that Jesus was actually born at *Sukkoth*. The traditional date of twenty-fifth December to celebrate Jesus' birth was purportedly chosen to steer people away from the pagan feast of Saturnalia, where the sun god Saturn was worshipped. This coincides with the Winter Solstice when we have the shortest day and longest night, signaling the beginning of the period when the days begin to lengthen and the light triumphs over the dark. We also know now that the calculations about the year of Jesus' birth are wrong and that it did in fact take place at least 4 years earlier than originally thought, based on Herod's death occurring in 4 BC.

It's interesting therefore that there are two different sets of calculations for Jesus' birth, one of which does take it approximately to the December date but the other, interestingly takes it to *Sukkoth*. One of the calculations for *Sukkoth* surrounds the conception and birth of John the Baptist, based on the Priestly rota.[141] On this basis, John's birth is calcu-

---

140. Matt 24:36.

141. 'We know that the priest Zechariah was serving in the Temple when the angel came to him to announce the birth of John the Baptist. Zechariah was assigned to

lated to be at Passover, which would mean that when Jesus was born six months later it would be *Sukkoth*. Other more speculative reasons given for the *Sukkoth* date include the suggestion that if Jesus had been born in December it would be too cold for sheep and shepherds to be out in the fields, which forms part of the birth narrative in Luke. Furthermore, the Angels' announcement to the shepherds that they were bringing "Good news of great Joy" is also understood to indicate *Sukkoth*, the festival most associated with joy. A further suggestion for the *Sukkoth* date is that it would explain why there was "no room at the inn" As *Sukkoth* is a pilgrim festival and as Bethlehem is only 5 miles outside Jerusalem it's quite likely that it would also be full with pilgrims. If this were so, and Jesus was born at the beginning of *Sukkoth* it would also mean that his circumcision, 8 days after his birth would have taken place on the eighth day of the festival, which is known as *Shemini Atzeret*.

Shemini Atzeret

Sukkoth was also known as the 'feast of the nations' signified by the 70 bulls that were sacrificed.[142] However on *Shemini Atzeret* only one bull was sacrificed, just for Israel. In Lev 23:36 it says: "For seven days [of Sukkoth] you shall bring a fire offering to God. On the eighth day, it shall be a holy convocation for you . . . it is a day of detention." This was interpreted by Rashi[143] as God saying to Israel "I have detained you with me" suggesting a special time of intimacy between God and Israel as God's chosen, his "son"[144] If this were the date of Jesus' circumcision, it would add even more significance to the occasion. Rashi comments: "You may compare it to a King who had held a festival for seven days and invited all of the country's inhabitants (the nations of the world) to the seven days of feasting. When the seven days of feasting were over, he said to his friend (Israel), 'Let us now have a small meal together, just you and I.'"[145]

---

the eighth group of *Abia* and served during the week of the 12th *Sivan*. If we add the forty weeks for a normal pregnancy, we reach the 14th *Nisan*; this means that John the Baptist, was born at the beginning of Passover. According to Judaism, the herald of the Messiah is expected in a Passover night.' Keegstra, *God's Prophetic Feasts*,18.

142. Representing the 70 known nations of the world at the time.

143. One of the best known Jewish Commentators.

144. "When Israel was a child, I loved him, and out of Egypt I called my son" (Hos 11:1).

145. *Bemidbar Rabbah* 21, *Sukkah* 55b. Midrash on Numbers (*Bemidbar* means

In the Middle Ages, *Shemini Atzeret* was also associated with the completion of the cycle of Torah readings, that is, the old Torah cycle was completed and a new one begun. This one day festival is called *Simchat Torah*.[146] Although this is well after the time of Jesus, it is interesting that this is also the day that celebrates God's word, the word that Jesus, the Word said he had not come to do away with but to fulfill. As we have already noted, the eighth day is significant within Judaism, since the eighth day signifies a new era, namely a complete week, plus one new day. Therefore if Jesus was born at *Sukkoth* it would mean that the one who was to renew the covenant had been sealed with the sign of the old covenant, that is circumcised on the eighth day, the beginning of a new era. Furthermore, if Jesus had been born at *Sukkoth* it is possible that his conception would have been at *Hanukkah*, the Feast of Dedication, also known a the Festival of Lights, which would be an appropriate time for the Light of the World to be conceived. Finally, we saw that in John's Gospel Jesus is described as "tabernacling" with us, that is, he is "God with us." Immanuel, as the Isaiah prophecy foretold. He is God, tabernacling in flesh amongst us, fully man and fully God, which would also lend further weight to the proposition that Jesus was born at *Sukkoth*, the Feast of Tabernacles. There is a further link between Jesus and *Sukkoth*, in that at the transfiguration, Peter asks whether he should build a *sukkah* for Jesus, Moses and Elijah who are also talking with Jesus about his death. As his death, is specifically spoken about in this instance as his "Exodus" the major redemption event for Israel, which lies behind the festival of *Sukkoth*, *Sukkoth* seems an attractive suggestion, especially as there is no scriptural basis for the traditional date of 25th December. Nonetheless a number of these suggestions are disputed and we will consider the cosmic significance in the traditional date in chapter 6.

"In the desert," the first Hebrew words of the book of Numbers, each of the five books of the Torah are known by the words they begin with.

146. "Joy in the Torah"—the Torah scrolls are carried whilst completing seven circuits around the synagogue accompanied by joyful dancing. In Israel this is celebrated on the same day as *Shemini Atzeret* but is celebrated on two separate days in the Diaspora.

Chapter 4

DAY OF ATONEMENT

HIGH PRIEST IS ONE of Jesus' titles, and the second major paradigm of his death and resurrection in the New Testament, is that of the High Priest on the Day of Atonement. In order to understand this properly, therefore, we need to determine just who the High Priest was and what in particular his role entailed on the Day of Atonement.

The High Priest

The details for keeping the festival are found in Leviticus 16 and the only explanation given is that the instructions are for Aaron, the High Priest concerning how to enter the Most Holy Place of the Tabernacle, because previously two of his sons died when they approached the LORD.[1] "Tell your brother Aaron that he is not to come whenever he chooses into the Most Holy Place behind the curtain in front of the atonement cover on the Ark, or else he will die. For I will appear in the cloud over the atonement cover."[2] In Exodus 28 there is a detailed version of the garments, that the High Priest was to wear. They were to consist of a breast-piece, an ephod, a robe, a woven tunic, a turban and a sash. They are to be made of gold, blue, purple and scarlet yarn and fine linen. Details about the High Priest's turban are also given: "On the turban that Aaron is to wear there

---

1. There is an earlier, though less detailed reference to the festival in Exod 30:9–10.

2. Lev 16:2.

is to be a plate of pure gold with the words "Holy to the LORD" engraved on it as a seal, which he will wear on his forehead "and he will bear the guilt involved in the sacred gift the Israelites consecrate, whatever their gifts may be. It will be on Aaron's forehead continually so that they will be acceptable to the LORD."[3] On the Day of Atonement however, the High Priest wore only the white linen garments. "He is to put on the sacred linen tunic, with linen undergarments next to his body; he is to tie the linen sash around him and put on the linen turban. These are sacred garments; so he must bathe himself with water before he puts them on." Another unusual feature of the High Priest's garments was that they were not sewn, but woven so that they were seamless.

The main events of the festival described in Leviticus 16 are as follows: having bathed and put on the sacred linen garments, the High Priest presents two goats, which must be identical, before the LORD at the entrance of the tent of meeting. He then casts lots; one goat is to be "for" the LORD, the other, also termed the scapegoat is to be "for" *Azazel*.[4] The High Priest sacrifices a bull for his own sins and along with a censer full of burning coals and incense for the altar, he takes the bull's blood and sprinkles it on the atonement cover, in Hebrew the *kapporet*, also called the mercy seat. This is the cover of the Ark of the Covenant which housed the tablets of the law, where God was enthroned between the Cherubim.

The High Priest then exits the Holy of Holies, slaughters the goat for the LORD and takes its blood up into the Holy of Holies as a sin offering. He subsequently emerges from there on clouds of incense and sprinkles the blood in other parts of the Temple. The High Priest then places his hands onto the goat for *Azazel* and confesses over it "all the wickedness and rebellion of the Israelites—all their sins"[5] The goat is led out and released into the wilderness. If the ritual was effective the crimson wool which had been tied onto the Temple[6] turned white in accordance with the words from Isaiah: "though your sins be as scarlet, they shall be as white as snow; though they be red like crimson, they shall be as wool."[7]

---

3. Exod 28:29.

4. We will look at a slightly different understanding of this below.

5. Lev 16:21.

6. Crimson wool was also tied onto the scapegoat.

7. Isa 1:18.

We know from the statement in the *Mishnah*, that as stipulated in Leviticus 16, the Day of Atonement took place once a year[8] and it was the only time in the year that the High Priest could enter the Holy of Holies.[9] That this was still considered to be dangerous is evident from the detail found in a later Jewish writing, the Talmud, namely that the High Priest had to have a rope tied round his ankle in case he died whilst in there. The details given are quite sparse and without the help of some of the inter-testamental texts such as 1 Enoch[10] as well as the writings of Philo,[11] Josephus[12] and the *Mishnah*[13] we would have little understanding of the ceremony during the second Temple period, and in particular the symbolism which was an important part of it. For example, in 1 Enoch there is a longer version of the story of the fallen angels that we read about in Genesis 6. In 1 Enoch we learn that the angels were led by *Azazel* (also named *Semihaza*), the chief of the fallen angels. They rebelled and came to earth and married human women, bringing with them heavenly knowledge which was then used to corrupt the earth, namely, the arts of metallurgy which allowed weapons to be made, the art of make-up,[14] and the abuse of women. This was the start of the events that led to the Flood. We also learn that *Azazel* is bound hand and foot and cast into the darkness in the desert by the angel *Raphael*,[15] which sheds further light on the goat being cast into the wilderness.

Further evidence from the Second Temple period also throws light onto the ceremony itself, thereby illuminating our understanding of it. It

8. That is before the destruction of the Temple in 70 AD.

9. The temple equivalent of the Tabernacle's Most Holy Place.

10. *1 Enoch* is part of a series of Jewish writings dating from second century BC to first century AD. 1 Enoch is thought to emanate from the second century BCE although the portions which are designated the Similituces or Parables may be a later addition. The suggested date for these vary, particularly as this portion of 1 Enoch was not found amongst the Dead Sea Scrolls. However a consensus was reached amongst the experts of the Third Enochic Seminar (Camaldoli, Italy 2005) that it was a pre-Christian text.

11. Philo of Alexandria, Jewish writer c. 20BC—50AD.

12. Flavius Josephus, a Jewish writer c. 37—100 AD.

13. Oral Torah compiled c.190 AD which although it was written after the destruction of the Temple, nonetheless contains information on the Temple services and rituals which are deemed to be authentic.

14. Interestingly, considering the current trend, the painting of eyebrows is mentioned!

15. *1 Enoch* 10:4–5.

suggests that rather than "Holy to the LORD," it was in fact the name of the LORD, the Tetragrammaton (YHWH) that was written on the High Priest's turban,[16] indicating that the High Priest, *the* Anointed was functioning as the LORD in the Temple, just as the King (who was also High Priest) and *the* Anointed was understood to be the earthly manifestation of Yahweh in the pre-exilic enthronement ceremony. In addition, rather than the goats in the ceremony being "for" *Azazel* and the LORD, which suggests they were sacrifices 'for' them,[17] the Hebrew can be translated "as," that is, the goats in fact represented *Azazel* and Yahweh. Therefore the blood of the goat that represented the LORD (Yahweh) was taken up into the Holy of Holies by the High Priest, who was the earthly manifestation of the LORD. This meant that in effect the LORD was taking his own blood into the Holy of Holies to effect atonement.

> It was therefore the life of the LORD himself that renewed the broken covenant and restored the creation to unity with the Creator.[18]

Although, as mentioned above, the biblical account details the colors for the High Priests' robe and the veil of the Temple which was also made up of the same four colors, no explanation is given for them. Nonetheless, we do know from accounts given by Philo and Josephus that these colors were symbolic: each of them represented one of the four elements of which the material world was made. The blue represented air, purple, the sea, red represented fire and white the earth.[19] In contrast the white linen garments were representative of the heavenly, angelic body. During the Day of Atonement ritual the High Priest removed his outer vestment made up of the four colors and wore just the linen garments. We noted in chapter 2 that the Temple represented/was the cosmos, the outer courts, the sea and the earth and the Holy of Holies, heaven. Therefore, the curtain that separated the Holy of Holies from the rest of the Temple, separated the invisible world from the visible. This meant that when the High Priest entered into the Holy of Holies through the curtain, having removed his outer garment he was leaving behind the material world and

16. *Letter of Aristeas*, 43:5. The date of this is uncertain but it was written in Greek, possibly by a Jewish writer living in Alexandria.

17. Barker has pointed out that this is how Origen, one of the Early Church Father's understood it. *Against Celsus* 6.43. Barker, *The Great High Priest*, 75.

18. Barker, *The Great High Priest*, 75.

19. Josephus, *War* 5:212–3; *Ant.*3:138–4.

entering into heaven. That is, he was passing through from the material world, represented by the curtain and his outer clothing that he had discarded, into the heavenly realm hence the warnings against the danger this involved. As observed in the Leviticus instructions, coming into the presence of the LORD without the right preparation could be fatal.[20]

> The High Priest was the only person who were an outer vestment made of the same fabric as the veil of the Temple and presumably, with the same significance: it veiled the glory of the Lord. The vestment represented the matter in which the Lord clothed himself when he appeared with his people, so the veil and the vestment became symbols of the incarnation . . . the High Priest wore this colored garment only when he was functioning in the visible creation as an incarnation of the Lord: within the veil, he wore the white linen robe of an angel.[21]

Jesus the High Priest

In the book of Hebrews, Jesus is presented as the High Priest who has made the final Day of Atonement sacrifice, that is, his death and resurrection are understood to be the ultimate fulfillment of what the Day of Atonement ritual only foreshadowed. As *the* Anointed, the one who had been foretold, as we have seen throughout the prophets, Jesus was the true High Priest who took, not a substitute for his own blood as the High Priest had done into the man-made Holy of Holies, but his own blood into the *actual* Holy of Holies—heaven.

> But when Christ came as high priest of the good things that are now already here, he went through the greater and more perfect tabernacle that is not made with human hands, that is to say, is not part of this creation. He did not enter by means of the blood of goats and calves; but he entered the Most Holy Place once for all by his own blood, thus obtaining eternal redemption."[22]

As we have seen, in the laws given in Leviticus, the High priest was the only person who could enter the Holy of Holies and he could do this only once a year. Entering the Holy of Holies was entering into the

---

20. This is evident in other places e.g. the warning in Exodus that the Israelites shouldn't approach the mountain because the LORD's presence was there.

21 Barker, *The Great High Priest*, 75.

22. Heb 9:11–12.

presence of God, that's why the High Priest entered in his heavenly garb. Direct access to God therefore was only available to the High Priest and then only once a year. The High Priest therefore, as the Anointed was the mediator between God and the people. When Jesus died, John tells us that the curtain in the Temple was torn in two.[23] The writer of the book of Hebrews comments:

> Therefore, brothers and sisters, since we have confidence to enter the Most Holy Place by the blood of Jesus, by a new and living way opened for us through the curtain, that is, his body, and since we have a great priest over the house of God, let us draw near to God with a sincere heart in full assurance of faith, having our hearts sprinkled to cleanse us from a guilty conscience and having our bodies washed with pure water.[24]

As a result of Jesus' death, his sacrifice, taking his own blood as the Anointed, the LORD, into the heavenly tabernacle, he opened the way for everyone to have direct access to God. His body was torn so that everyone could come into God's presence at any time, not just the High Priest, on one day of the year. The curtain tearing in two was a physical manifestation of the spiritual reality that had taken place. The material world no longer hid God's presence, he was accessible to all because Jesus' material body had been torn. The High Priest's outer garments, made up of the same colors as the veil of the Temple were symbolic of this. They were the material world that concealed the presence of God. It was not just his body, but the earth that was torn: "And Jesus cried again with a loud voice and yielded up his spirit. And behold, the veil of the Temple was torn (*eschisthe*) in two, from top to bottom; and the earth shook and the rocks were torn (*eschisthesan*)."[25] Pitre states: "Notice the twofold consequence of Jesus' death: with the yielding up of his spirit, it is the Temple and the earth that are both 'torn asunder' (Greek: *schizo*). In other words, the effects of his death are both cultic and cosmic."[26] Jesus had carried out the final Atonement, that the Day of Atonement ritual prefigured:

> Nor did he enter heaven to offer himself again and again, the way the high priest enters the Most Holy Place every year with blood that is not his own. Otherwise Christ would have had to

23. Matt 27:51.

24. Heb 10:19–22.

25. Matt 27:50–51.

26. Pitre, Brant, "The New Temple," 63.

suffer many times since the creation of the world. But he has appeared once for all at the culmination of the ages to do away with sin by the sacrifice of himself. Just as people are destined to die once, after that to face judgement, so Christ was sacrificed once to take away the sins of many.[27]

The book of Hebrews does not mention the scapegoat with respect to Jesus. However both goats had to be identical, suggesting that they represented the one entity. Furthermore, the High Priest as *Yahweh* transferred the sins of Israel onto the goat, suggesting that in fact he bore the sins. Jesus was *Yahweh* in the flesh, he was "the image of the invisible God."[28] The fact that Israel's sins were transferred to the scapegoat or goat "as" *Azazel* and then sent away into the wilderness resonates with Jesus bearing all our sins on the cross,[29] where, at the point of death, he felt himself totally separated from God. "*Eloi eloi, lama sabacthani.*"[30] It is also interesting to speculate whether this lies behind the incident during Jesus' trial, when Pilate asks the people who they want him to release and who they want crucified. The crowd choose to release Barabbas, the wicked "son of the father" and choose Jesus to be crucified.[31] According to Matthew, Barabbas, was in fact called Jesus Barabbas, which meant that the people had a choice between two men, named *Yeshua*, "salvation;" one "son of the father" who wanted to "save" the Jewish people from the Romans by the use of violence, the other "Son of the Father" who wanted to save everyone from the impending wrath, by dying in their place.

Understanding the symbolism that lies behind the biblical narrative, explains so much more clearly what is actually happening; it also helps to uncover the connections that the first Christians and the New Testament writers were aware of between Jesus and his foreshadowing in the Jewish festivals. So far though, we have only just begun to discover some of the symbolism and the underlying theology as well as some of the ways that this all links to Jesus.

27. Heb 9:25–28.

28. Col 1:15.

29. 1 Pet 2:24.

30. Mark 15:34.

31. Barabbas was an insurrectionist and a murderer (Luke 23:19). His name means "son of the father."

The Letter of Barnabas[32] gives us further insight into what happens after the sacrifice. "Let them eat of the goat which is offered for their sins at the fast and let all the priests, but nobody else, eat of its inwards parts unwashed and with vinegar."[33] This is significant as one of the charges against Christianity is that as a Jew, Jesus would never tell his followers to drink his blood[34] This was also linked by Barnabas to Jesus' drinking vinegar on the cross.[35] As we saw in chapter 2, this was said of the King in an enthronement Psalm: "They put gall in my food and gave me vinegar for my thirst."[36] It is also interesting in this respect, that the High Priest and his sons had originally been the only ones who could eat the Bread of the Presence. As Barker has pointed out the regulations for handling the bread suggest, that in fact, in some way, it acquired holiness by being set in front of the Lord[37] and it therefore was the means whereby the Lord's presence was imparted when it was eaten each week by the High Priest and his family.[38]

Priestly Garments

One of those who judged Jesus at his trial was Caiphas, who previously, "because he was High Priest that year" had understood that it was expedient for one man to die.[39] In other words, he understood what lay behind the Day of Atonement festival and what had happened in the original enthronement festival namely, that one man, *the* Anointed,[40] had to "offer his life" as a sacrifice in order that atonement could be made for the nation. As High Priest, he knew that what took place on the Day of Atonement was only a prefiguring of the final Atonement that had to be made by Melchizedek, the High Priest. He would have been aware of the

32. A Christian work dated c 130 CE.

33. *Barn* 7.

34. John 6:53–55.

35. Matt 27:48; Mark 15:36; John 19:29.

36. Ps 69:21.

37. Barker points out that in the *Mishnah*, although the bread was set on a marble table in the Temple, when it was brought out again it was set on a gold table suggesting it had gained status.

38. Barker, Margaret, *The Great High Priest*, 69.

39. John 11:49–53; 18:13–14.

40. Whether the King at the enthronement ceremony or the High Priest in the Day of Atonement ritual.

teaching of the suffering Messiah. It was the priests who knew this teaching. This explains why "a large number of them became obedient to the
faith" once they had been told that Jesus was the Messiah who had been
prophesied.[41] At his trial Jesus remained silent, even when falsely accused
by two witnesses, just as it was prophesied in the words of Isaiah "He was
oppressed and afflicted yet he did not open his mouth: he was led like a
lamb to the slaughter and as a sheep before its shearers is silent, so he did
not open his mouth."[42] At his silence, Caiphas said to Jesus "'I charge you
under oath by the living God: Tell us if you are the Messiah, the Son of
God.' 'You have said so,' Jesus replied. 'But I say to all of you: from now
on you will see the Son of Man sitting at the right hand of the Mighty
One and coming on the clouds of heaven.' Upon hearing Jesus' answer
Caiphas tore his clothes and said: 'He has spoken blasphemy. Why do
we need any more witnesses? Look, you have now heard his blasphemy.
What do you think?' 'He is worthy of death,' they answered."[43] It is de-
bated whether it was Jesus' indirect answer to the question of whether he
was the Christ the Son of God, that elicited the charge of blasphemy or
indeed his further claim that he was the Son of Man.[44] Nonetheless, Jesus'
answer not only draws on the Son of Man prophecies in Daniel, but also
take us by allusion to Psalm 110, in which the King, is told by God that he
is "priest in the order of Melchizedek" and told sit at his right hand that
is the right hand of God, both of which Scriptures, Caiphas would have
been familiar with.

According to the *Mishnah*, blasphemy only takes place if the Divine
Name is pronounced[45] following which, those judging are to stand up and
rend their garments; this meant all layers, including the undergarment.[46]
This is exactly what Caiphas did.[47] If we think back to the instructions in
Exod 28:32/Lev 39:22[48] it states that the undergarment of the High Priest

41. Acts 6:7.

42. Isa 53:7–8. These were the words the eunuch was reading as we saw in the
previous chapter and which Philip explained were referring to Jesus.

43. Matt 26:63–66.

44. We will look at the identity of the Son of Man as a divine figure further down
but this is also a possibility.

45. *m.Sanh* 7.5.

46. The act of *Kriah*, tearing of clothes because of the loss of a close relative involves only one item of clothing, carried out within modern day Judaism.

47. Mark 14:63.

48. "You shall make the robe of the ephod all of blue. It shall have an opening for

had to be woven in such a way that it was all of one piece and the opening of the neck finished in such a way as to stop it being torn. There are
also specific instructions in Leviticus that forbid the tearing of the High
Priest's clothing.[49] If the High priest's clothing was torn it meant that he
could no longer carry out his High Priestly function.[50]

In contrast, Jesus robe was not torn. Following his crucifixion, John
records that the soldiers who crucified him took his clothes and divided
them amongst themselves but the undergarment remained: "This garment was seamless, woven in one piece from top to bottom."[51] Jesus had
a seamless garment, just as was stipulated for the High Priest.[52] As High
Priest, his sacrifice on the cross was the final Day of Atonement sacrifice
which fulfilled what had previously been prefigured in the festival. This
was the LORD come to his Temple, as Matthew made clear,[53] to fulfill
all that had been prefigured in the festivals. We know from Josephus that
Caiphas continued as High Priest until removed in 36 AD. However, we
also know from the Talmud that 40 years before the destruction of the
Temple in 70 AD, that the Day of Atonement sacrifices were ineffective:
"Our Rabbis taught: During the last forty years before the destruction
of the Temple the lot ['For the Lord'] did not come up in the right hand;
nor did the crimson-colored strap become white; nor did the western
most light shine; and the doors of the Hekal [Temple] would open by
themselves"[54]

---

the head in the middle of it, with a woven binding around the opening, like the opening in a garment, so that it may not tear."

49. "The priest who is chief among his brothers, on whose head the anointing oil
is poured and who has been consecrated to wear the garments shall not let the hair of
his head hang loose nor tear his clothes." Lev 21:10.

50. There are 613 commandments *mitzvot* and *mitzvah* 445 states that a *Kohen*
(a priest) should not enter the sanctuary with a torn garment. *Mitzvah* 373 states that
he High Priest is forbidden to tear his garment. Mending the covenant has the connotation of mending a tear, as in a garment and it's interesting to speculate that just as
the Temple "represented" the cosmos, and the high priest's garments also as we have
seen represented the material world, the fact that his garments couldn't be torn or
the priests couldn't wear torn garments in the sanctuary was because the garments in
effect would then represent a break in the covenant.

51. John 19:23.

52. Exod 28:32, 39:22, Lev 21:10.

53. Matt 3:3.

54. *b.Yoma* 39b. That is the tractate on the Day of Atonement in the Talmud.

The Lot cast for the goats on the Day of Atonement determined which would be for the LORD and which for *Azazel*. Prior to 30AD the black and the white stones, although picked by chance came up evenly, however from 30—70 AD only the black stone came up which was not only virtually impossible mathematically, but it was deemed to be a bad omen. The Red strip refers to the crimson wool, part of which was tied on the goat for *Azazel* and part tied on the Temple door, again for the last forty years that the Day of Atonement service was carried out, this remained red indicating that the sacrifice had not been accepted. The Temple doors swinging open every night of their own accord was also seen as a bad sign and that also occurred for the 40 years prior to the destruction and after Jesus had opened the way for all to come into the presence of God. Finally the menorah (the Western light), that which had been the subject of the Hanukkah miracle and which was supposed to remain alight at all times, also for those forty years went out each night, despite all attempts to keep it alight. The Menorah has lots of associations—the seven planets as well as the tree of life, but it was also associated with God's presence in the Temple, suggesting that God was no longer present in his Temple.

We mentioned in the previous chapter that Jesus' birth and therefore his death are earlier than originally thought due to a miscalculation[55] (Herod died in 4BC and this therefore gives an earlier date than the actual millennium, ironic as that is). We cannot also be sure, that the 40 year period of which the *Talmud* speaks, is an exact figure or whether it represents the symbolic use of numbers prevalent in the Bible.[56] Nonetheless, the fact remains that following the death of Jesus, the Day of Atonement ritual was no longer effective. Therefore although Caiphas' priesthood continued for a few years following Jesus' trial, symbolically and spiritually with the tearing of his garments, his priesthood had come to an end, replaced by the High Priest whose undergarment wasn't torn. Consequently just as the tearing of the curtain, made of the same material as the High Priestly robes, had a symbolical and spiritual meaning, the physical tearing of the High Priestly robes also reflected the spiritual

---

55. Carried out by a sixth century Monk named *Dionysius Exiguus*.

56. Forty is a symbolic number signifying purification. In the Flood, the rain lasted 40 days, Moses fasted and prayed on the mountain for 40 days and Israel wandered in the desert for 40 days whilst a new generation emerged. Jesus spent 40 days in the desert fasting and praying and then 40 days with his disciples before he ascended to heaven. What is particularly interesting is that the *mikveh*, the ritual bath is to be filled with 40 *se'ah* of water (approximately 150 gallons).

reality; one priesthood had ended and the other begun; the High Priest-hood in the order of Melchizedek. But who was Melchizedek?

Melchizedek

Melchizedek is mentioned only twice in the Old Testament, once in Gen-esis 14 following Abram's defeat of Kerderlaomer, "Then Melchizedek King of Salem brought out bread and wine. He was priest of God Most High, and he blessed Abram"[57] then Abram gave him a tenth of the pos-sessions he gained from the battle.[58] The second time is in Ps110:4. It is perhaps not surprising then, that the Jewish writers view the Christian claims made in the book of Hebrews as a stab in the dark, particularly as the claim is also made there, that this is a superior priesthood to that of the Levitical priesthood instituted in the Torah. Nonetheless, this is what is claimed in the book of Hebrews:

> If perfection could have been attained through the Levitical priesthood—and indeed the law given to the people established that priesthood—why was there still need for another priest to come, one in the order of Melchizedek, not in the order of Aaron? For when the priesthood is changed, the law must be changed also. He of whom these things are said belonged to a different tribe, and no one from that tribe has ever served at the altar. For it is clear that our Lord descended from Judah, and in regard to that tribe Moses said nothing about priests. And what we have said is even more clear if another priest like Melchize-dek appears, one who has become a priest not on the basis of a regulation as to his ancestry, but on the basis of the power of an indestructible life.[59]

In other words the Melchizedek priesthood is not handed down through a family line as it was with Aaron and his sons, but on the basis of "an indestructible life." What did this mean? We know from Genesis 14 that Melchizedek, was priest of *El Elyon*, God Most High in Jerusalem and from Ps110, that the King was also proclaimed "Priest forever in the or-der of Melchizedek." This is an enthronement Psalm which is thought to depict the "birth" of the new King, i.e his becoming "Son of God" (as

57. Gen 14:18–19.
58. Gen 14:20.
59. Heb 7:11–16.

it says of the King in Ps 2:7) in the Holy of Holies and his subsequent enthronement.[60] Verse three is particularly obscure and is translated in various ways, one of which is "From the womb of dawn, as Dew I have begotten you." It has been suggested that Dawn may refer to *Sahar* (Dawn) an Ugaritic goddess. The Hebrew word for dew is *Tal*, which is the name of a Canaanite fertility god and which throughout the Old Testament is connected with resurrection. It is interesting that there is a specific prayer for dew which is still said at Passover in the Synagogue which is also connected with themes of resurrection, re-creation and fertility.

If this was all that we had to go on, and before the discovery of the Dead Sea Scrolls, it was—it would still leave us very much in the dark. However, amongst the scrolls at Qumran, the scroll designated 11QMelch also talks about Melchizedek as an exalted figure, "a god-like being" who will atone for the sins of the people. Melchizedek's name has been substituted for the name of the LORD in the scroll which quotes Isa 61, so instead of reading "In the year of the LORD's favor" it reads "in the year of Melchizedek's favor." Ps82 is also quoted and its application to Melchizedek again suggests his divinity. In the text, the Melchizedek figure is expected to make the Great Atonement at the end of the tenth Jubilee, that is 490 years from that date, in the first "week" that is during the first seven years of the tenth Jubilee which it has been estimated would be around 19—25 AD. This would then coincide with the beginning of Jesus' ministry.[61]

Before he carried out his role as *the* Anointed on the Day of Atonement the High Priest had to undergo ritual cleansing. At the beginning of his ministry Jesus was fully immersed in the Jordan at this baptism and consequently anointed in the Holy Spirit, that is before he took up his role as the Anointed, the High Priest which he was to fulfill with his death and resurrection. Following his anointing with the Spirit and his subsequent testing in the wilderness, Jesus began his ministry in the Synagogue at Nazareth with an inaugural speech, which not only set the agenda for his ministry, but also declared who he was:

> He stood up to read and the scroll of the prophet Isaiah was
> handed to him. Unrolling it, he found the place where it is

60. Margaret Barker has written extensively on this, see for example, Barker, *The Great High Priest*.

61. Barker, *The Great High Priest*, 71. As mentioned earlier Jesus was born before 4BC when Herod died, and began his ministry at 30 according to Luke and therefore his ministry would have begun in the first seven years of the tenth jubilee.

written: The Spirit of the Lord is on me because he has anointed me to proclaim good news to the poor. He has sent me to
proclaim freedom for the prisoners, and recovery of sight for
the blind, to set the oppressed free, to proclaim the year of the
LORD's favor.[62] Then he rolled up the scroll, gave it back to the
attendant and sat down. The eyes of everyone in the synagogue
were fastened on him. He began by saying to them, 'Today this
scripture is fulfilled in your hearing.[63]

This is one of the scriptures that is quoted in the Melchizedek text
from Qumran, the text that foretells the coming of the Melchizedek Priest
who will make the Great Atonement. This text is made up of quotations
from the Old Testament which speak of the year of Jubilee with explanations and expansions of them. Jesus was announcing that this had come
to pass "Today this scripture is fulfilled in your hearing." It is possible that
the hostile reaction of the crowd was in response to his claim that he was
Melchizedek, that is, he was claiming that he was the Righteous King, the
High Priest, the Anointed—that is the Messiah. Identifying himself as
the Melchizedek priest is also thought to lie behind the first of the seven
signs that revealed Jesus' glory, in John's gospel.[64] This was at the wedding
at Cana, when he turned water into wine. Whilst there is more than one
conclusion to be drawn from this sign,[65] Jesus changing water into wine,
and thereby offering wine instead of water, takes us by allusion to Genesis
14 where Melchizedek offered, not the usual hospitality gift of bread and
water to Abram, but that of bread and wine (as Jesus was to offer his
disciples on the eve of the Great Atonement) and thus Jesus was, in fact
announcing himself as Melchizedek, just as he did in the Synagogue at
Nazareth. This is further confirmed when John sent his disciples to ask
Jesus if he was "the one who is to come or shall we expect someone else?"

62. The Year of the LORD's favor is the Year of Jubilee.

63. Luke 4:18–21.

64. I think we need to understand that glory has several connotations, most of
which fit what is meant here but glory also conveys the sense of meaning the visible
manifestation of an invisible reality. Each of the signs that John records, reveals a little
bit more of who Jesus actually is, so that, however inadequately we can grasp a little
more of the heavenly reality.

65. The wine replacing the water, has been said to illustrate that the wine of the
new kingdom, the Spirit, has replaced the laws of the old covenant which required
ritual ceremonial washing John 2:6. It is also understood to point to Jesus who in
this capacity acts as the bridegroom as he oversees the wine for the guests, which is
normally the bridegroom's task and that this is foreshadowing the heavenly wedding
banquet to come, when Jesus the bridegroom comes back for the church his bride.

Jesus replied by quoting from Isaiah: "Go and tell John what you have seen and heard; the blind receive their sight, the lame walk, lepers are cleansed and the deaf hear, the dead are raised up, the poor have good news preached to them,"[66] demonstrating that the miracles he was carrying out were those expected of the Messiah, and therefore that he was the Messiah, "the One who is to Come."

Son of Man

As well as being identified with Melchizedek Jesus also refers to himself as Son of Man; in fact, this is his preferred self-designation, which would suggest that by using it he meant something specific. Despite this, Son of Man is one of the most controversial titles; ideas about its meaning ranging from its being an Aramaic circumlocution,[67] in other words another way of saying "I," to it designating a heavenly redeemer figure which is certainly the case in 1 Enoch. The book of Enoch is mentioned in the book of Jude (yes that is actually in the New Testament!) It's in chapters 37—51, known as the Similitudes or Parables, that we meet the Son of Man. He is a heavenly figure expressly identified with the Anointed (1 En 48:10, 52:4). He is also called "the Elect one"[68] and the "Righteous One,"[69] which is a title applied both to Yahweh[70] and to Jesus.[71] The name of the Son of Man was given before the creation of the earth (1 En 48:3), which sounds very much like what is said of Jesus in John 1:1. Furthermore, although represented as two distinct persons there is also a parallelism in the text between the Son of Man and the Lord of Spirits (a designation of God in 1 Enoch), which suggests a close association, just as Jesus claims in John 10:30.

The Son of Man is also a heavenly figure in the book of Daniel and there are a number of correspondences between the figure here and that in the book of Enoch as well as the similarity in the throne room visions in both books. The imagery used of the throne in Daniel resonates with

66. Luke 7:20–23. As well as elements of Isa 61:1–4, this also incorporates elements of Isa 35:5–6.

67. Vermes, *Jesus the Jew*, 186.

68. 1 En 40:5; 45:3; 49:2; 61:8; 62:9.

69. 1 En 38:2

70. See Isa 24:16, Prov 21:12.

71. Acts 3:14, 22:14, 1John 2:1.

that used in 1 Enoch and in Ezekiel, where God's throne is spoken of as a chariot with fiery wheels. It is also the imagery used by the Jewish mystics who spoke of the *merkavah* (the chariot throne). The mystics made ascents into heaven very much like Paul's experience in the Temple. These ascents took them to the throne of God, which had a sea of crystal before it. They had to pass through the seven heavens to reach the throne, but could only do so by means of the seal, which was the secret name. Again, this sounds very like what is happening in Rev 7:3 when a seal which is the Name, is put on the Servants of God. This imagery is also observed in Rev 4:6 and 15:2 "Before the throne there was, as it were, a sea of glass, like crystal. I saw what appeared to be a sea of glass mingled with fire." This is also very similar to Moses' account of seeing God on Mt Sinai: "Under his feet was something like a pavement made of lapis lazuli, as bright blue as the sky."[72] The point is, these are all visions of the throne room of the holy of holies, heaven. The same vision that Isaiah saw when he saw the LORD seated on his throne who we learn from John 12:41 was Jesus and the creatures around the throne sing "Holy Holy Holy, is the Lord God Almighty, who was and is and is to come." The same song which is sung in Rev 4:6 and the same song we sing before going up to the throne room to partake of the body and blood of Jesus administered by the High Priest in his/her heavenly garment.[73]

In Daniel's vision he sees "one like a son of man coming with the clouds of heaven." He approached the Ancient of Days and was presented before him. He was given authority, glory and sovereign power; all nations and peoples of every language worshipped him. His dominion is an everlasting dominion that will not pass away and his kingdom is one that will never be destroyed.[74] All promises that were given to the Davidic Messiah. It's been suggested that rather than "presented before" the Hebrew *qrb,* which literally means "brought near" is the term used for a Temple offering and could be understood as "offered as a sacrifice,"[75] thus providing a Day of Atonement link for the book of Daniel and the Son of Man. The fact that the Son of Man also comes with the "clouds of heaven" is also suggestive of the High Priest's exit from the Holy of Holies, which

---

72. Exod 24:10.

73. That is before communion in the Anglican liturgy, that is if you attend a church that still uses the liturgy.

74. Dan7:13–14.

75. Barker, *The Revelation of Jesus Christ,* 382.

would have been surrounded by clouds of incense.[76] A Day of Atonement link is also suggested by the fact that in both visions from Enoch and Daniel, books are opened[77] in the midst of "Thousands upon thousands"' in a judgement setting which is very suggestive of the Books of Life and Death that are written and sealed on the Day of Atonement, when it is believed that God has judged the fate of his people for that year.

Both Daniel and 1 Enoch pre-date the Christian era. There are, however, later Jewish texts in which the Son of Man is actually called "My Messiah" and "My Servant Messiah."[78] In 1 Enoch, the Son of Man is enthroned.[79] He is righteous and makes the elect ones righteous.[80] He will be a light to the Gentiles and overthrow Kings and their kingdoms (1 En 46:5). As a result of the Son of Man's role, the wicked will be condemned and judged, the new Jerusalem will be established, gentiles will be converted and the exiles will be gathered in (1 En 90:28–38). In addition, the righteous dead will be resurrected (1 En 51:1–2), all of which parallels what is said of the Day of the Lord and what is expected when the Messiah comes. Therefore, the outcome of the Son of Man's role is the inauguration of the Day of the Lord. That is exactly what Jesus said he had come to do when he read from the Isaiah scroll in the Synagogue at Nazareth. In 1 En 55:4 the Son of Man is also the one who will judge *Azazel* and the Watchers (the fallen angels), which provides a further link with the Son of Man and the Day of Atonement ritual.

Again, the parallels with Jesus are startling he is called Messiah;[81] he is enthroned (Col 3:1) he is righteous (1 Pet 3:18) and makes other righteous (Rom 5:1), he is a light to the Gentiles (Luke 2:32), he overthrows Kings and their kingdoms (Dan 2:44; Luke 1:52; Rev 11:15), the wicked will be condemned and judged (John 5:29–30), the new Jerusalem will be established (Rev 21:10), the Gentiles be converted (Acts 15:3), the exiles will be gathered in (Matt 28:19), the righteous dead will be resurrected (John 5:28–29) and Satan and the fallen angels will be judged as a result

76. We noted earlier that the High Priest took a censer of hot coals and incense into the Holy of Holies to hide God's presence.

77. Dan 7:10; 1 En 47:3.

78. 2 Esdras 13. The date is uncertain but it thought to be late first century/early second century AD.

79. 1 En 45:3, 1 En 46:3, 1 En 48:6.

80. 1 En 45:3, 1 En 46:3, 1 En 48:6.

81. Jesus is called Christ throughout the New Testament, that is the Greek word for Anointed.

of his fulfilling the Day of Atonement ritual in his Great Atonement as the High Priest in the order of Melchizedek.[82]

Following Peter's acknowledgement of Jesus as "the Christ," that is recognizing that he is the Messiah, Jesus immediately begins to refer to himself as "the Son of Man" who "must suffer many things and be rejected by the elders, the chief priests and the teachers of the law, and that he must be killed and after three days rise again."[83] It is acknowledged that, just as you would find within present day Judaism, different ideas about the Messiah existed, within the Judaisms of Jesus time, all of which draw on elements associated with the Messianic idea in the Old Testament and all of which expected a Davidic Messiah. Nonetheless different strands of the concept were highlighted by the different groups that existed at the time of Jesus; we hear this in some of the questions that the crowd ask when trying to determine whether he is the Messiah or not. We also know this from the different inter-testamental texts and the Dead Sea Scrolls. The use of the Son of Man figure by Jesus as his preferred self-designation could simply have been the means to avoid being taken by the crowds and forcibly presented as the Messianic King:[84] "Jesus may have used the self-designation with the dual purpose of revealing his identity discreetly to those who had ears to hear and hiding it from those who had no ears to hear."[85] However, it is much more likely that he used this title as a means of identifying the kind of Messiah that he was, namely, the heavenly Redeemer, the Son of Man figure foretold in the inter-testamental texts that we have just considered. This also throws light on the question we raised above—whether the charge of blasphemy at Jesus' trial was in response to his acceptance of the title of Messiah and Son of God or because he spoke of himself as the Son of Man. In the New Testament Greek, the Son of Man is always written with the definite article, even though it would have been translated originally from Aramaic, it is translated in the "definite and literal form" not the idiomatic form,[86] that is *the* Son of Man. Consequently it has been noted that by using this form "our Gospels faithfully

82. Heb 7:1—10:22.

83. Mark 8:31.

84. "After the people saw the signs Jesus performed, they began to say 'Surely this is the Prophet, who is to come into the world' Jesus, knowing that they intended to come and make him King by force, withdrew again to a mountain by himself." John 6:14–15.

85. Seyoon, *The Son of Man*, 35–36.

86. Seyoon, *The Son of Man*, 35.

convey the sense of something unusual that Jesus intended with his self designation of *bar nasha* (Aramaic, Son of Man)."[87] When Jesus uses the term it is often in reference to Dan 7.13, which we have mentioned above, is where a heavenly redeemer figure is given all authority and an everlasting kingdom, that will never be destroyed. Therefore, Jesus is saying: "I am *the* son of Man whom Daniel saw in a vision. He is claiming to be the heavenly, divine being who appeared to Daniel in a vision.

Given the foregoing evidence that the Son of Man was in fact a heavenly figure, not only associated with Yahweh, but also with the Anointed, it is possible that Jesus' self-designation as the Son of Man, has warranted the charge of blasphemy at Jesus' trial. This is in fact what we see in the stoning of Stephen in Acts 7:55–58; it is only when he mentions the Son of Man that the crowd start to stone him. It would suggest, therefore, that Son of Man was a title and not, as some scholars want to suggest, "an Aramaic circumlocution" and that it was also a heavenly redeemer figure. This is also apparent in Matt 9:2–6 when Jesus claims that the Son of Man has authority to forgive sins, which only God can do.[88]

Jubilee

We said above that Jesus announced at the beginning of his mission that he had come to inaugurate the Year of the LORD's favor, that is the year of Jubilee. As well as the Isaiah 61 text, which Jesus read from in the Synagogue, the Melchizedek scroll at Qumran is made up of a number of other texts from the Old Testament which speak of the year of Jubilee. This was the period designated in Leviticus 25 when Hebrew slaves were to be set free, all debts between Israelites were cancelled and any land that had been leased was returned to the owners. The land itself was to remain fallow and only that which grew naturally was to be harvested. In effect, therefore, the people, the land and the animals were to return to the state that prevailed at creation, where food was not worked for but was there for the taking.

Jesus was announcing, that he was the righteous King whose sacrifice would reverse the effects of the fall. At his crucifixion he wore a crown of thorns, a symbol of the fact that he bore the consequences of the Fall: "cursed is the ground because of you through painful toil you will eat

---

87. Seyoon, *The Son of Man*, 35.

88. Matt 9:3.

food from it all the days of your life. It will produce thorns and thistles for you."[89] Jesus was announcing the Jubilee year, that all would be free from debt. A Jubilee was always announced on the Day of Atonement (Lev 25:9), thereby suggesting that they were linked; that the renewal of the covenant through the Day of Atonement ritual, set in motion the effects of Jubilee. Reading from this section of the Isaiah scroll, the section that is quoted in the Melchizedek text from Qumran, Jesus was saying that the Great Atonement would be fulfilled with his high priestly sacrifice that fulfilled the Day of Atonement sacrifice once and for all and that this would be the catalyst for the beginning of the real Jubilee. The Day of Atonement was a covenant renewal festival and Jesus is saying (as he was later to say to his disciples) that his body and his blood were for the remission of sins and the renewing of the covenant,[90] as Jeremiah had foretold.[91]

Jesus' final Day of Atonement sacrifice would renew the everlasting covenant and reverse the affects of the Fall. The thorns and thistles would give way to the harvest and new creation, and God would provide, as he had during the Exodus, a double portion of manna on the sixth day, so that Israel could keep the Sabbath and do no work, not even collecting manna. The Sabbath year occurred every seven years and had the same stipulations as the Jubilee year; food could only be gathered, but nothing sown. However, a Jubilee year meant that this would happen over two years, the Sabbath Year followed directly by the Jubilee year. God said to the Israelites: "You may ask, 'What will we eat in the seventh year if we do not plant or harvest our crops?' I will send you such a blessing in the sixth year that the land will yield enough for three years. While you plant during the eight year, you will eat from the old crop and will continue to eat from it until the harvest of the ninth year comes in."[92] So God would provide. Jesus was proclaiming the year of Jubilee. He said:

> Therefore I tell you, do not worry about your life, what you will eat or drink; or about your body, what you will wear. Is not life more important than food and the body more important than clothes? Look at the birds of the air; they do not sow or reap or

89. Gen 3:17–18.

90. "This is my blood of the new covenant, which is poured out for many, for the forgiveness of sins." Luke 22:20; Matt 26:28 (some manuscripts have "new" covenant, others just "covenant.")

91. Jer 31:31–34, quoted in Heb 8:8–12.

92. Lev 25:20–22.

store away in barns, and yet your heavenly Father feeds them. Are you not much more valuable than they? Can any one of you by worrying, add a single hour to your life?[93]

This doesn't mean that we don't have to work and we do not have to plan. I am not suggesting a prosperity Gospel, but ultimately, no matter what we do, God is the one who provides and this Year of Jubilee has also liberated us from our slavery to sin:

> But thanks to God that, though you used to be slaves to sin, you have come to obey from your heart the pattern of teaching that has now claimed your allegiance. You have been set free from sin and have become slaves to righteousness [94]

We are able to return home, to access Eden again:

> Whoever has ears, let them hear, what the Spirit says to the churches. To those who are victorious, I will give the right to eat from the tree of life, which is in the paradise of God.[95]

We will reap the harvest that he has sown:

> I have sent you to reap what you have not worked for. Others have done the hard work and you have reaped the benefits of their labour.[96]

and our debts are forgiven:

> Forgive us our debts as we also have forgiven our debtors.[97]

Jesus inaugurated the Jubilee. He set us free from our slavery to sin, paid our debt and gave us a heavenly home. However, the provisions for Jubilee have a practical element too and this will be discussed further in chapter 7.

Day of Atonement and the Anointed King

We noted at the beginning of this work that Kingship was the framework which encompassed all of Jesus' life, ministry, death and resurrection

93. Matt 6:25–27.
94. Rom 6:17–18.
95. Rev 2:7.
96. John 4:38.
97. Matt 6:12. See also Matt 18:23–35.

and this explained not only who he was and what he came to do but it also elucidated the other titles applied to Jesus, which for centuries have caused so much dispute. This being the case, how then does the title of High Priest fit into this framework? We noted from the outset that the sacral King also functioned as High Priest and therefore straight away we have a connection. We observed too, that the High Priest "bore" Yahweh's name, in effect, he was functioning as Yahweh in the Temple. The goat that was sacrificed was also the goat "as" Yahweh; consequently the sacrifice of the goat was within Temple theology, Yahweh's own sacrifice, his blood renewing the covenant. Therefore, just as the pre-exilic King, as *the* Anointed "had been" the earthly manifestation of Yahweh at his enthronement, post-exile the High Priest as *the* Anointed "was" Yahweh. The Day of Atonement brought about the same conditions as the Enthronement Ceremony, namely, atonement, renewal of the covenant and renewal of creation through the application of the blood with its life,[98] in different parts of the Temple, which in the temple-as-cosmos theology renewed the earth. Therefore with the demise of the monarchy and the High Priest having taken over the role as *the* Anointed as well as the absence of the bronze laver in the Temple which formed part of the Enthronement ritual, the High Priest as *the* Anointed achieved through the Day of Atonement ritual what the King as *the* Anointed had achieved through the Enthronement ritual—the renewing of the covenant, the binding of Chaos and the renewal of creation.

It could be argued that this provided the rationale for the New Testament designation of Jesus as High Priest, because not only were the twin roles of King and High Priest incorporated into the role of the Messiah, *the* Anointed, but also post-exile, as the High Priest became *the*Anointed it was necessary to connect Jesus in a clear manner to this title too. However, as we noted above, it was not just the *title* that Jesus was understood to fulfill, but the *actual* festival of Day of Atonement, which was the major post-exilic festival that the High Priest carried out. The link between the two offices is further confirmed in the book of Hebrews which not only portrays Jesus as the High Priest, but also associates this role with that of the King. As well as giving a detailed description of how Jesus fulfills

---

98. According to Lev 17: 11 "the life of a creature is in its blood." The word for life here, *nephesh,* can also mean spirit. Further on it stipulates that the blood of an animal that is to be eaten for food must firstly be drained, which lies behind the kosher rules of ritual slaughter. Lev 17:11 (in conjunction with other scriptures) also lies behind the Jehovah's Witness attitude towards blood transfusions.

the High Priestly role of the Day of Atonement, a number of Psalms used at the King's enthronement are also quoted and applied to Jesus. For example Ps 2.7: "You are my Son, today I have become your father"[99] as well as Ps 45:6,7 where the King is also called God, "Your throne O God, will last for ever and ever," is applied to Jesus. As we might expect, Ps 110 is also applied to Jesus as this is not only an enthronement Psalm, in which God says to the King: "Sit at my right hand until I make your enemies a footstool for your feet" but is also the Psalm in which God says to the King: "You are a priest forever in the order of Melchizedek."[100] Ps 22:2 is also quoted and applied to Jesus. This Psalm which was mentioned in chapter 3, speaks of the King's suffering and foreshadows events at the crucifixion.[101] Furthermore, a passage which forms part of the Messianic promise to David: "I will establish the throne of his kingdom forever. I will be is father and he will be my son"[102] is quoted and applied to Jesus. Therefore the book of Hebrews not only associates Jesus with the role of the High Priest, and in particular with his role on the Day of Atonement, but also links Jesus with the role of the King at the pre-exilic Enthronement Ceremony at *Sukkoth.*

In chapter 2 we noted that part of the Enthronement festival in the ancient near east was the *hierogamy,* that is, the sacred marriage of the King and his consort, representing the god and goddess and bringing about regeneration and fertility. In Israel this is transposed into the relationship between Yahweh and Israel, which is spoken of in terms of a marriage.[103] It is interesting, therefore, that at the Day of Atonement, the following practice used to be carried out, which we alluded to briefly in chapter 2: "There were no happier days for Israel than the fifteenth of Av and the Day of Atonement, for on them the daughters of Jerusalem used to go forth in white raiments." The "white raiments" had to be borrowed and ritually immersed. "And the daughters of Jerusalem went forth to dance in the vineyards. And what did they say? 'Young man, lift up thine eyes and see what thou wouldest choose for thyself.'"[104] In other words, they were dancing in the vineyards in order to attract a man to marry.

---

99. Heb 1:5; 5:5.

100. Heb 5:6; 7:16, 21.

101. Heb 2:12.

102. 2 Sam 7:13–14 and 1 Chr 17:13.

103. Jer 31:32. We will consider this in more detail in the following chapter.

104. *m. Ta'anith* 4:8

The fifteenth of Av is also known as a minor holiday *Tu B'Av* which in Israel is currently celebrated as a day of love, almost like Valentine's day and it is thought to be an auspicious day on which to get married. It is interesting, therefore, in light of the Day of Atonement replacing the New Year Enthronement ceremony, that a custom linked with marriage was performed. It is also interesting, that the girls are to wear white linen robes, which have been ritually immersed which is suggestive of the High Priest's angelic garment for entering the Holy of Holies on the Day of Atonement. The white robes also feature in Revelation. We read there that "nothing impure will enter the new creation but only those who are written in the Lamb's Book of Life"[105] and they will wear white robes.[106]

Present Day Festival

The present day ceremony falls within the autumn cycle of festivals, between *Rosh Hashanah* and *Sukkoth*. It is considered the holiest day of the year and the day upon which the judgement is made for that year, namely when the final decision is made by God regarding whose name goes into the Book of Life or into the Book of Death.[107] A 25 hour fast begins at nightfall on 9 Tishri. This is a complete fast including no water. Other abstentions are also required during this period: leather shoes are not to be worn, no lotions or perfume applied, no washing or bathing and no marital relations to take place. The time is spent in prayer and at the Synagogue and each person is meant to focus on their own *avodah*.[108]

Men will often visit the *Mikveh* (the ritual bath) before attending the first Day of Atonement services (there are five and it is usual to attend all of them). Some also wear a white *Kittel* (robe) and a white *Tallis* (prayer shawl). It is said that this is to remind people that they are mortal.[109] However, it is interesting to speculate whether the white garment replicates that of the High Priest on the Day of Atonement before he entered the Holy of Holies. This is further suggested by the emphasis on each person

105. Rev 21:27

106. Rev 4:4.

107. We noted earlier that these books were opened at *Rosh Hashanah* and the intervening ten days each person could make amends and consequently change their fate.

108. *Avodah* means worship but can also mean work.

109. A *kittel* is also worn at Rosh Hashanah and by the leader of the Passover Seder and it also is used as a burial shroud.

focussing on their own *avodah*. The fast undertaken is in itself a form of sacrifice, not just because of the deprivation of food, but because the fat of each person is being burned up in place of the animal sacrifice. They are, therefore, in effect carrying out their own sacrifice. The restriction on wearing shoes[110] and marital relations—all of which applied to the High Priest, suggests that each person is now acting as their own High Priest, offering prayers and *avodah*, making their own sacrifice. In the men's case, they are also wearing the white angelic robes, having ritually bathed, and making *aliyah*, that is going into the presence of God. Making *aliyah*, is the practice of "going up" to read from the Torah scroll; during *Yom Kippur* there are 6 (7 on a Sabbath) *aliyot*. This is the same term that was used for 'going up' to the Temple when it stood and still used for "going up" that is emigrating to Israel, all suggesting that the "going up" actually refers to going up to the presence of God and in this case indicating that God is somehow present in the Torah. This is further strengthened by the holiness attributed to the Torah. The Torah scrolls are housed in the *Aron Kodesh* (the holy ark—where God's presence was said to be, between the cherubim, in the Temple), hidden by the *paroket,* a curtain which hides the scrolls from the rest of the Synagogue (this is the same name used for the curtain in the Temple). The scrolls themselves wear the accoutrements of the King and High priest—a crown and a breastplate. The symbolism is obvious, the scrolls are now the "dwelling place" of God. Just as God's presence had been mediated by the King and High Priest, now it is mediated by the Torah. To be called up, to make *aliyah*, is a real privilege, since, they are, in effect, going up into the presence of God. Further indications of the holiness of the scrolls is the use of a *yad*[111] which avoids the scrolls being touched by human hand. Furthermore, if the scrolls are inadvertently dropped, the whole congregation has to fast and indeed once the scrolls are no longer fit for use, they are not merely discarded, but buried—the reason given is that they contain the Name of God. In the Old Testament God says 'I will make a place for my Name," and his Name was the means by which he was present in his Temple,[112] therefore God's Name in the Torah, is the means by which he is present. We said at the beginning that the Temple *avodah* sustained the world and this surely lies behind the rationale for the Torah being read every day

110. The High Priest did not wear shoes when ministering in the Temple.

111. Literally "hand." It is a pointer that is used, usually shaped into a hand at the end, which the person reading the Torah scroll uses to follow the text.

112. 1 Kgs 8:29.

and the complete Torah being read throughout the cycle of a year. This is further strengthened by the fact that the emphasis seems to be on reading it aloud rather than it being heard. This is evidenced by the general chatter in the women's gallery whilst it's being read. The fact, that much of the Temple symbolism is also transferred to the Synagogue—the *ner tamid*, the everlasting light replacing the Menorah or Western Light that was always to be kept lit; the Synagogue built facing east, towards Jerusalem and the bimah, the raised platform where the Torah is read, replicating the altar, the place where *avodah* now takes place. A sacrifice of the lips rather than an animal sacrifice.[113]

The Book of Jonah is read on the Day of Atonement, which is interesting on a number of counts. Firstly, it shows God's mercy to a gentile nation, which underscores the message throughout the Old Testament, that he is the God not just of Israel, but the whole world and that the whole world is included in his plan of salvation. It is also interesting because Jesus quotes Jonah as a prefiguring of what will happen with himself: "For just as Jonah was three days and three nights in the belly of the great fish, so the Son of Man will be three days and three nights in the heart of the earth." This is particularly interesting because Jonah contains *chaoskampf* motifs, particularly relevant to the Day of Atonement. In the book of Jonah, Yahweh sends out a great wind *ruach* that stirs up the sea which threatens to overwhelm the ship that Jonah is on. Lots are cast to see whose fault it is and the lot falls to Jonah. The sailors ask who he is and where he is from and Jonah answers that he is a Hebrew and his God is the creator of heaven and earth. Jonah tells them to sacrifice him, to throw him into the sea and the waters will become calm, which is what happens. A large sea monster then swallows Jonah and whilst in its belly he sings a Psalm that resonates with the enthronement Psalms of the King. "From deep in the realm of the dead I called for help." (Jonah 2:2). "You hurled me into the deep into the very heart of the seas, and the currents swirled about me all your waves and breakers swept over me" (Jonah 2:3). Here the word deep is *Tehom*, the same word used in Gen 1:1. Jonah was in Sheol, "the realm of the dead" for "three days and three nights" (Jonah 1:17). He is eventually spewed out by the fish and goes to Nineveh where the people repent. Unhappy with this, Jonah leaves the city and makes himself a shelter—a *sukkah*.

---

113. Heb 13:15.

Therefore, Jonah, a Hebrew prophet, is sent to the gentiles for their salvation. Lots are cast, (as they were for the goats on the Day of Atonement and for Jesus' clothing). Jonah is thrown into the deep as a sacrifice to pacify the Chaos waters, is swallowed by a large fish, which we have noted is also a representation of the Chaos waters (Leviathan). He remains in the deep, the place of the dead (Sheol), for three days and nights and is then raised up by Yahweh, as a result of his message of repentance, the gentiles (in Nineveh) were saved. A *sukkah* is built (as a reed hut was at the enthronement ceremony of the surrounding cultures, representing the Temple/Cosmos) and Jonah rests in it.

During *Yom Kippur* the *paroket* is replaced by a white curtain and the doors of the *Aron Kodesh* are left open until the end of the festival. According to Jewish tradition the gates of heaven swing open on *Rosh Hashanah*, the court of heaven is convened and the books of Life and Death are open for judgement to take place. A medieval prayer for *Rosh Hashanah* states: "All mankind will pass before you like members of the flock. Like a shepherd pasturing his flock, making the sheep pass under his staff, so, too, will you review, count, calculate and consider the soul of all living beings. At this time you will decide the needs of all Your creatures and inscribe their verdict . . . ,"[114] which sounds very much like Ezekiel 34:17 "As for you, my flock, this is what the Sovereign Lord says: 'I will judge between one sheep and another . . . '" In the *Mishnah* too we read: "On Rosh Hashanah all mankind will pass before G-d like *b'nei maron*," that is a flock of sheep, which, in turn, reminds us of both the courtroom scene in the vision of Enoch and the book of Daniel, in which the Son of Man is seated on the throne of Glory and "ten thousand thousand" stand before the Ancient of Days and the books are opened. This further suggests that these are Day of Atonement visions. It also reminds us of Matthew 25:31–33 "When the Son of Man comes in his glory, and all the angels with him, he will sit on his glorious throne. All the nations will be gathered before him, and he will separate the people one from another as a shepherd separates the sheep from the goats. He will put the sheep on his right and the goats on his left."

We saw above that *kpr*, the Hebrew word for atonement also has connotations of covering from danger and as we learned above, entering into the presence of God is dangerous without the correct rituals or "covering." It is suggested that this is also the case with Adam and Eve,

---

114. Stolper, *Living Beyond Time*, 82.

that having sinned they then try to "cover" themselves with fig leaves, because they are afraid to enter the presence of God, but their own "covering" is inadequate. God, therefore, provides his covering for them of animal skin. Therefore, the covering of Adam and Eve has necessitated a sacrifice, the first sacrifice recorded in the Bible. Covering and atonement also feature in the story of Moses and the second lot of tablets, which is linked in Jewish tradition to the Day of Atonement. Moses had thrown down and broken the tablets following the apostasy of Israel worshipping the Golden Calf. He ascended Mt Sinai again to the presence of God, and fasted and interceded for Israel, asking if he could make atonement for them, offering himself in place of them. He asked God to forgive their sin "or blot me out of the book you have written," God answered, "Whoever has sinned against me I will blot out of my book."[115] Moses also asked to see God's glory, but God said to him 'I will cause all my goodness to pass in front of you and I will proclaim my name, the LORD, in your presence . . . But . . . you cannot see my face, for no one may see me and live." He then told Moses to stand in a cleft in the rock and he would cover him with his hand while he passed by (Exod 33:21–23). Moses is then told to prepare two more stones for the ten commandments and the LORD comes down in a cloud, proclaiming his name and then passes in front of Moses saying: "The LORD, the LORD, the compassionate and gracious God, slow to anger, abounding in love and faithfulness, maintaining love to thousands, and forgiving wickedness, rebellion and sin. Yet he does not leave the guilty unpunished; he punishes the children and their children for the sin of the parents to the third and the fourth generation" (Exod 34:6–7). This is known as the Thirteen Attributes of God and its repetition forms part of the Day of Atonement service. Following this God makes a new covenant with Israel.

Covering and atonement, therefore, are closely linked in the Day of Atonement, not just observed in the Temple ritual as we noted above, but also in subsequent Jewish tradition. We observed at the beginning, that in the Temple at Yom Kippur, the *kapporet* (the cover of the Ark of the Covenant) between the Cherubim where God was enthroned, was covered with the blood of the sacrifice, which was in effect a substitute for Yahweh's own blood. The same root *kpr* for *kapporet* is also the root of Yom Kippur, that is the day of Atonement (or covering). The smoke of the incense, which the High Priest took in with him, was to conceal

---

115. Exod 32:33.

the atonement cover from the priest "so that he will not die,"[116] because as we saw in the story of Moses, and in the instructions for the priests at the beginning of this chapter, it was dangerous to be in God's presence "uncovered." "Since it [atonement cover] stands as the boundary between the enthroned God and the tablets of the covenant, figuratively speaking, Yahweh looks down on the covenant through the blood dabbed on the Atonement Slate, leading him to govern his people out of mercy and forgiveness."[117] The *kapporet* or atonement cover was also called the mercy seat. In chapter 2 it was stated, that the Rabbis interpreted *Yahweh* as God's aspect of mercy (whereas *Elohim* was his aspect of justice). As the real High Priest, therefore, who made atonement with his own blood, Jesus, who is Yahweh incarnated, fully man and fully God, as God's aspect of mercy, has covered the mercy seat with his own blood. Thus, when the Father looks down on his creation, he sees us through the blood of Jesus. It is the blood of Jesus, which covers us and protects us and which has given us robes of righteousness, white linen robes, like those of the High Priest so that we can enter God's presence directly ourselves.

The Covenant

The everlasting Covenant, the Covenant of *hesedh* and the knowledge of God underlies all of the biblical Covenants[118] and all of the biblical narrative. We have noted in the previous chapters that the cosmos, our word for the universe derived from the Greek word *Kosmos*[119] was created once Chaos, its polar opposite was overcome and its boundaries set. Chaos always threatens to return, to overcome the cosmos (order) again. The work of the Priests in the Temple, its rituals and the festivals were to maintain order, to stop Chaos breaking through, which was possible whenever the covenant bonds were breached by sin or impurity. The Name sealed the covenant and the High Priest wore the Name on his forehead, therefore when the High Priest functioned in the Temple, he was functioning as the LORD. This was particularly true in the Day of Atonement ritual in which the High Priest as the LORD and thus the Creator, was re-creating

116. Lev 16:13.

117. Hartley, *Leviticus*, 234.

118. Barker, *The Everlasting Covenant*, 1.

119. Which means order and is the same Greek word for the service, that is the 'order' of the Temple.

the cosmos, using blood that represented his own blood to renew the
covenant and "bring times of refreshing"[120] to the earth. The renewal
of the covenant as a result of the Enthronement Ceremony resulted in
the renewal of creation, witnessed empirically as the grape harvest and
the coming of the late rains; post-exile this now depended on the Day
of Atonement. The dependence on the Temple for fertility is evident in
the foregoing quotation from the Mishnah:'The world stands upon three
things: the Torah, the Temple service and deeds of loving kindness.'[121]
"Loving kindness" translates the Hebrew word *hesedh*, and is in fact one
of the names of the everlasting covenant. *Hesedh* has the connotation
of loving kindness within a close, covenant, marital-type relationship.
It is used most often in the Hebrew Bible of the relationship between
God and Israel. Although it implies a two-way relationship, it also can
infer when used of God's relationship with Israel, a loving-kindness that
is not deserved, that has within it an element of grace and mercy. The
Day of Atonement ritual in the Temple therefore was a covenant renewal
ceremony whereby Israel's sins were forgiven, the harvest and rains guaranteed and the covenant renewed.[122] This is the covenant that the writer
of Hebrews declared had been fulfilled, by Jesus as High Priest.[123]

---

120. Acts 3:19.

121. *m.Aboth* 1:2.

122. Jer 31:31–34. We will consider this further in the following chapter.

123. Heb 8:8–12, 9:15.

Chapter 5

PASSOVER

Introduction

ALTHOUGH IN THE PREVIOUS two chapters we have observed that the
themes of kingship and the Enthronement Festival are still evident in
the festivals of *Sukkoth* and Day of Atonement, it is arguably at Passover
which we will consider in this chapter, that kingship and the enthronement ceremony are *most* evident. This is not just because it is during this
festival that Jesus, through his actions, actually declares himself as Messianic King but also because we will see that the *chaoskampf* motifs which
underlie the enthronement ceremony are also part of the Exodus story.
This of course, provides the rationale for Passover. As well as considering how Passover links with the Enthronement Festival we will also be
considering our third and final paradigm of Jesus' suffering, death and
resurrection—that of the Passover Lamb.

Jesus is called "the Lamb of God who takes away the sin of the
world,"[1] specifically identified with the Passover lamb and we will see
below the numerous parallels with the lamb itself. However, that is not
where the foreshadowing ends. The Passover celebrates the Exodus from
Egypt, which is the foundational salvation story of Israel. Jesus' death is
spoken of as an Exodus and therefore Jesus is understood to be leading a
second Exodus. There are numerous parallels, particularly in John's Gos-

1. John 1:29.

pel between Jesus and elements of the Exodus story. There is also a whole Jesus/Moses typology, especially in Matthew's gospel, which identifies Jesus as the Prophet, that Moses foretold would come. Finally, the Messiah was (and still is within Orthodox Judaism) expected to come at Passover, preceded by Elijah and we will see that Jesus, does in fact ride in as King Messiah at Passover, having been announced by John the Baptist, who is acknowledged by Jesus as "Elijah." We will also consider whether Jesus' last supper was in fact a Passover Seder and look at the symbolism within the current Passover Seder. Although the Exodus story should be familiar to us all, it is worth recapping it in order to ensure we understand all the allusions to it that we will find in the New Testament portrayal of Jesus.

Exodus

The Exodus is *the* redemption story of the Old Testament, as God constantly reminds the Israelites "I am the LORD your God, who led you out of Egypt."[2] However, in order to understand the Exodus properly we need to go right back to the beginning of God's call to Abram, the LORD (Yahweh) says to Abram:[3] "Go from your country, your people and your father's household to the land I will show you"[4] and he does.[5] The LORD makes a covenant with Abram and says that his offspring will be as numerous as the stars,[6] that he will be the father of many nations (hence his name change to Abraham) "and Kings will come from you."[7] He also tells Abraham, 'through your offspring (or seed) all nations on earth will be blessed because you have obeyed me."[8] This is the real beginning of the story of the restoration of our relationship with God.[9] The obedience that God is referring to is the sacrifice of Isaac, which we looked at in chapter 3. Isaac's son Jacob has twelve children who become the twelve tribes of Israel. Joseph, Jacob's favourite is sold into captivity by his jeal-

2. There are in total 87 references, some examples are: Exod 20:2, Lev 26:13, Deut 5:6.

3. "Exalted father."

4. Gen 12:1.

5. This is later to be known as the Promised Land, that is the land promised to Abraham, Isaac and Joseph and the cause of so much conflict in the Middle East.

6. Gen 15:5.

7. Gen 17:4–6.

8. Gen 22:18

9. This is why Abraham is referred to so often in the New Testament.

ous brothers. What is interesting to note here is that the story of Joseph also mimics the dying and rising motif of the Enthronement ritual. He is thrown down into a cistern (used for storing spring/rain water) by his brothers, but then, rather than being allowed to die, is rescued, raised up from the pit and sold to passing traders who take him to Egypt where he rules as second in command to the Pharaoh. As a result Egypt has 7 years of great fertility (which counteract the 7 subsequent years of famine). Joseph, therefore, the beloved son, is thrown into water, rescued, raised up out of the pit and is "enthroned" as Pharaoh's right hand man. The outcome of this is fertility. It is then because of the famine that Joseph's brothers come to Egypt to buy grain and they are reconciled with Joseph and all move to Egypt. Jacob dies and eventually so does Joseph and the Israelites become enslaved for 400 years, just as the LORD told Abram, they would.[10] Genesis ends with the death of Joseph and we then learn in the first chapter of Exodus that a new Pharaoh 'to whom Joseph meant nothing' came to power in Egypt. Realizing how numerous the Israelites had become he enslaved them in case they joined forces with Egypt's enemies. The Pharaoh also told the Hebrew midwives to kill any male babies born. Despite this they became "even more numerous" so Pharaoh gave an order that all male Hebrew babies would be thrown into the Nile. Cue Moses.

His mother hid him for as long as she could and then he was put into a basket and placed into the Nile. Moses, whose name means "drawn out" (*Moshe*) is so called because he is literally drawn out (*meshitihu*) of the water, that is the Nile, he will also be the one who "draws out" the Israelites from the Red Sea.[11] He is rescued by a daughter of Pharaoh and raised in the Pharaoh's household. Once again we have the Enthronement theme. Moses is put into the waters, rescued "raised up," and became part of the Egyptian royal household. The Hebrew word used for the basket that Moses was placed in is *tebah* which is used on only one other occasion in the Old Testament, namely for the Ark Noah builds. This further confirms the enthronement theme as the Flood narrative, is also a reca-

10. "Then the LORD said to him: 'Know for certain that for four hundred years your descendants will be strangers in a country not their own and that they will be enslaved and mistreated there. But I will punish the nation they serve as slaves and afterward they will come out with great possessions.'" (Gen 15:13–14).

11. This is often rendered Reed Sea now as the original Hebrew name *Yam Suph*, means Sea of Reeds, however the Septuagint rendered this Red Sea and there is evidence to support either reading. Nonetheless the New Testament writers have continued with the rendering of Red Sea and we will use that throughout.

pitulation of the original creation story. After killing an Egyptian, Moses goes into exile, marries and becomes a shepherd. It is whilst minding the sheep that he has the burning bush encounter. God gives him the commission to go back to Egypt to save his people. God therefore uses Moses to bring his people from slavery in Egypt to freedom in the Promised Land, that is the land he promised to Abraham.[12] It is here that God reveals his name. He instructs Moses to tell the Israelites that he is "the God of your fathers, the God of Abraham, Isaac and Jacob" and that his name is *ehyeh asher ehyeh*, 'I am who I am.'"[13]

This is where the story of the Exodus itself begins. Moses goes to Egypt with Aaron but Pharaoh won't let the people go and God visits ten plagues upon the Egyptians. What is significant here is that these are not just random acts that God carries out (sending frogs, lice, boils etc) to beat Pharaoh and the Egyptians into submission, they are much more than that. They are deliberately chosen to show that Yahweh, the Holy one of Israel, whose people Pharaoh has enslaved, is the one true God. Each of the plagues is a direct challenge to one of the many Egyptian gods.[14] This is made clear in Yahweh's statement to Moses about the final plague. "On that same night I will pass through Egypt and strike down every firstborn of both people and animals, *and I will bring judgement on all the gods of Egypt.* I am the LORD'" (Exod 12:12). Yahweh is demonstrating, that he is the creator God in control of his creation. The plagues brought a reversal of creation as a precursor to the new creation, which the Exodus would bring about.[15] Just as God created through ten sayings ("And God said . . ." Gen 1:3–29), he demonstrated that he could undo these by ten plagues.[16] Similarly, as he destroyed life through the ten plagues, God

12. "God heard their groaning and he remembered his covenant with Abraham, with Isaac and with Jacob. So God looked on the Israelites and was concerned about them." Exod 2:24–25.

13. Exod 3:14–15.

14. Plague one, the Nile turned to blood which challenges *Hapi*, God of the Nile. Plague two - frogs - challenges *Heket* Goddess of fertility, with the head of a frog, and so on, until the 10th plague which challenges the "son of God," Pharaoh's son and heir—Pharaoh as we saw in chapter 2 was understood to be a god.

15. On the six days of creation, God separated the waters, created vegetation, livestock and creatures that crawled along the ground, and finally human beings. The plagues, saw the life giving waters of the Nile turned to blood, livestock died, vegetation destroyed by hail and locusts and resulted finally in the death of the firstborn of the Egyptians.

16. *m.Aboth* 5:1

would re-create new life, his new creation, Israel, through the Ten Words, *Aseret Ha-Devarim*.[17] He would raise her up out of the waters of Chaos and give her life through the ten commandments.[18] Yahweh, therefore, demonstrated that he was the one true God, the God of Israel, the creator God. He had heard their cries and had come to rescue his people. It is the tenth plague, however, after which the festival is named. The tenth and final plague, that was visited on the Egyptians was the death of the first-born. God says to Moses: "Tell the whole community of Israel that on the tenth day of this month each man is to take a lamb for his family, one for each household."[19] The instructions continue: "The animals you choose must be year-old males without defect . . . take care of them until the fourteenth day of the month, when all the members of the community of Israel must slaughter them at twilight."[20] They are then to dip a bunch of hyssop into the blood of the lamb and place it on the sides and tops of the door frames of the houses, where they eat the lambs. "The blood will be a sign for you on the houses where you are, and when I see the blood. I will pass over you"[21] The lamb is to be roasted whole, with none of its bones broken and all of it to be eaten before sunrise. It is to be eaten with bitter herbs and bread without yeast. "And when your children ask you what does this ceremony mean to you, then tell them, 'It is the Passover sacrifice to the LORD, who passed over the houses of the Israelites in Egypt and spared our homes when he struck down the Egyptians.'"[22] This then is the background to the Passover Festival.

Passover Lamb

By the first century, the Passover had become a pilgrim festival and the sacrifice of the Passover lamb had, therefore, to be carried out in the Temple.[23] The lambs would be chosen according to the Passover instructions

17. Exod 34:28.

18. "See I have set before you today life and prosperity, death and destruction. For I command you today to love the LORD your God , to walk in obedience to him and to keep his commands, decrees and laws, then you will live and increase and the LORD your God will bless you in the land you are entering to possess." (Deut 30:15–16).

19. Exod 12:3.

20. Exod 12:5–7.

21. Exod 12:13.

22. Exod 12:26

23. Deut 16:5

just quoted, on the tenth day of Nissan and the priests would check that
they were without defect or blemish and they would then be held by the
families who had purchased them until they were sacrificed on the fourteenth Nissan, the Passover eve. Jesus, who at the beginning of his ministry is twice identified by the John the Baptist as "The Lamb of God who
takes away the sin of the world"[24] entered into Jerusalem on the day the
Passover lambs were chosen, to the shouts of 'Blessed be he who comes
in the name of the Lord' the greeting in Ps 118:26, part of the *Hallel*,[25] as
a greeting to the King; the crowd thereby establishing their acceptance,
their "choice" of Jesus. He would also later be subjected to questioning
by the priests and elders, trying to establish "by what authority" he was
carrying out the teaching and the miracles, that they had seen him do.[26]
In other words, they were looking for defects in him, as they were to do at
his trial when trying to ascertain whether he was the Messiah, the King,
as the crowds claimed.

The Passover lambs were sacrificed on the day of preparation for
the Passover, in the Temple. They were killed at three in the afternoon,
that is the ninth hour,[27] according to Hebrew time-keeping during which
the Levites sung the *Hallel*. The lambs were then hung on iron hooks
and flayed (that is whipped or beaten so that their skin was removed).[28]
In the original instructions in Exod 12:9–10 the lamb had to be roasted
whole on a spit made from pomegranate wood,[29] and none of its bones
were to be broken. Following his arrest and trial, Jesus, the Lamb of God,
chosen by the people, found to be "without blemish or defect,"[30] by the

---

24. John 1:29. Although it has been argued that the Passover sacrifice is not
apotropaic, that is, it doesn't remove sin, the stipulations set out in Num 9:13 suggest otherwise. "But if anyone who is ceremonially clean and not on a journey fails to
celebrate the Passover, they must be cut off from their people for not presenting the
LORD's offering at the appointed time. *They will bear the consequences of their sin.*"
This is also the view of Rashi, one of the great medieval rabbinic commentators whose
commentary on this has God saying: "I see the Paschal blood and propitiate you. *Ex.
Rab.* 15.35b and " . . . I will have pity on you and for the sake of the Passover blood and
the circumcision blood I will atone for you." *Ex. Rab.* 15.12

25. The *Hallel* is also recited at *Sukkoth* as we saw in chapter 3.

26 Matt 21:23–27, Mark14:43–65.

27. *m.Pesh* 5.1.

28. *m.Pes* 5.9.

29. *m.Pesh* 7.1.

30 1 Pet 1:19.

priests and the elders, and proclaimed as such by Pilate,[31] is whipped and beaten[32] and hung on a wooden cross. He is crucified at nine a.m[33] and died at three in the afternoon, the ninth hour[34]; his sacrifice therefore taking place at the same time as the Passover lambs were being slaughtered and whilst the *Hallel* was being sung. The people had actually shouted the final part of the *Hallel* as they greeted Jesus only days before and Jesus, himself, would have sung it at his last supper with his disciples. At his crucifixion, although the legs of the other two men crucified with Jesus were broken, Jesus' legs were not, fulfilling, as John tells us,[35] the Scripture which states: "Not one of his bones will be broken." The Scripture quoted is found both in Num 9:12 and Exod 12.46 where it is referring to the Passover lamb.[36] However, as we noted in chapter 2, this is also said of King David in Ps 34.20. Therefore Jesus is explicitly linked in the first two instances with the Passover lamb, as well as, in the last instance, with King David. Jesus' side is pierced and blood flows from him.[37] His blood is poured out, as he said it would be to his disciples, for the renewal of the covenant and the forgiveness of sins.[38] The blood of the Passover lamb was caught and poured against the base of the altar and had to be free flowing not congealed.[39] During the crucifixion Jesus was offered wine vinegar on a sponge on a stalk of a hyssop plant,[40] the same plant, that was used to daub the blood of the Passover lamb on the doorways of the houses of the Israelites to protect them, so that the Angel of Death would pass over them.[41] No portion of the Passover lamb was to be left over, but

31. John 19:6b.

32. Matt 27:26, John 19:1.

33. Mark 15:25.

34. Matt 27:45.

35. John19.36.

36. It forms part of the passage giving instructions on how to observe the Passover. "They must not leave any of it till morning or break any of its bones." Num 9.12.

37. We noted in chapter 3 that this in fact resonated with the wine and water which were poured out together as a libation at *Sukkcth*.

38. Matt 26:28.

39. *m.Pes* 5:5–6.

40. John 19:29.

41. We saw in the previous chapter that vinegar was to be mixed with the Day of Atonement sacrifice before the priests ate it. Vinegar was also offered to the suffering king in Ps 69:21.

if it was, it had to be burned.[42] Later Christian tradition would ensure that none of the Eucharist, the bread or wine, that is the body and blood of Jesus, the Passover lamb could be left over from this ritual. If any of it is left over it has to be consumed. In the Catholic tradition, if any falls to the floor it has to be buried.

Jesus is explicitly identified as the Passover lamb by Peter "you were redeemed . . . with the precious blood Christ, a lamb without blemish or defect . . . chosen before the creation of the world"[43] and Paul "Christ, our Passover lamb, has been sacrificed."[44] Just as the blood of the Passover lamb was daubed on the doorposts to protect the Israelites, the blood of Jesus "our Passover lamb" is also a means of protection.[45] (Heb 10:19). The Passover themes, however, don't end there. As well as being identified with the Passover lamb, Jesus is also associated with Moses. However, in order to understand the rest of the allusions we need to revisit the next part of the Exodus story.

As a result of the last plague, the death of the firstborn, Pharaoh releases the Israelites telling them to "Go worship the LORD as you have requested."[46] So the Israelites leave Egypt "with their dough before the yeast was added"[47] and "with articles of silver and gold and clothing"[48] just as God had told Abram they would.[49] Moses then leads them towards the Red Sea. However, Pharaoh has a change of heart and pursues them with his soldiers and chariots and the Israelites find themselves literally "between the devil and the deep blue sea." Then the LORD tells Moses to raise his staff across the sea to "divide the water" and the LORD drove back the sea "with a strong east wind and turned the water into dry land." All the Israelites pass through the divided sea "with a wall of water" on either side.' (Exod 21–23). The Egyptian chariots and horsemen follow them into the sea, but the LORD tells Moses to stretch out his hand again

42. Exod 12:10, Deut 16:4.

43. 1 Pet 1:19–20. We noted in chapter 3 that this was also said about the "lamb that God would provide" instead of Isaac's sacrifice, that it was created before the foundation of the world.

44. 1 Cor 5:7.

45. Heb 10:19.

46. Exod 12: 31b.

47. Exod 12:34.

48. Exod 11:2; 12:35–36.

49. Gen 15:13–14.

over the sea, which sweeps back over the Egyptians. "Not one of them survived."[50]

Moses

When Jesus rides into Jerusalem as King at Passover he is also identified, not just as 'a prophet' but, as "*the* prophet" "*ho prophetes,*" signifying that he was the prophet that was expected, the prophet whom Moses foretold: "The LORD our God will raise up for you a prophet like me from among you, from your own people. You must listen to him."[51] As the Rabbis were to say "As the first redeemer so shall the second redeemer be."[52] In other words the Messiah will be "like unto Moses" and in Matthew in particular, Jesus is depicted in terms of a second Moses. Nonetheless, what Moses does, Jesus fulfills and surpasses.[53]

In Exod 7–12 Moses is the instrument of ten plagues, in Matt 8–9 Jesus carries out ten miracles. Moses is "god-like"[54] but Jesus *is* God (John 1:1). Moses was considered to be King,[55] but Jesus is the King Messiah, the King of Kings (Rev 17:14). Jesus and Moses are mediators of covenants sealed with blood (Exod 24:8; Matt 26:28), but the covenant Moses mediated is just for Israel, whereas Jesus' covenant encompasses all who believe in him and it is with his own blood that this covenant is sealed. Moses brings out the twelve tribes from Egypt and Jesus appoints twelve disciples who will judge the twelve tribes.[56] Jesus though, also has "sheep who are not of this pasture."[57] Moses is given the law on the mountain by God,[58] but the people cannot approach the mountain or they will die because they can't approach God.[59] Jesus, who is God himself, gives his teaching on the mountain,[60] where the people have followed him and

50. Exod 14; 28.

51. Deut 18:15.

52. *Eccl.Rabbah* 1:28.

53. See Heb 3:1–6.

54. Exod 7:1.

55. Philo, *Mos*1.1,8–9, 18–32, 48, 158; Ezekiel the Tragedian 68–82.

56. Matt 5:21–48.

57. John 10:16.

58. Exod 20:1–17.

59. Exod 19:23.

60. Matt 19:27–28.

are able to approach him and his teaching brings eternal life.[61] Moses
parted the Red Sea; Jesus walked on the Sea. Jesus not only demonstrated
his mastery over the waters,[62] but he also demonstrated that he was in
fact, not just a prophet, but Yahweh himself, as his statement to his disciples confirmed. When the disciples saw him walking on the lake, "they
were terrified" but Jesus immediately said to them: "Take courage! It is
I. Do not be afraid."[63] The "It is I" translates the Greek "*ego eimi*," which
in fact should be rendered "I am." It is the *ehyeh asher ehyeh* of Exod
3:14, the "I am who I am,"—the answer we noted earlier that God gave
to Moses when he asked for his name. Jesus was demonstrating that here
was one greater than Moses. He didn't have to part the waters, he walked
over them, because he was Yahweh himself,[64] the one who had from the
beginning mastered the Chaos waters, separating them at creation and
who parted them again at the Red Sea to lead his people from slavery to
freedom. The one who will lead them again following his Exodus[65] from
slavery to sin, into freedom.[66]

Matthew's Gospel is structured in five sections imitating the five
books of the Torah.[67] For Matthew, Jesus is the new Moses, bringing a
new teaching, or new interpretation, which was also expected of the Messiah. There were differing opinions held as to whether there would be a
new Torah in the Messianic Age/Age to Come[68] or a new interpretation
of it. In his "sermon on the mount" Jesus takes the teaching of Moses
and extends it.[69] The rabbis spoke of the yoke of Torah and tried to dis-
suade people from converting because of the difficulty in keeping the
commandments. Jesus, however, said "my yoke is easy and my burden

61. John 6:68.

62. Mark 4:35–41.

63. Matt 14:27.

64. This is also demonstrated at his arrest. When Jesus says "I am" (*ego eimi*) the
guards fall down on their backs, the same reaction that took place at the temple when
the High Priest pronounced the divine name.

65. We will see below that Jesus death is spoken of as an Exodus at his
transfiguration.

66. "It is for freedom that Christ has set us free. Stand firm, then, and do not let
yourselves be burdened again by a yoke of slavery" (Gal 5:1).

67. Moses, *Matthew's Transfiguration Story*, 162.

68. See Davies, *Torah in the Messianic Age*.

69. At one time these sayings in Matt 5:21–48 were called antitheses, "you have
heard it said. . .but I tell you . . . " However, they don't t contradict the law, but expand
it and make it even more stringent.

is light." In the Jewish mystical tradition it says of the Torah: "when it descended into this world, it put on the garments of this world, otherwise the world could not have endured it."[70] As the living Word, Jesus *is* the Torah incarnated: "Do not think that I have come to abolish the Law or the Prophets; I have not come to abolish them, but to fulfill them."[71] "The new incorporates the old. There is no antithesis."[72]

It could be argued that as the most "Jewish" of the Gospel writers, Matthew would naturally have emphasized the fact that Jesus was pre-figured in both the Exodus and Moses. However, we also see parallels between Jesus and the Exodus in John's Gospel. Here Jesus says:

> I am the bread of life. Your ancestors ate the manna in the wil-derness, yet they died. But here is the bread that comes down from heaven which people may eat and not die. I am the living bread that came down from heaven. Whoever eats of this bread will live forever. This bread is my flesh which I will give for the life of the world.[73]

Jesus has just performed the miracle of feeding the 5000 with bread that he blessed and was multiplied, which happened "as the Jewish Pass-over was near" so that this and his subsequent actions of walking on the water are imbued with that association. Twelve tribes were gathered up out of Egypt and taken to the Promised Land; twelve baskets of leftovers were gathered up "so that none be wasted." Jesus is saying that in the Exodus, the people ate the manna, which "rained down from heaven" yet they died. Jesus, born in Bethlehem (*Beit Lechem* - house of bread) is the living bread from heaven, which gives eternal life, "whoever lives by believing in me will never die."[74] He also promises to give some of the hidden manna "He who has an ear, let him hear what the Spirit says to the churches. To him who overcomes, I will give some of the hidden manna."[75]

Jesus' followers are the unleavened bread, without yeast, that is sin (the Rabbis associate leaven with sin). "Clean out the old yeast so that you may be a new batch, as you really are unleavened, for our Passover

70. Zohar, *Be'ha'alotkh* 111, 152a.

71. Matt 5:17.

72. Allison, *The New Moses*, 232.

73. John 6:48–51.

74. John 11:25.

75. Rev 2:17.

lamb, Christ has been sacrificed."[76] Jesus is the Rock[77] that provided the
water in the desert for the Israelites in the Exodus[78]; he gives living water,
as he said at *Sukkoth*[79] and as he promises in the new creation.[80] Jesus
also draws a comparison between his crucifixion and exaltation and the
bronze serpent that was lifted up in the desert by Moses (Num 21:8–9).
"Just as Moses lifted up the serpent in the wilderness, so the Son of Man
must be lifted up that everyone who believes may have eternal life in
him."[81] The serpent as we know is associated with sin and bronze in the
Bible, also represents sin and judgement.[82] Jesus on the cross, bore all our
sin, and so was identified with sin. "We implore you on Christ's behalf; be
reconciled to God. God made him who had no sin to be sin for us, so that
in him we might become the righteousness of God."[83] There were 40 years
between the Exodus from Egypt and Israel's entry into the promised land,
the beginning of the development of the new creation, the new community that God had chosen and there were 40 days between Jesus' Exodus[84]
and his ascension into heaven,[85] following which the new community of
God's people was created by the Holy Spirit.[86] Moses called his generation
a "perverse generation without faith" (Deut 32:5) as did Jesus (Luke9:41).

The typology is further confirmed at the transfiguration. During
the Exodus, Moses ascends Mt Sinai which is covered by a cloud for six
days. On the seventh day God calls from the cloud and Moses enters the
cloud and remains there 40 days and 40 nights. God then gives him the

76. 1 Cor 5:7.

77. "They were all baptized into Moses in the cloud and in the sea. They all ate
the same spiritual food and drank the same spiritual drink; for they drank from the
spiritual rock that accompanied them, and that rock was Christ." 1 Cor 10:2–4.

78. Exod 17:6.

79. Echoing Isa 55:1, and as he said to the Samaritan woman at the well (John
4:10).

80. "To the thirsty I will give freely from the spring of the water of life" (Rev 21:6).

81. John 3:14–15.

82. Gold represents God's holiness and glory—all the items inside the Tabernacle
were made of gold and those outside of bronze, the bronze laver etc. Silver represents
redemption.

83. 2 Cor 5:20b–21.

84. Luke 9:31.

85. Acts 1:3.

86. Acts 2:3, 41, 47.

instructions for building the tabernacle,[87] *skenas*,[88] so that he can dwell among his people. When Moses comes down from the mountain with the two tablets of the law his face is radiant "because he had spoken with the LORD."[89] Following Peter's declaration that Jesus is the Messiah, Jesus immediately identifies himself as the Son of Man and says: "For the Son of Man is going to come in his Father's glory . . . Truly I tell you some who are standing here will not taste death before they see the Son of Man coming in his kingdom."[90] "After six days" and therefore on the seventh day, following this declaration, Jesus takes Peter, James and John "up a high mountain." Here he is transfigured, that is, "his face shone like the sun and his clothes became as white as the light."[91] Moses and Elijah appear next to Jesus and they are covered in a cloud, out of which God speaks saying: "This is my son, whom I love, with him I am well pleased. *Listen to him!*" echoing the words that Moses had said: "The Lord your God will raise up for you a prophet like me. . .*You must listen to him.*" confirming that Jesus is that prophet. In Luke's gospel we learn that Elijah and Moses talk to Jesus about his departure. This is the usual English translation but, the actual Greek word means Exodus (*exodcn*). Jesus' death was to begin the new Exodus that would free all those who followed him.[92] Peter asks Jesus whether he should build a shelter for each of them, again the English translation obscures the fact that the Greek word here (*skenas*) means Tabernacle. Moses had gone up the mountain, and "on the seventh day" (recalling that the Exodus resulted in a "new creation"), he entered the cloud and God spoke with him and gave him the instructions for making the Tabernacle (*skenas*). The Tabernacle was in itself a minicosmos, a replica of creation, as we noted in chapter two. Jesus, who has come to tabernacle amongst his people '*skene*,'[93] ascends a mountain "on the seventh day" enters a cloud and God acknowledges him as his Son and

---

87. Exod 24:15–25:8.

88. Exod 25:8 Septuagint.

89. Exod 34:29.

90. Matt 16:27–28.

91. Matt 17:2.

92. Jesus said " . . . everyone who sins is a slave to sin . . so if the Son sets you free, you will be free indeed ." (John 8:34–36).

93. John 1:14.

the Messianic King[94] whose Exodus will also result in a new creation,[95] and a new Temple.[96] This is also therefore a Tabernacles moment, when the Messianic King was revealed in all his glory as Zechariah prophesied. *Sukkoth*, the feast of Tabernacles was a celebration of the Exodus as we observed in chapter 3, it was the time that God dwelt amongst his people in the Tabernacle. Furthermore, the presence of Moses who prophesied about the Messiah and Elijah, who was to be the forerunner of the Messiah, also confirm Jesus' status as Messiah.

Therefore, Jesus "departure" his death is the new Exodus which will redeem all those who believe in him, he is the fulfillment of the Law (hence the presence of Moses) and the Prophets (hence the presence of Elijah) who had spoken of him, just as he was to explain on the road to Emmaus to the disciples after his resurrection when they didn't recognize him and what he had done "'How foolish you are and how slow to believe all that the prophets have spoken! Did not the Messiah have to suffer these things and then enter his glory?' And beginning with Moses and all the Prophets, explained to them what was said in all the Scriptures concerning himself."[97]

Peter, John and James had witnessed a "preview" of Jesus, the Son of Man coming in his glory[98] as they were later to attest. James refers to him as "our glorious Lord Jesus Christ."[99] John said: "We have seen his glory, the glory of the one and only Son."[100] Peter said: "We were eyewitnesses of his majesty. He received honor and glory from God the Father when the voice came to him from the Majestic Glory, saying, 'This is my Son, whom I love; with him I am well pleased.' We ourselves heard this voice that came from heaven when we were with him on the sacred mountain."[101] They had seen the Son of Man 'coming in his Kingdom' as Jesus had prophesied (Matt 16:28).

---

94. Remembering that Messiah, means Anointed, and these are the same words that God spoke to Jesus at his anointing, his baptism, reminding us that he is the Messianic King.

95. "If anyone is in Christ, he is a new creation." 2 Cor 5:17.

96. John 2:19–21.

97 Luke 24:25–27.

98. Luke 9:29.

99. James 2:1.

100. John 1:14.

101. 2 Pet 1 16b–18.

The Passover Seder

Having considered how Jesus is prefigured in the Exodus story at which Passover was instituted, we will now consider how elements of Jesus' life and death are evident in the Passover Seder itself, which forms the main celebration of Passover. As the Passover lambs could no longer be sacrificed in the Temple following its destruction in 70 AD, the *matzot* (unleavened bread) became a substitute for the lamb. As it celebrates the major redemption story of Israel, the Seder, as we might expect, is rich with symbolism, ritual and meaning. The words *Ma nishtanah ha-lailah ha-zeh mi-kol ha-leilot?*—"why is this night different from all other nights?" is embedded in the psyche of all Jewish children. Not only is the whole story told during the course of the Passover Seder, with appropriate symbolic foods eaten at particular points as the story unfolds, but the story is told as though it had happened within living memory. One of the instructions for the festival is that "In every generation a man must so regard himself as if he came forth himself out of Egypt, for it is written. 'And thou shalt tell thy son in that day saying. It is because of that which the Lord did for me when I came forth out of Egypt' (Exod13:8)."[102] That is, each person must feel as if they personally had come out of Egypt. This is a collective event, linking not just those taking part in the Passover now, wherever they are in the world, but linking the present generation with their physical and spiritual ancestors; a really powerful way to re-live the reality of the freedom from all that Egypt represented. Before Passover begins however, the house has to be totally cleansed of leaven (yeast) and this is turned into a game with the children searching for and "finding" the leaven, that has been placed there by their parents. This is then burned the next morning as a symbolic gesture. This takes place on the fourteenth day of the first month, at the time of morning prayer, which is the same time that Jesus was crucified.[103] The rabbis have associated leaven (yeast) with sin and Jesus at his death removed our sin, our spiritual leaven. This is why Paul says "Clean out the old yeast so that you may be a new batch, as you really are unleavened for our Passover lamb, Christ has been sacrificed."[104] Therefore sin (leaven) is removed from the

---

102. *m.Pesh* 10.5.

103. He was crucified at 9 a.m.(Mark 15:25) but died at 3 p.m. in the afternoon (Mark 15:34–37).

104. The important point here is that it was the custom for a 'starter dough' from the last batch of bread to help the new batch rise. If anything was wrong with that

house and burnt at the same time and on the same day that Jesus died to remove sin.

At the Passover meal, therefore, only unleavened bread *matzah* is eaten along with the ritual foods, which are all symbolic of elements of the Exodus itself. There is some variation in the symbolism applied to the foods, but they each represent a part of the Exodus story. The *charoset*, for example, a mixture of apples, dates/sultanas, nuts and, red wine, symbolizes the mortar the Israelites used when they were forced to build as slaves for the Egyptians. The whole evening has a set order (hence the name *seder*) during which the *haggadah*, the recital of the Exodus story is told and at appropriate points the symbolic foods are eaten and the four cups of wine drunk. There are also songs and Psalms as well as the four questions asked by the child chosen to do so. The meal is eaten at night, reclining—indicating that the people are now free (slaves stood to eat). The 4 glasses of wine correspond with the four different phrases God uses to describe how he will redeem Israel. They are commonly known as the cup of sanctification ("I will bring you out of Egypt"), the cup of deliverance ("I will deliver you from Egyptian slavery"), the cup of redemption ("I will redeem you with my power") and the cup of restoration[105] ("I will take you as my people").[106]

There is little consensus about whether Seder practice today mirrors that of its original institution. However, it is agreed that the major elements of the unleavened bread, the bitter herbs and the wine would have been present from the beginning, as the first two form part of the instructions in Leviticus and wine always features at Jewish festivals. Although the following describes what takes place at a modern Passover Seder, it is thought to date back at least to the medieval period and possibly, much earlier, some suggesting as early as the first century. As part of the Seder, three *matzot* are placed in a white bag called a *matzahtash*. During the

---

dough, it would therefore be passed on to all the new loaves. Therefore the unleavened bread both physically and symbolically represented a break with the past and a new beginning.

105. This is also known as the "cup of completion," depending upon which *Haggadah* is followed.

106. Ex. 6:6–7 "Say, therefore, to the sons of Israel, 'I am the LORD, and I will *bring you out* from under the burdens of the Egyptians, and I will *deliver you* from their bondage. I will also *redeem you* with an outstretched arm and with great judgments. 'Then I *will take you* for My people, and I will be your God; and you shall know that I am the LORD your God, who brought you out from under the burdens of the Egyptians.'"

Seder, the leader takes the middle *matzah* out breaks it in two, covers the larger piece in a linen cover and whilst the children close their eyes it is hidden outside the room. Later on the children search for it and once found it is handed over to whoever is leading the Seder, usually the father, who "redeems" it with cash. The cloth is then removed from the *matzah*, which is broken up and a small piece given to everyone to be consumed following the final glass of wine. The *matzah* then is the last thing to be eaten. There are different Rabbinic interpretations for this ritual; one suggests the *matzot* represent the patriarchs: Abraham, Isaac and Jacob, which would mean that the middle piece would represent Isaac, whose sacrifice we saw earlier foreshadows that of Jesus. However, that does not explain the rest of the ritual. Messianic Jews on the other hand understand the three *matzot* to represent the Trinity, hidden from view by the material (world) of the *matzahtash*.[107] The middle piece taken out is then the Son, Jesus, whose body, like the *matzah* is broken, wrapped in linen, hidden (in the tomb) and resurrected; his sacrifice, his brokenness redeeming the world. This middle *matzah* which is broken and hidden is called the Afikomen, which means "the *coming* one."[108] John the Baptist sent his disciples to ask Jesus: "Are you the one who is *to come*, or are we to expect another?" As we saw in chapter 4, the "One who is to come" is a title of the Messiah. The Seder, therefore, contains a ritual of obscure origin, which would seem to be directly linked to the New Testament Messiah, Jesus, "the Coming One" and his death and resurrection.[109] Furthermore, the broken unleavened bread of the Afikomen, being passed round to all the participants along with the final cup of wine, the cup of restoration, closely parallels what happened at the Last Supper. Jesus took the unleavened bread,[110] broke it and said to his disciples: "Take and eat, this is my body" and took the final cup of wine and said: "This is my blood of the covenant, which is poured out for many."[111] Just as the Seder celebrates the Passover and the Exodus, the major redemption story of the Jewish people, the Eucharist, likewise, instituted at the Last Supper,

107. Just as the curtain in the Temple hid God's presence.

108. There is some debate about this, however the word (albeit in Hebrew here) appears in the *Mishnah, m.Pesahim* 10:8 and despite the differing Jewish claims that it means desert, or an after dinner song, it does mean "the Coming One."

109. See also John 3:31; 6:14; 11:27.

110. This was during the festival of unleavened bread and whether or not this was a Passover meal, the bread would have been unleavened.

111. Mark 14:22–24.

a Passover Seder,[112] celebrates the Exodus of the Passover Lamb, the redemption story of all people who follow Jesus, the new Moses.

The parallels don't end there—the *matzot*, by rabbinic decree, have
to be made in such a way as to appear bruised, striped and pierced in
line with the prophecies from Zech 12:10 and Isa 53:5, both of which
are understood to be Messianic prophecies within Judaism. As we noted
in chapter 3, they are also both applied to Jesus in the New testament. It
could be argued, of course, that this is perfectly in line with normative
Jewish Messianic expectation as these are read as Messianic prophecies
in the *Targumim,* but it fails to explain the other elements of the ritual
and suggests a suffering Messiah which the *Targum* is at pains to reject.[113]
The fact that it was unleavened bread which Jesus gave his disciples is also
significant. We have seen above that leaven is associated with sin, therefore this was Jesus' sinless body that he was passing round. Furthermore,
unleavened bread was later to become a replacement for the Passover
sacrifice, once the Temple was destroyed. The unleavened bread, therefore, that Jesus said was his body, in effect, came to replace the Passover
lamb, a lamb that was without defect, just as Jesus was the Passover Lamb
without defect, that is the lamb without sin. Therefore Jesus was associated with both elements of the Passover sacrifice, the Lamb and the bread
which came to replace it.

As a final part of the ritual of the Seder, the door is opened for Elijah
(a fifth and final cup is also set for him) in accordance with the *midrash*
on Mal 4:5 (3:23 Hebrew Bible) "Look I will send Elijah the prophet before the coming and great day of the LORD." This is the day that Jesus
announced had arrived in the Synagogue at Nazareth.[114] Elijah is, therefore, understood to be the forerunner of the Messiah. An expectation,
which was also evident in Jesus' time as we see from the questions the
disciples ask Jesus following his transfiguration.[115] The fifth cup is also

---

112. We consider this below.

113. Rather than explicating the Isaiah 53 passage by adding the word Messiah
or just re-wording the verse, according to the usual practice adopted, when it comes
to this passage which clearly speaks of the Servant suffering vicariously for the sins
of others, the Targumist completely changes the obvious meaning, so much so, that
Levey actually comments on it: "This is an excellent example of Targumic paraphrase
at its best . . . a reworking of the text to yield what the Targumist desires it to give forth."
Levey, *The Messiah,* 67.

114. Luke 4:16–19

115. "Why then do the teachers of the law say that Elijah must come first?" Jesus
replied: 'To be sure, Elijah comes and will restore all things. But I tell you Elijah has

called the "cup of wrath" and when the door is opened the leader of the Seder shouts: "Pour out your wrath on the world!" We noted in chapter 3 that throughout the Old Testament there are allusions to God's cup of wrath which will be poured out. The fifth cup then is also called the cup of wrath—the cup that the nations are meant to drink, of which Jeremiah speaks: "This is what the Lord, the God of Israel, said to me: 'Take from my hand this cup filled with the wine of my wrath and make all the nations to whom I send you drink it.'"[116]

The Last Supper

The question still remains whether the Last Supper of Jesus and his disciples was in fact a Passover meal. One suggestion is, that it was in fact the *seudah maphsehket*, which was traditionally celebrated by Galileans and was followed by a fast (*Ta'anit Bechorot*) held in memory of the firstborn. As a Galilean and first born of Mary, this would be plausible, particularly as it took place on the evening preceding the Passover, which would also then tie in with John's dating of the Last Supper. The variant dating of the Last Supper between John and the synoptic Gospels is one of the reasons that casts doubt on whether it was a Passover meal.[117] If John's dating is accepted this would mean that there would not be a lamb at the meal since the sacrifice of the lambs had not yet taken place. The lamb, as we have observed in the instructions from Leviticus formed a major part of the Passover meal prior to the destruction of the Temple. Another suggestion is that Jesus and his disciples followed the Qumran calendar but again this has also been disputed.[118] However, if they did follow the Qumran practice, whose participants saw themselves as the true Temple, this could also explain why there would not have been a lamb that had

---

already come and they did not recognize him but have done to him everything they wished, in the same way the Son of Man is going to suffer at their hands.' Then the disciples understood that he was talking to them about John the Baptist." (Matt 17:9–13). Also in Matt 3:4 John is described as wearing a garment of camel's hair and a leather girdle around his waist which echoes what was said about Elijah in 2 Kgs 1:8.

116. Jer 25:15–17.

117. Nonetheless the variant dating has also been questioned.

118. The Qumran calendar was proposed by Jaubert, *The Date of the Last Supper* and critiqued by Benoit, *Jesus and the Gospel*, 87—93, although there are many more works on the subject.

been sacrificed at the meal.[119] There are, however, convincing arguments for both sides, but the fact that it occurred during the Passover period and more importantly because Jesus told his disciples to "Go and make preparations for us to eat the Passover,"[120] as well as specifying it as a Passover meal[121] rather suggests that is, in fact, what it was. As all the other evidence points to the sacrifice of the Passover lamb and the whole Exodus theme prefiguring Jesus, not to mention that Jesus self-identified with various elements of the Exodus, it would seem to me that there must be a way to reconcile both.[122]

There are a number of elements that would suggest it was a Passover Seder: the disciples were reclining,[123] it was held at night,[124] the cup of wine that Jesus lifts up could quite easily, given the order of the meal,[125] represent the cup of salvation. Jesus dips a morsel and passes it to Judas, which forms part of the Passover Seder.[126] The fact that when Judas leaves, the other disciples think he is going to give alms to the poor[127] and the hymn sung at the end of the meal could well have been part of the *Hallel*, the Psalms sung during the Seder.[128] The bread that is broken by Jesus, would have been unleavened and could well have been the Afikomen, which as we have noted above is full of Messianic symbolism. It has, in fact, been argued that the Afikomen was already part of the Passover

119. Again this matter is disputed, some scholars believe that there were sacrifices made at Qumran as there were bones found there, nonetheless these included the bones of deer and they were cooked rather than roasted (as a sacrifice would have been). It is considered that the daily prayers at Qumran replaced the Temple sacrifices as they were to do in the Synagogue, but yet again, this has been disputed. The main fact to keep hold of was that Jesus' death took place at Passover instituting a new Exodus for all people who would follow him.

120. Luke 22:8.

121. "I have eagerly desired to eat this Passover with you before I suffer, for I tell you, I will not eat it again until it finds fulfillment in the kingdom of God." Luke 22:14b.

122. This has been attempted by Brant Pitre whose endeavor to reconcile both ideas is quite convincing. Pitre, *Jesus and the Jewish Roots*.

123. Luke 22:14.

124. Mark 14:17.

125. Mark 14:23.

126. Mark: 14:20. Although here it is a piece of bread.

127. Giving to the poor, as well as inviting the needy or strangers along, is an integral part of any Jewish festival meal, but particularly the Passover meal.

128. Mark 14:26.

Seder at the time of Jesus.[129] If that were the case, when Jesus was offering the broken bread to his disciples, saying "Take and eat, this is my body,"[130] he would be offering the Afikomen, which was already a symbol of the Messiah, 'the Coming One,' bruised and pierced as he would be.

There are also differing opinions on how many cups of wine are visible in the Gospel stories of the Last Supper; some people see four altogether, with Jesus taking the third cup, the cup of redemption when he utters the words, "Drink from it all of you. This is my blood of the (new) covenant, which is poured out for many for the forgiveness of sins."[131] It is then suggested that it was the fourth cup of wine, the wine of restoration or completion which he did not drink but of which he said: "I tell you, I will not drink of this fruit of the vine from now on until that day when I drink it anew with you in my Father's kingdom."[132] A further suggestion is, that the fourth cup which Jesus did not drink at the Supper, is represented by the wine mixed with myrrh, that is offered to Jesus on the cross.

There is, however, no mention of the fifth cup, the cup for Elijah. Elijah of course, has already been and pointed the way to the Messiah as Jesus explained to his disciples following his transfiguration.[133] However, as we have noted, the cup is also called the cup of wrath, and in the Garden of Gethsemane, Jesus fell with his face to the ground and prayed: "My Father, if it is possible, may this cup be taken from me. Yet not as I will, but as you will."[134] When Peter wielded a sword at Jesus' arrest, Jesus commanded "Put your sword away! Shall I not drink the cup the Father has given me?"[135] This is the cup of wrath for the nations, that is the *goyim*. This is the cup, which was meant for us, which Jesus drank in our place so that we could be reconciled with the Father: "Since we have now been justified by his blood, how much more shall we be saved from God's wrath through him!"[136]

The fifth cup of the Passover, the one that is missing from the Last Supper, is the cup of wrath, which Jesus "drank" on the cross. Whether

129. Eisler, 'Das Letzte Abendmahl', 5—37.

130. Matt 26:29.

131. Matt 26:28. Some manuscripts have "new covenant" and some just "covenant."

132. Matt 26:29.

133. That is John the Baptist, "A voice of one calling in the wilderness, prepare the way for the LORD." Matt 3:3, quoting Isa 40:3 and applying it to John.

134. Matt 26:39.

135. John 18:11.

136. Rom 5:9.

the Last Supper was a Passover Seder or not is uncertain, nevertheless what we can be sure of, is that we are meant to connect Jesus' act of redemption, his Exodus, with God's original act of redemption, the Exodus from Egypt; we are meant to realize that Jesus fulfilled the original Exodus. Israel's redemption was a foreshadowing of the redemption of the whole world. Israel, a Holy Nation and a Royal Priesthood[137] were the ones interceding for the world, being a light to the nations, until the Light of the World[138] emerged from their midst to make all his followers a Holy Nation and a Royal Priesthood.[139] When we celebrate the Last Supper, therefore, that is the Eucharist, having understood its origins, it becomes enriched with all the symbolism, that we have just uncovered. Jesus is the Passover lamb, the Afikomen, striped, bruised and pierced, the unleavened bread without sin, the living bread from heaven, the Rock which gives the life giving water of the Spirit. The prophet like Moses, the one greater than Moses, whose death, the new Exodus, redeems his people from slavery to sin and brings them into the Promised Land where he will tabernacle with them, the firstfruits of the new creation.

Habikkurim

When Israel entered the promised land, following the Exodus, they were commanded to offer the firstfruits of their harvest to the LORD. The LORD said to Moses "Speak to the Israelites and say to them: When you enter the land I am going to give you and you reap its harvest, bring to the priest a sheaf of the first grain of your harvest. He is to wave the sheaf before the LORD so it will be accepted on your behalf; the priest is to wave it on the day after the Sabbath.'"[140] Passover is immediately followed by the week-long festival of unleavened bread, *Hag haMatzot,* which has almost become synonymous with it.[141] During this period, on the seventeenth Nissan, the festival of Firstfruits, *Habikkurim,* is celebrated on the day following the weekly Sabbath, that is on the first day of the week.

---

137. Exod 19:6.

138. John 8:12.

139. 1 Pet 2:9.

140. Lev 23: 9–12.

141. This is one of the reasons that makes it difficult to pinpoint the date of the last supper, as "Passover" and "Unleavened Bread" appear to be used interchangeably in the New Testament as they often are now.

In John's Gospel, we are told that "early on the first day of the week,"[142] that is on the Festival of *Habikkurim*, Firstfruits, Mary Magdalene, one of Jesus' followers, went to the tomb where Jesus had been buried only to find it empty. She found the stone had been removed from the entrance and ran to tell Simon Peter and the other disciples. They also went to the tomb and found the grave clothes, but no body. Jesus had said that on the third day he would rise again, but as John explains "they still did not understand from Scripture that Jesus had to rise from the dead."[143] Mary stood outside the tomb weeping and upon turning saw Jesus but didn't recognize him, "thinking he was the gardener" (Jn20:15). By allusion, we are taken back to Genesis 1 and the Garden of Eden, just as we were at the beginning of John's Gospel. This time, however, this is the new Adam, the second Adam,[144] the firstfruits of the new creation: "But Christ has indeed been raised from the dead, the firstfruits of those who have fallen asleep. For since death came through a man, the resurrection of the dead comes also through a man. For as in Adam all die, so in Christ all will be made alive. But each in his own turn: Christ the firstfruits; then, when he comes, those who belong to him."[145] This is the first day of the new week. Day 8 symbolic within Judaism, signifying a full week (seven days) plus one, the beginning of a new week, and symbolically the beginning of a new era and in this case a new creation. On the cross Jesus cried out "it is finished" (*tetelestai*), that is the work of salvation, which corresponds with the work of creation.[146] Jesus died at 3 p.m. just before the Sabbath started, therefore, he finished his work of new creation on the sixth day, just as he had "in the beginning." Creation and Salvation are two sides of the same coin. Furthermore, Mary had set out for the tomb "while it was still dark"[147] symbolizing the darkness before creation in Genesis 1 and before the dawn of the new day, both physically and spiritually. Mary had seen who she thought was the Gardener, which in effect he was, this was the new Adam, the firstfruits of the new creation, this was Yahweh, his work of new creation finished, having overcome the forces of Chaos.

142. John 20:1.

143. John 20:9.

144. 1 Cor 15:45.

145. 1 Cor 15:20–23.

146. In the Greek translation of the Septuagint written third century BCE for Jewish people in the Diaspora, the word used for God finishing his work comes from the same root as *tetelestai*, (*stotelesten*).

147. John 20:1.

In the beginning all things were made through Jesus (Jn 1:3) and at the end, in Jesus all things are made new. "Therefore, if anyone is in Christ, the new creation has come: the old has gone."[148] The day of the resurrection therefore was not just day one of the new week, the eighth day, it was also the festival of firstfruits, *Habikkurim*. We have, therefore, exactly the same sequence of events as in the Old Testament salvation. Israel, rescued from slavery, had carried out the Passover sacrifice, undergone the Exodus, risen up from the waters of Chaos of the Red Sea, a new creation, which entered the Promised Land and offered the firstfruits of the harvest to God. Jesus, the Passover lamb had been slain at the feast of Passover, had undergone his Exodus, overcame the forces of Chaos, death and sin, rose up from them, which resulted in freedom from slavery to sin, the firstfuits of the new creation, where no distinction was made in terms of class, gender, ethnicity or social status.[149]

Firstfruits, as the name implies is another of Israel's festivals connected with a harvest, in this case the barley harvest. On this day a sheaf of barley (an *omer*) was "waved before the Lord,"[150] signifying that once the firstfruits had been waved and offered to the LORD, the rest of the harvest would be acceptable. Jesus as the firstfruits of the new creation, the new harvest, makes all who believe in him acceptable through his sacrifice. *Habikkurim* (Firstfruits) is also known as *reshit katzir* (the beginning of the harvest). As the opening words of Mark's gospel declare, this is "the beginning of the good news about Jesus the Messiah,"[151] and his resurrection on the Festival of Firstfruits, *reshit katzir,* is the beginning of the harvest, that we are all part of. Jesus said to his disciples: "The harvest is plentiful but the workers are few. Ask the Lord of the harvest, therefore, to send out workers into his harvest field."[152] As new creations, helping to bring in the harvest, we are the continuation of the good news spoken of by Mark.

---

148. 2 Cor 5:17.
149. Gal 3:28.
150. Lev 23: 15
151. Mark 1:1.
152. Luke 10:2.

Shavuot

The festival of Firstfruits, though, is not the end of the Exodus story. The *omer* (the sheaf of barley), which is waved on the feast of Firstfruits, begins the 50 day count to the next festival of *Shavuot*, with the period in-between known as *sefirat haOmer* "counting the *omer*."[153] This is viewed within Judaism as a period for personal reflection, but also as a time of anticipation, as though you were awaiting a special visitor. *Shavuot* was a pilgrim festival celebrated in the Temple at Jerusalem and, therefore, during the second Temple period, Jewish males from across Israel and the Diaspora would travel to Jerusalem to take part in the festival there. It was also known as Pentecost because of the 50 day period of counting the *omer*, which precedes it. Originally a harvest festival, *Shavuot* came to be associated with the giving of the Torah at Sinai; that is, the spiritual fulfillment of the physical redemption of the Exodus and the birth of the Jewish nation. Israel, God's chosen people, had been given the Torah to enable them to be in relationship with God. The *halakhah*, the laws derived from the Torah[154] is normally translated as 'law.' However, it actually stems from the root *halalkh* which means "go," as Neusner has pointed out: a better translation would be "the way." "The *halakhah* is the 'way'; the way man lives his life; the way man shapes his daily routine into a pattern of sanctity, the way man follows the revelation of the Torah and attains redemption."[155]

Jesus' resurrection was not the end of his Exodus either. Jesus rose on *Habikkurim*, the Festival of Firstfruits and 50 days later his disciples were in Jerusalem for the feast of *Shavuot* (Pentecost) waiting for the gift of the Holy Spirit, as Jesus had commanded them to do.[156] This would be the spiritual fulfillment of the physical redemption of Jesus' Exodus. Jesus had said he had not come to do away with the Law (Torah) but to fulfill it. When asked, which were the greatest commandments, Jesus gave the two which summed up all the others: "Love the Lord your God with all your heart, and with all your soul and with all your mind." This is the

---

153. Lev 23.13–14.

154. That is both the written and oral Torah.

155. Neusner, *The Way of Torah*, 25.

156. On one occasion, while he was eating with them, he gave them this command: "Do not leave Jerusalem, but wait for the gift my Father promised, which you have heard me speak about. For John baptized with water, but in a few days you will be baptized with the Holy Spirit." Acts 1:4–5.

first and greatest commandment. And the second is like it: 'Love your neighbor as yourself.' All the Law and the Prophets hang on these two commandments."[157] He also said to his disciples "A new Command I give you: Love one another. As I have loved you, so you must love one another. By this everyone will know that you are my disciples, if you love one another."[158] As Paul later said: "Love is the fulfillment of the law."[159] Jesus also declared himself to be "the Way, the Truth and the Life," that is he *is* the *halakhah*, the *way* for his chosen people,[160] his new creation to be in relationship with God. At *Shavuot* Jesus sent the Holy Spirit which would enable the new creation, his chosen ones to keep the commandments, to walk in the way. "If you are led by the Spirit, you are not under the law."[161] At Pentecost his disciples were given the Firstfruits of the Spirit,[162] the means by which they were able to be in relationship with God and to bear fruit.[163] Just as the giving of the Torah, celebrated at Pentecost, was considered to be the birth of the Jewish nation, the giving of the Spirit at Pentecost is understood to be the birth of the Church. Pentecost is not a "new" Christian festival but rather the fulfillment of the original Jewish festival.

The Torah was given with thunder and lightning and the Lord descending with fire on Mt Sinai.[164] The Spirit was given with a sound like the blowing of a violent wind and with tongues of fire descending on Mt Zion (Jerusalem), as Joel had prophesied would happen on "The Day of the LORD," as Peter explained: "Then Peter full of the Spirit stood up and said that this was in fulfillment of Joel's prophecy that 'in the last days, God says I will pour out my Spirit on all people . . . and everyone who calls on the name of the Lord will be saved, for on Mount Zion and in Jerusalem there will be deliverance.'"[165]

The Torah was given during the Exodus to the newly redeemed people of Israel who had just carried out the Passover. The Holy Spirit

---

157. Matt 22:37–40.

158. John 13:34.

159. Rom 13:10b.

160. "You did not choose me, I chose you and appointed you that you might go and bear much fruit" (John15:16).

161. Gal 5:18.

162. Rom 8:23.

163. Gal 5:22–23.

164. Exod 19:16–18.

165. "Joel 2:28–32 quoted in Acts 2:17–21.

was given following the Passover sacrifice of Jesus, his Exodus, to his
newly redeemed people. The Torah was given on tablets of stone, but the
Holy Spirit was to write the law on people's hearts: "This is the covenant
I will make with the people of Israel, after that time," declares the Lord
"I will put my law in their mind, and write it on their hearts. I will be
their God, and they will be my people. No longer will they teach their
neighbor, or say to one another, 'Know the Lord,' for they will all know
me, from the least of them to the greatest declared the LORD, for I will
forgive their wickedness and will remember their sins no more."[166]

Following the giving of the Torah and the apostasy of the Golden
Calf, 3000 died, whereas at the giving of the Holy Spirit, 3000 were given
eternal life. However, this is not a simple dichotomy between the Law
and the Spirit. Jesus said: 'Do not think that I have come to abolish the
Law or the Prophets, I have I have not come to abolish them but to fulfill
them."[167] The Spirit, the giver of life, breathed life into the law: "And you
show that you are a letter from Christ delivered by us, written not with
ink but with the Spirit of the living God, not on tablets of stone but on
tablets of human hearts."[168] The Spirit sealed the new covenant (or the
renewed covenant). Jeremiah prophesied this would happen even though
God brought his chosen people out of Egypt "with a mighty hand and an
outstretched arm"[169] they did not keep their side of the covenant: "The
days are coming," declares the Lord, "when I will make a new covenant
with the people of Israel and with the people of Judah. It will not be like
the covenant I made with their ancestors when I took them by the hand
to lead them out of Egypt, because they broke my covenant, though I was
a husband to them, declares the Lord.[170]

Shavuot is also associated with marriage and, as it says in Jeremiah,
Yahweh was Israel's "husband." The giving of the second Tablets of the
Law at Sinai[171] is understood to be God's betrothal to Israel. In ancient
Israel the betrothal was preceded by a ritual immersion and then made
under the *chuppah*[172] the wedding canopy, where the *ketubah*, the mar-

166. Jer 31:33–34.

167. Matt 5:.17

168. 2 Cor 3:3.

169 Deut 26:8; Ps 136:12.

170. Jer 31:31–32.

171. Moses had smashed the first lot of tablets following the incident with the
Golden Calf.

172. In current Jewish weddings the ritual immersion takes place before the wedding

riage contract was also agreed. This set out the terms and conditions of the marriage. A period of separation, usually a year, would take place while the groom prepared a place for them to live and then he would come back for his bride. At Sinai, God tells Moses that the people are to prepare themselves before they meet him "on the third day." Moses consecrates them and they wash their clothes.[173] Tradition has it that Mt Sinai was lifted over the heads of the people as a *chuppah,* so that the betrothal between Israel and God took place at Sinai. The *ketubah,* the terms and conditions of the marriage, was therefore the Torah. God's proposal to them was: "If you obey me fully and keep my covenant, then out of all nations you will be my treasured possession."[174] To which the people responded: 'We will (do everything the LORD has said').[175] The Temple was understood to be the place that the "groom" Yahweh, was preparing for his bride, although others have said that the wedding, the *nissuin* would only take place in the Messianic Era/Age to Come. As Christians we believe we are living in the Messianic Era, in the period of the betrothal, when the bridegroom,[176] Jesus has gone to prepare a place for us: "My Father's house has plenty of room, if that were not so, would I have told you that I am going there to prepare a place for you? And if I go and prepare a place for you, I will come back and take you to be with me . . ."[177] Both the groom[178] and the bride[179] have been ritually immersed. Our *ketubah* is sealed with the Holy Spirit,[180] which was also given at Pentecost/Shavuot and our bridegroom will return to take us to the wedding feast of the Lamb, to which all are invited.[181] "Let us rejoice and be glad and give the glory to Him, for the marriage of the Lamb has come and his bride has made herself ready."[182]

---

and the wedding is conducted under the *chuppah.*

173. Exod 19:14.

174. Exod 19:5.

175. Exod 19:8.

176. John 3:29, Matt 9:14–15.

177. John 14:2–3.

178. Matt 3:13–17.

179. Eph 5:26–27.

180. "When you believed, you were marked in him with a seal, the promised Holy Spirit." Eph 1;13b.

181. Joel 2:28–32 quoted in Acts 2:17–21.

182. Rev 19:7.

Passover and the Anointed King

Jesus is the Passover Lamb, he is the prophet that Moses said would come, the new Moses leading a new Exodus and creating a new people. However we noted at the outset that Jesus, first and foremost, is King and that the elements of his death and resurrection, even though portrayed in different images, namely Servant, Passover Lamb and High Priest, are all still elements of his kingship. This is also the case here, because the original Exodus, is in itself, a recapitulation of the original creation story, which is portrayed in terms of sacral kingship. This is articulated in the Psalms:

> The waters saw you, God
> the waters saw you and writhed;
> the very depths were convulsed.
> Your path led through the sea,
> your way through the mighty waters
> though your footprints were not seen.
> you led your people like a flock
> by the hand of Moses and Aaron.[183]

Thus the parting of the Red Sea is equated with the chaos waters "the very depths (*Tehomoth*) convulsed." In other places Egypt is associated with *Rahab*: "For Egypt's help is worthless and empty, therefore I have called her, "*Rahab* who sits still,"[184] which in turn is associated with the Chaos waters/evil forces:

> You rule over the surging sea;
> when its waves mount up, you still them,
> you crushed *Rahab* like one of the slain;
> with your strong arm you scattered your enemies
> the heavens are yours, and yours also the earth
> you founded the world and all that is in it.[185]

Rahab is also associated with the dragon: "Awake, awake, put on strength, O arm of the Lord! Awake, as in days of old, the generations of long ago! Was it not you who cut *Rahab* in pieces, who pierced the dragon?" [186]

---

183. Ps 77:16, 19–20.

184. Isa 30:7.

185. Ps 89: 9–11.

186. Isa 51:9. See also Job 9:13, 26:12.

Therefore the Exodus, contains all the same Enthronement/king-ship motifs that we saw in chapter 2 and which we have been identify-ing in the subsequent chapters: the overcoming of the chaos waters, new creation and fertility. Israel, a holy nation and royal priesthood, rises up out of the Red Sea, the waters of Chaos, a new creation and enters the Promised Land, a land flowing with milk and honey. This is the founda-tional salvation story and it is itself a recapitulation of the creation story. In later Jewish writings Moses is identified as King, he offers himself as an atonement for the people following the incident of the Golden Calf. The "new song" that Israel sang to the LORD following the overcoming of the chaos waters is called the song of Moses and Miriam, or the Song of the Sea, it celebrates Yahweh as King[187] and also contains the very same line that is found in Isa12:2:

"The LORD is my strength and my song he has become my salva-tion." which is also found in Ps 118:14: the enthronement Psalm, which forms part of the *Hallel*, sung at Passover, but also at *Sukkoth*, which con-tains the lines proclaiming Jesus as King when he rode into Jerusalem at Passover. Words so important that they are said every day in the Jewish Morning Prayer:

Blessed is he who comes in the name of the Lord.

That this was a new creation is reinforced by the fact that this also consti-tuted the beginning of a new year: "This month is to be for you the first month, the first month of your year."[188] Therefore new creation and new year are linked as we've seen throughout. The New Year festival celebrates the original creation which it recapitulates and creation is once again re-newed. The creation motif is also laid out in the first chapter of Exodus when we learn that the Israelites "have been fruitful and multiplied and the land was filled with them,"[189] echoing the command to Adam and Eve.[190] The two reasons given for observing sabbath—commemorating Exodus (Exod 20:9–11) and commemorating creation (Deut 5:15) also suggests a connection between creation and the Exodus.

In the creation story in Genesis, God overcame the waters of Chaos, created over six days and then rested on the seventh day, in his temple,

---

187. "The Lord reigns for ever and ever" (Exod 15:18).

188. Exod 12:2.

189. Exod 1:5–7.

190. Gen 1:28.

the cosmos. In the Exodus story, God parted the Red Sea and Israel rose up a new creation and God gave instructions to build a Tabernacle in which he would dwell amongst his people. The fact that the instructions for the building of the Tabernacle, mimic the sequence of the original creation again reinforces the fact that Israel is a new creation

On the seventeenth Nissan, the Ark came to land, recapitulating the original Creation, when God had overcome the forces of chaos and created. On the seventeenth Nissan, Israel rose up again from the Chaos waters of the Red Sea, a new creation. On seventeenth Nissan, Israel brought before God the firstfruits of the Promised Land. On seventeenth Nissan, Jesus, rose from his battle with the forces of Chaos, the firstfruits of the new creation. The Exodus, therefore, not only looks back to God's victory over Chaos in the beginning, but points forward to his final victory. It's vitally important therefore that we grasp the whole concept of myth in the bible, itsplace and its power to convey symbolically the reality of what is happening. I would suggest therefore that the movement that sought to demythologize the Bible, and the movement that now seeks demythologize the church, rather than helping people to understand it and to make it more "relevant" has in fact hindered our understanding of it.[191]

> In myth primeval event and eschatological event merge *Urzeit wird Endzeit*. Thus the myth provides assurance that the outcome of the struggle between creator and Chaos is certain that the power of evil has been broken. The day is imminent the prophet (Ezekiel) assures the reader when God and the dragon will meet for the final battle. In the end God will prevail and confirm his rule symbolized in the rebuilding of the Temple palace within the eschatological Jerusalem.[192]

191. "In the past many readers of the Bible have expended considerable energy reading myth out of the Bible. Fidelity to biblical tradition would seem to demand just the opposite attitude however." Batto, *Slaying the Dragon*, 171.

192. Batto, *Slaying the Dragon*, 172.

Chapter 6

FESTIVALS, KINGDOM
AND CORONATION

Introduction

THE JEWISH FESTIVALS NOT only tell the story of God's chosen people and their redemption, they tell the story that God chooses everyone and all can be redeemed; everyone is chosen but not everyone will respond. The festivals foreshadowed what would one day take place for real. *Yom Kippur*, the Day of Atonement was fulfilled at the tenth Jubilee by the High Priest in the order of Melchizedek, taking his own blood, not a substitute into the real Holy of Holies "not made with human hands." The harvest festival of *Sukkoth* was fulfilled when the *real* King, the *real* Son of God rode into Jerusalem to cries of "Hosanna to the Son of David," with palm leaves strewn at his feet and the words of Psalm 118, ringing in his ears. This was Yahweh the King coming to his Temple as the prophecies had foretold, coming to renew the covenant, coming to complete the festivals that had awaited their fulfilment, which were "only a shadow of things to come."[1] This was *the* Anointed who *really* died and rose again and is enthroned at the right hand side of God. This was the prophet like Moses foretold in Deut 18, leading a new Exodus, his body and blood the *real* bread from heaven and the living water from the Rock, making a way for his chosen people into the promised land, the eternal city. This was

1. Col 2:17.

140

the Lamb of God, entering Jerusalem at the time of the selection of the Passover lambs, the King Messiah entering Jerusalem as expected from Bethany, over the Mount of Olives, riding from the East on a donkey and on a colt the foal of a donkey, fulfilling *Pesach*, the festival of Passover and the prophecies of Zechariah. The lamb that was inspected and found to be without defect, who was flailed and hung up to die; whose blood protects from the Destroyer and, whose body, the unleavened bread, striped and bruised as the prophecies foretold, is eaten as communion, as eucharist, thanksgiving. *Habikkurim*, the Festival of Firstfruits was fulfilled when the firstfruits of the new creation rose from the dead, from the tomb, between the Cherubim, a wave offering, that made the rest of the harvest acceptable to God. The author of the new creation, rising on the first day of the new week, the new era. The *reshit ketzir*, the beginning of the harvest that will be completed in the new creation, when the King with the golden crown, the Son of man, descends on clouds of glory with his sickle in his hand, not to the Temple built on the threshing floor of Araunah but the Temple he created. The festival of *Shavuot*, Pentecost, 50 days from *Habikkurim*, the spiritual fulfilment of the physical redemption of Israel, through the Exodus, when Yahweh once again divided the waters and Chaos was overcome again. When the *Aseret HaDibrot*, the ten commandments were given, so that we could walk again with God and he could dwell in our midst, fulfilled at Pentecost the spiritual fulfilment of the physical redemption of Jesus' Exodus, when the Holy Spirit was given and the church was born. These feasts tell the story of Israel's redemption, who as a light to the nations, foreshadowed the redemption of the whole world, God's plan from the beginning. Each of these festivals are still celebrated within Judaism; God's chosen people keep the *moadim*, the appointed times with God but for those of us who believe that Jesus is the Messiah, and fulfilled these festivals, we now have our own *moadim*, that tell the story of our redemption, that began with Genesis and will end with Revelation.

Christian Festivals

Following the split between those who believed Jesus was Messiah and the other Jewish groups of the time toward the end of the first century, for followers of Jesus the celebration of the Jewish festivals gave way to the development of Christian festivals which continued to develop their own traditions. Unfortunately the aftermath of the Enlightenment coupled with our increasing industrialization has meant our faith has been divorced from the natural world it grew out of, the temple decorated with motifs from Eden, the festivals following the agricultural year. The metaphors of nature, sewing, reaping, harvesting, watering have lost their meaning because they've been removed from their original setting. These were not just part of the Jewish festivals, but part of *our* festivals until recent times. Forest church is a noble attempt to redress the balance but we need much more. We need to fill the imaginations of our children with the story of the King with the tattooed thigh, on a white horse, coming to rescue us from the dragon. To fill their mouths with the seasonal tastes of food prepared for a banquet with the King, celebrating his festivals. To punctuate their years with times of joy and thanksgiving and awe and wonder. To make them part of God's family, to understand community exists not just in communion, in sharing bread and wine at the altar, but in sharing all God's bounty with each other and with those who have nothing.

The fact that Jesus was foreshadowed and prefigured in each of the Jewish festivals is not coincidental. These are the *moadim*, the appointed times to meet with God to eat with him and before him, to dance and sing and be joyful before him. Of course, for both Jews and Christians, every day is a time to meet with God,[2] but we also need to observe our appointed times with him, our "date nights." *Sukkoth* is the most joyful of all the Jewish festivals—full of dance and music; singing, feasting, and drinking, because God ordained it so, but it seems so far removed from the majority of our festivals, even the traditionally joyful celebrations of Christmas and Easter Sunday. The Spiritual significance of our festivals is understood by Christians, but the actual celebration of them has been reduced, for the most part, to a number of church services, which often lack imagination. I believe it is crucial that we revive our festivals by recovering their ancient meaning and expression and then invest them with our own traditions—to revive the "festive" part of festivals. One writer has noted:

2. That is why Jewish men wear a kippah, that reminds them, that they are in God's presence always, and why they pray three times daily, but it is also in every aspect of Jewish life, eating kosher is a constant reminder of God's presence, but the point I'm making here is that the festivals are a real celebration of our relationship with God, like a "date-night" that keeps the relationship, fresh and on track, a reminder of our first love.

"The word 'festival' is now reserved for occasions when people who are young, or would like to be, huddle together in a field to listen to music in the rain and shop for ethnic clothing and candles. And get inebriated. Some 1,500 years ago, our Anglo-Saxon and Celtic ancestors had a much better idea. They celebrated regularly to mark the passage of the seasons that governed the natural world around them and the cycle of the sun, which gave them light and warmth."[3]

The writer's answer to this however is not to embrace the existing church festivals or to revive those we've discarded, but to "get together at regular intervals, with family or with friends, to take stock and commune." Of course that *is* what happens at family parties, for birthdays, weddings, even Bank Holidays but there is no sense of being part of a wider community. There is no deeper sense of purpose to that gathering or the belief that it is part of a bigger picture. Furthermore, there is no sense that these gatherings form part of a cycle which gives meaning and structure to our lives. In fact the writer frowns on the idea of reverting to the liturgical calendar[4] neither is he suggesting that we should be worshipping anything, "neither God nor Mammon."[5] He identifies the problem, but rejects the most obvious answer, even though he has nothing with which to supplant it. Although he recognizes the deep seated need placed within us to celebrate, to come together, to express gratitude and celebrate nature, and community, giving a rhythm to the year, what he fails to acknowledge, is who it is we're grateful to, and why we have that need in the first place. Nonetheless he does appreciate the importance of marking the seasons and the equally depressing effect of not doing so:

> In a country like Britain with real seasons, the annual cycle of the earth's movement around the sun has significance. It was only as I was considering this topic that I remembered that the word "equinox" refers to the two days a year when night and day are the same length. If we don't mark such moments, then I fear that our years will just become a featureless smudge in time.

Exactly! This is what the Jewish cycle of festivals and the life cycle rituals achieve; they imbue not only each individual year with meaning and purpose, but also each individual life. Not only are they linked to the liturgical calendar, celebrating the great salvation history between God

3. Shakespeare, *A Point of View.*
4. He is to be fair, equally dismissive of druids parading at Stonehenge.
5. Shakespeare, *A Point of View.*

and the Jewish people, they are also linked to the agricultural cycle, to nature and the celebration of the harvests, as well as the astrological year. Passover occurs at the spring equinox and Day of Atonement takes place at the autumn equinox.

So rather than our years becoming a "featureless smudge in time," they are filled with meaning and fellowship and joy. This is exactly what the Christian liturgical year is also about, but we seem to have lost our way a little. Christianity has its own cycle of festivals with symbolic meanings that speak, not just to our spirit, but to our flesh as well and which also cohere with the annual cycle of the sun. Unfortunately many of these have been cast aside in the misguided attempt to modernize the church. I feel it is up to us to revive them, to get in tune again with the seasons, and the rhythm of nature because that's part of *our* created nature.

It's been argued that because Easter takes its name from the pagan Goddess *Eostre*, and because Jesus' birth is celebrated at the winter solstice, that Christianity has taken over the pagan festivals and in so doing, it is argued, ousted what were popular, *life affirming* celebrations and replaced them with church festivals in a form of imperialism. As a consequence, pagan festivals are seen to be the only ones "legitimately" linked to nature and the seasons. However, the need to mark the seasons and the cycle of the sun is not just the prerogative of pagans. How sad that those who have the "Good News," who are themselves New Creations, are the ones who rather than embracing creation and all its bounty are seen to be the biggest kill-joys. We need to reclaim what is legitimately ours:

> . . . much of what modern audiences view as 'pagan'—solstices, the healing power of plants, astrology, and so on—were standard parts of medieval science, religion, and medicine.[6]

Jesus didn't just use parables about seeds and harvests, about reaping and sewing because he lived in a predominantly agrarian society but because that's the language of creation, it's *his* language, he created the earth, the cosmos, the sun and the moon to keep the appointed times, the festivals so that his creation could come together and rejoice with him and enjoy all that he has provided for our pleasure and our sustenance. He came to give us "life in all its fullness" and he came to set us free. "To live entirely on the timeline is to be a slave; to step onto the spiral of sacred time is to begin the slow journey to freedom, the wide sublime

---

6. A Clerk of Oxford, *A Little History of Lammas.*

highlands we were made for."[7] I would argue that the decline in church membership is not because church is not relevant in the sense of not able to speak to this generation in its own language, it's not relevant because it's forgotten how to speak in *its* own language.

Compared with the medieval church, we have stopped celebrating so many festivals. For example, one important festival we seem to have lost from our calendar is that of John the Baptist. This is one of the oldest festivals and yet, here in England, for the most part, it has fallen by the wayside. In other parts of the world it's still celebrated all day and night with lots of different traditions attached to it. Although ostensibly a church festival, the celebration is also for the summer solstice and so in Europe particularly there are bonfires and feasting and in the Nordic countries, garlands of flowers are worn and people spend time in nature which is right at the heart of what the Bible is trying to tell us. These two are linked—creation and salvation. This is especially so with *this* festival, which links, not just the solar calendar, but also the prophecies of the Old Testament fulfilled in the New.

The Feast of John the Baptist

Isaiah prophesied that there would be *"a voice of one calling in the wilderness, prepare the way for the Lord,* make straight paths for him."[8] In the final book in our canon[9] of the Old Testament, the LORD says through Malachi: "I will send my messenger, *who will prepare the way* before me." We also learn that this will be the prophet Elijah,[10] and that the *'sun of righteousness will rise with healing in its wings."* [11]

At John the Baptist's birth, his father Zechariah prophesied over him: 'And you my child will be called a prophet of the Most High; for *you will go on before the Lord* to *prepare the way for him,* to give his people the knowledge of salvation through the forgiveness of their sins, because of the tender mercy of our God, by which t*he rising sun will come to us from heaven to shine on those living in darkness* and in the shadow of death . . .

---

7. Hill, *Holidays and Holy Nights,* 15.

8. Isa 40:3.

9. Although the same books are present, the Jewish canon is set out differently.

10. Mal 4:5.

11. Mal 4:2.

"[12] Coming out from the wilderness,[13] John preaches a baptism of repentance for the forgiveness of sins.[14] He is expressly identified by Luke with the Isaiah prophecy. He is the *"voice of one calling in the wilderness,"* he is the one *"preparing the way of the LORD."*[15] John also fulfills the Malachi prophecy, not just because that also says that the LORD will send a messenger "to prepare the way before me," before he comes to his Temple but also because Malachi says that the messenger will be Elijah and John is expressly identified with Elijah by Jesus[16] who is Yahweh incarnate, come to his Temple.

Furthermore, Jesus is "the light that shines in the darkness and the darkness has not overcome it."[17] He is also, therefore, understood to fulfill the Isaiah prophesy: "The people walking in darkness have seen a great light on those living in the land of deep darkness a light has dawned."[18] John was a witness to the light, "the sun of righteousness." The "rising sun" as his father prophesied: "There was a man sent from God whose name was John. He came as a witness to testify concerning that light, so that through him all might believe. He himself was not the light; he came only as a witness to the light."[19]

So we celebrate John the Baptist's birth because he was the one "who prepared the way of the Lord," he was the forerunner of the Messiah as was, and still is expected. There is more to it than that, however, there is also a cosmic significance. John the Baptist was conceived at the autumn equinox when night and day are equal, just before the sun finally begins to *decrease* and there is more darkness than light. His birth, therefore, nine months later, occurs at the Summer Solstice, the point at which the sun has reached its pinnacle and is beginning to decline. These days in the Roman calendar were known as *dies descrentibus* (the declining days). Jesus is conceived at the spring equinox when night and day are again equal but the darkness begins to lessen and daylight *increases* and he is born at the winter solstice when the Sun begins its triumph over darkness. These

---

12. Luke 1:76–79.

13. Luke 1:80.

14. Luke 3:3.

15. Luke 3:4–6.

16. Mat 17:10–13.

17. John 1:5.

18. Isa 9:2, quoted and applied to Jesus in Matt 4:16.

19. John 1:6–8.

days are known as the *dies crescentibus* (the growing days).[20] John said of Jesus "he must increase, but I must decrease."[21] The light has triumphed over the darkness, and the sun of righteousness has risen with healing in its wings. If we no longer celebrate these festivals, not only is all of this symbolism lost, we lose our connection to the seasons and the significance of the sun's cycle.

Michaelmas and Lammas

Michaelmas and Lammas are other festivals, which were linked to the harvest and therefore the sun's cycle. They each had their own traditions which mostly now, particularly in urban societies, have fallen by the wayside.[22] Michaelmas falls at the autumn equinox and celebrates St Michael, the Archangel and the expulsion of the Devil from heaven. This is linked to one of the traditions of the festival—a legend which states that when the Devil was expelled from Heaven by Michael he fell on a blackberry bush and cursed them. Michaelmas, therefore is traditionally the last day for picking blackberries and so they feature in recipes associated with this festival. There are other traditions such as the Goose Fair, associated with it and it was the time for hiring of agricultural laborers. The special foods and the harvest and the traditions all give a deeper meaning to the seasons which are also tied in with our faith. Michaelmas ends the harvest season that began with the wheat harvest at Lammas. Loaves were baked from the first of the wheat and taken to church to be consecrated which is where the name originates. It is a corruption of the Old English for loaf and mass. There were also traditions attached to this festival, whereby the Lord's prayer was written on crosses and hidden in barns to protect the harvested wheat. "Although to modern eyes this kind of ritual often looks like pagan folk-magic, it's part of a complex picture of popular and learned devotion in early medieval England; this particular ritual might well have been performed by a priest and it's made up of explicitly Christian symbols and practices."[23] Although many churches still celebrate Harvest festival, unfortunately as I said in chapter 1, these

20. O Carragain, *Ritual and Rood*, 83.

21. John 3:30.

22. However, a vestige of its importance remains in that Michaelmas is one of the "Quarter days," and is also the beginning of legal and university terms.

23. A Clerk of Oxford, *A Little History of Lammas*.

are often devoid of anything remotely to do with the harvest and provide little connection between our lives and the seasons and leave no lasting impression on young minds.

The Year of the Lord that we celebrate in the festivals, the liturgical year is about the journey we take with the Son, his advent, birth, epiphany, his being presented in the temple. His baptism, miracles, and testing in the wilderness. His death, resurrection and ascension. The gift of the Holy Spirit to his disciples, the growth of the church, the harvest as a foretaste of what will come, culminating in the festival of Christ the King. A cycle that is completed in a solar year; we track the journey of the Son who gives us life in all its fullness, as we orbit round the sun that gives the whole earth life. Our spiritual life and our physical life interwoven, dancing together, following the Lord of the Dance. "The Year of the Lord shows our hearts, sense and imaginations what there is to love about God. If we don't know how to dance, how can we invite others to join in?"[24] We need to learn how to dance again, to hear his song and sing a new song so that others can join the dance, that the Father, Son and Spirit are already dancing, *perichoresis*, a circle dance that we are all invited into. "The Greeks called the universe cosmos . . . meaning something that has beauty, order, harmony. It means that the space around earth is alive with rhythms and the moon, the planets, the sun and the earth itself are, one could say, 'dancers' to the music of these rhythms."[25] We also share in those rhythms, not just people, but animals, even the tiniest cell is governed by circadian rhythms that follow a 24 hour pattern that reflects the 24 hours of a day, the time it takes the earth to do one full rotation on its axis. "Without this internal temporal compartmentalization and it synchronization to the external environment our biology would be in chaos."[26] When God created, he brought order out of Chaos, that order is not just part of the world around us, but part of our very being.

This means that we too are part of that dance, following the same rhythm, the same music, the same song that the morning stars sang at creation. "The dances of early man were not for fun: they had a religious significance. In ancient times men felt instinctively their connection with the cosmic rhythms, with the 'cosmic dance' and the human dance was

24. Hill, *Holidays and Holy Nights*, 3.

25. Kovacs, *The Spiritual Background*, 28.

26. Foster and Kreitzman, *Circadian Rhythms* ,1.

an act of worship of the cosmic dance."[27] We have forgotten the dance and we've stopped singing the song. It's suggested that the increase in ill-health, particularly heart disease is because we have forgotten this rhythm, that we are living 'a-rhythmical' lives. "The first step to regaining a connection with the healing, life-giving power of rhythm is to learn to live consciously with the rhythm of the year and with the festivals of the seasons."[28]

The festivals give us sacred time, just as do Sabbath and Jubilee, all of which present us with time to celebrate our relationship with God, with creation, with one another. They are all part of the "now and not yet," but it's important we are not too focussed on the not yet, that we forget to enjoy the "now." Every holiday was originally a "holy day." a festival day that harmonized the seasons of the year with the seasons of the Lord. The seasons of the church, just like the natural seasons, have their own colours: purple for kingship but also for sorrow, penitence and, preparation used for Lent and Advent. White, symbolizing innocence, purity, victory, joy and, resurrection for Easter and Christmas. Red, for sacrifice, but also the fire of the Holy Spirit for Palm Sunday, Good Friday and Pentecost and green a sign of hope, growth and joy for "Ordinary time" (which suggests that all the other times, all the festivals should be extraordinary!) The stripping of the church on Maundy Thursday in readiness for Good Friday is also symbolic of the cosmos entering the liminal period, when right order is reversed, when the King is stripped of his insignia, when it appeared for a short time that the Light of the world *had* been overcome by the darkness but the flowers and the white and gold of the altar cloths and the candles of Easter Sunday all demonstrate that the Light burst forth from the darkness and "the darkness has not overcome it."[29] The readings from the Bible also take us through the story, covering each of the seasons, so that the whole story is told throughout the course of the year, not just the story from Series 2 but how this was foretold in the Series 1. Attempts to modernize the church by doing away with vestments, set readings and liturgy but not replacing it with any other form of symbolism leave a void. "I think there is a growing sense that the future of the Church lies with all those people who want ritual,

27. Kovacs, *The Spiritual Background*, 30.

28. Kovacs, *The Spiritual Background*, 32.

29. John 1:5.

sacred experience, transformation and a way to live in harmony with the patterns and rhythms of existence."[30]

I believe we need to recapture the joy of these celebrations and to re-capture the vision of the kingdom, to keep both things in tension, the joy and pleasures of this world that God created for us but also to remember that he called us to be warriors but gentle warriors,[31] to remember that our King, with the tattooed thigh rides a white horse and keeps back the forces of Chaos and it's our job, till he comes again to guard the shore, to advance the Kingdom.

The Kingdom

"Narnia has come to Liverpool!!" This was the message I received from my daughter a year ago. It was the "Narnia Experience" that a local church had put on in St George's Hall in Liverpool. I can't say her enthusiasm was matched my mine but I went anyway, because I knew what it meant to her. It wasn't some childish whim (she was 24 at the time!) but one of the ways that God communicated his kingdom message to her. For her, watching the Chronicles of Narnia was a genuinely spiritual experi-ence. As it turned out, we both felt a bit stupid, sitting on the "railway platform" waiting for it to start, as there were only two other families and they both had young children. As God would have it though, these families each had boys in them and so when it came to the choice of Lucy or Edmund's path, it was just us two that choose Lucy's. Whilst being lectured by the "housekeeper" in the professor's library, the door opened slightly and two creatures from Narnia beckoned us out, whispering "Lucy, Lucy." That was it. We were already captivated. Going through the "wardrobe" of fur coats and out into the fir decked landscape we startled Mr Tumnus. Picking up the parcels he had dropped, he hesitantly asked us "Are you Daughters of Eve?" Already in tears, we answered "Yes." This sense of wonder continued throughout our time in his house and then again when Mrs Beaver said: "The prophecy is coming true—Aslan is on the move!" we were nodding like fools and crying again. By the time we reached the "'frozen river" all rationality had gone, (I actually looked round when they said it was beginning to thaw). I hope you have not

30. Hill, *Holidays and Holy Nights*, 5.

31. "Let your gentleness be evident to all. The Lord is near." Phil 4:5. I love *War-rior Daughter*, by Wild Wood Kin which really illustrates this message.

switched off at this point; this was a deeply spiritual experience, one of the most profound I've had, and the fact that I got to share it with my daughter, just the two of us, and that God had arranged that, was humbling. I could go on—about Father Christmas' sledge and handing "Lucy" her weapon—the frozen creatures waking up and joining them for battle. Finally, watching Aslan being killed and coming back to life. It was draining and invigorating at the same time.

It was only later that we found out that this was the same night that the Enemy was at work on my other daughter. The coiling, twisting serpent taking what should be good and inverting it, as he does, into something evil. She was saved, but not before he had struck her. The timing was not coincidental and for some people would leave a massive question mark that could lead away from God, but in my experience, and I don't say that lightly, I know that God will always bring good, out of bad. The point of sharing this, is that Narnia enables us to see the Kingdom just as Jesus said through childlike eyes,[32] to see the reality of the battle. We need to keep in view, the truth that the things of this world are less real than those of the spiritual world. That as Lewis was demonstrating, there is a clash of kingdoms. We need to know that the enemy doesn't function alone, that there are principalities and demons and other "kingdoms" that try to overthrow the Most High King,

> For we do not wrestle against flesh and blood, but against principalities, against powers, against the rulers of the darkness of this age, against spiritual hosts of wickedness in the heavenly places.[33]

We know there's a spiritual battle, it's made clear in the Bible, but we so easily forget and it is only when something happens to jolt us out of our comfortable, material lives where we are lulled into a completely false sense of security, that our memories are stirred and we acknowledge again the temporal nature of this life and the eternal reality of the spiritual life. That's what Lewis knew and that's why Narnia is brilliant. But it's a battle for which we've been equipped, not just with one weapon, like the four in Narnia had, but with the whole armor of God:

> Therefore put on the full armor of God, so that when the day of evil comes, you may be able to stand your ground, and after

32. "Truly I tell you, unless you change and become like little children, you will never enter the kingdom of heaven." Matt 18:3.

33. Eph 6:12.

you have done everything to stand. Stand firm then with the belt of truth buckled around your waist, with the breastplate of righteousness in place, and with your feet fitted with the readiness that comes from the gospel of peace. In addition to all this, take up the shield of faith, with which you can extinguish all the flaming arrows of the evil one. Take the helmet of salvation and the sword of the Spirit, which is the word of God.[34]

The greatest weapon is left till last:

Pray in the Spirit at all times and on every occasion.[35]

Not just praying, but praying in the Spirit. There is a real movement of prayer happening particularly amongst the young, the LORD is raising up prayer warriors and Prayer Storms.[36] We have weapons, we have armor and we have a supernatural force—that is so much better than Luke Skywalker—because ours is real. What is even better, is that God uses the most unlikely, the ones that the world rejects, those who are considered the 'least'—Israel, the least amongst the nations, David, the youngest of the sons of Jesse, Gideon, whose clan was the weakest in Manasseh and him the least in his family. God chooses the 'foolish things of the world to shame the wise . . . the weak things of the world to shame the strong."[37]

The kingdom then is a place where the first is last and the last is first, a place where the meek inherit the earth, where the pure in heart will see God, where gentleness is strength. It's a place where there's finally justice, where the Daniel Clark's are finally listened to, before it's too late and people are no longer "trafficked." A place where there's no more hunger, or oppression. It's a place with a real King, the King of Kings who sits enthroned in a golden city with jeweled gates. Where there is a happily-ever-after. It's what we pray for—for his Kingdom to come "on earth as it is in heaven," that God will reign here, not just in people's hearts but in the reality of their lives—that God's kingdom would become a reality here while we wait for the King to come for the final episode.

Some of us, already live in a Kingdom, unfortunately not yet a place of equality or justice or plenty for everyone, but nonetheless it's a Kingdom, with a Monarch who believes they reign only by God's grace.

34. Eph 6:13–17.

35. Eph 6: 18.

36. Prayer Storm in Manchester, led by a gifted young prophet, James Aladiran is such a movement which is awakening a new generation to prayer and fasting.

37. 1 Cor 1:27.

Unfortunately not many people seem aware of that, or how important it is that at the heart of our democracy, we have a sovereign who understands their first duty is to God. As this is a book about the King of Kings, and particularly about his connection with Ancient Israelite kingship and its enthronement ceremony, it seems appropriate to look at our Coronation ceremony as it is, in fact, entirely based on the ancient Israelite enthronement ceremony, not to mention the fact that the Queen is *Fid.def.* that is Defender of the Faith.

The Coronation

The Queen is not just nominally the Supreme Governor of the Church of England but is (as far as anyone can say that about another person) a real Christian. Whilst you may think that goes without saying, the placement of someone in high office, even in the Church, as we know, isn't always a guarantee of that. I have been particularly impressed by the series *The Crown*. Not only does it show the vast amount of work that the Queen in particular does, and how it impacts her life, but also, against popular opinion, demonstrates what influence she still has on the politics of this country. It also gives insight into the depth of her own Christian faith and the absolute necessity of the Monarchy continuing to exist in Britain, despite its many detractors.[38] Although the Queen's own commitment to Christianity is important, there's more to it than that. The Coronation and enthronement of our Kings and Queens is based entirely on the ancient Israelite Coronation and Enthronement Ceremony. The Coronation of English Kings and Queens began to be held in Westminster Abbey in 1066 using a liturgy written by St Dunstan in the tenth Century which has remained, with occasional adaptations, the basis for all Coronations which are carried out, with the Eucharist as the basis for the service. We were fortunate in that Queen Elizabeth II's Coronation was televised, with the exception of the Anointing ceremony, and that's still available to watch. The ceremony itself, the words used from scripture and the regalia, as well as the blowing of trumpets, which we noted at *Yom Teruah*, signified the entrance of the King, all mimic the ancient Israelite

---

38. The series also covers the Queen's life long friendship with Billy Graham and the influence he had on her faith. Unless you're of the post-war generation he might also seem an anachronism (as many think the Queen is) but in fact Billy Graham, apart from his numerous campaigns in Britain and all over was also the founder of one of the most relevant youth organizations that exists today - Youth for Christ.

ceremony. This is evident even from the beginning, as the opening words which are sung when the Monarch enters the Abbey are from Ps122, one of the Songs of Ascent, sung at *Sukkoth* when the pre-exilic New Year Enthronement ceremony originally took place. Psalm122 prays for the peace of Jerusalem, suggesting perhaps an intentional correspondence between England and Jerusalem, as Blake's poem also suggests.[39]

The Monarch is then presented to the people, with the words, "I here present to you, Queen Elizabeth, your undoubted Queen" and they are asked if they will do homage and serve her. The people signify their willingness and shout "God Save Queen Elizabeth." When Samuel presents Saul as King to the people he asks: "Do you see the man the LORD has chosen? There is no one like him among all the people, and all the people shout 'Long Live the King.'"[40] Furthermore, the instructions in Deut 17:18–19 state that when a King is chosen, the Book of the Law is to be given to them to study. As part of the Coronation ceremony the Queen promises to maintain the Law of God and the true profession of the Gospel and is presented with the Bible accompanied by the words: "Our gracious Queen: to keep your Majesty ever mindful of the law and the Gospel as the Rule for the whole life and government of Christian Princes, we present you with this Book, the most valuable thing that this world affords."

It is the anointing in particular, however, that links our Coronation directly with the enthronement of the ancient Israelite Kings and therefore, with Jesus, as the concept of messiah is derived from the ideology of ancient Israelite kingship. As we have said from the beginning, the King and post-exile the High Priest were *the* Anointed, *ha-Mashiah*. Jesus is King of Israel and High Priest, he is *the* Anointed, the Messiah.[41] Anointing is the point at which the Holy Spirit comes upon the King, and he is changed, just as happened to Saul,[42] and David.[43] This is also understood to be the case in the British ceremony. As a prelude to the anointing, the hymn *Veni, Creator Spiritus* is sung, inviting the Holy Spirit to come, the

39. "Jerusalem" set to music by Hubert Parry, and serving almost as a second national anthem for England.

40. 1Sam 10:24. This also featured at Solomon's enthronement (1 Kgs 1:39) which we will see below.

41. Most often rendered Christ, the English transliteration of the Greek for Anointed, *Kristos*.

42. 1 Sam 10:1–7.

43. 1 Sam 16:13.

belief being, that at this point, the Queen is empowered from God. It is a sacred moment between her and God and therefore, as stated earlier, the cameras were not allowed to film. During the anointing, a golden canopy is held over the Queen by four Knights, evoking so many allusions—the *sukkah* at Tabernacles that formed part of the enthronement ceremony, the tabernacle representing the cosmos and, the *chuppah* under which Jewish weddings take place. In fact, one of the articles of the regalia is a sapphire ring engraved with a ruby cross of St George, the patron saint of England - the one who killed the dragon (!) This ring, which is also known as 'the wedding ring of England' is placed on the Queen's fourth finger of her right hand, signifying that she is wed to her people.

However in *The Crown*, we are privy to what the TV audiences of the Coronation were not. In the anointing scene, which follows the script of the actual ceremony, the Archbishop of Canterbury anoints the Queen on her head, breast and hands and then steps back searching the Queen's face. No explanation is given, but what he is looking for is some sign of change as there was when the Kings of ancient Israel were anointed, he is looking to see if the Spirit has come upon her. We have already been alerted to the significance of the anointing in an earlier flashback which showed the young Queen Elizabeth having it explained to her by her Father, just prior to his own Coronation.[44] This idea is also taken up in the commentary from Prince Edward who abdicated and who should have been the one anointed. He has been watching the Coronation on TV in France, where he is exiled and proclaims to his guests, at the point of Anointing, that the Queen "has been turned into a goddess" to which one of the guests watching responds "and you gave all that up—the chance to become God?" Of course this is a dramatization but the writers are obviously aware of the background of this ritual. The next part of the ceremony directly links the Coronation of our Monarch with that of the ancient Israelite Kings. As the Archbishop anoints the Queen, he prays:

> O Lord and heavenly Father,

44. In this scene, the soon to be, King George explains to the young Elizabeth the importance of the oath, saying: "It is a promise you can never break, a very sacred promise indeed." He then says to her "you have to anoint me otherwise I can't be king. Do you understand? When the holy oil touches me I am transformed, brought into direct contact with the divine, forever changed, bound to God. It is the most important part of the entire ceremony." It appears that the sacredness of the ceremony was felt by the Queen who as a child observing it wrote: "The arches and beams at the top were covered with a sort of haze of wonder as Papa was crowned, at least I thought so" suggesting perhaps, that even as a child of 11, she felt something of the numinous there.

the exalter of the humble and the strength of thy chosen

who by anointing with Oil didst of old

make and consecrate Kings, priests, and prophets

to teach and govern thy people Israel

Bless and sanctify thy chosen servant Elizabeth

who by our office and ministry is now to be anointed with oil.

Directly following the rest of the prayer and anointing the people stand and the choir sings the words from 1 Kgs 1:39–40:

Zadok the priest and Nathan the prophet

anointed Solomon King and all the people rejoiced and said

God save the King

Long live the King

May the King live for ever Amen. Hallelujah.

Before the anointing ceremony the Queen's crimson robe is taken from her and the *Colobium Sindonis*, a white linen robe is placed on her along with the *Supertunica,* and a girdle which are both made of gold. These are reminiscent of the vestments of the High Priest. Tradition states that the white linen robe represents the divesting of all worldly vanity and standing naked before God. In chapter 4 we saw that the High Priest wore his white linen robe to enter the Holy of Holies, divesting himself of the garments representing the material world (his garments were made from the colors representing the four elements) before entering into the presence of God. His normal regalia however also included a golden sash and a breastplate with 12 jewels representing the 12 tribes.

When the Queen is crowned, it is with St Edwards Crown which contains 12 stones around the base. Whether or not this was intended to replicate the stones on the High Priest's breastplate we are unsure. However, King Edward (the Confessor) was canonized as the name of the crown suggests and was therefore ostensibly at least (though some facts suggest otherwise) a "godly" man. The Queen is also given the *armillis,* "the bracelets of sincerity and wisdom." Israelite Kings also wore a golden crown set with jewels,[45] and a band on their arm.[46]

Another feature of the Coronation which is a direct link back to ancient Israel, is the Stone of Scone also known as the Stone of Destiny.

45. 1 Chr 20:2.

46. 2 Sam 1:10.

This is situated within the Coronation chair (St Edward's Chair) which was commissioned by King Edward in approximately 1300 AD to accommodate the stone. During the Coronation, the chair containing the stone is placed facing the High Altar. Legend has it that the Stone of Scone is the same stone that Jacob rested his head on at Bethel (Gen 28:18). The legend states that this was carried to Egypt by Jacob's sons, then to Spain, arriving in Ireland around 700BC. It was placed on the sacred Hill of Tara and was used from then on for the Coronations of Irish Kings until it was taken to Scotland and from 1292 all Scottish Kings were crowned on the stone. It was then brought to England by King Edward in 1296 and English Monarchs were crowned on it (that is under Edward's seat). In 1950, it was stolen by Scottish nationalists, but was returned to England until 1996 when it was officially restored to Scotland and now resides in Edinburgh castle. Although the earlier history of the stone is said to be legend, it is nonetheless documented on the Westminster Abbey official website. There is in fact, a whole movement called the British Israelites who believe that this is so—and much more—they believe that British Monarchs are direct descendants from David and that this is evidenced in the heraldic emblems of the harp, lion and unicorn (representing David, Judah, Ephraim). A document (MS43968) in the British Library purports to trace this line. Although the description of it suggests that it is not considered to be factual, nonetheless, the whole idea is interesting.[47]

Nevertheless, regardless of the tradition attached to the stone, the Coronation itself is deliberately based on the ancient Israelite Coronation. It is also overtly Christian. As well as being presented with spurs signifying chivalry, the Queen is also given a sword to defend widows and orphans, a rod, signifying justice and mercy, and a scepter. The Queen is robed in the Imperial Robe with the words: "Receive this Imperial Robe, and the Lord your God endow you with knowledge and with majesty and with power from on high; the Lord clothe you with the robe of righteousness and with the garments of salvation." She is then given the Orb, which has a cross mounted over it with the words: "Receive this Orb set under the Cross and remember that the whole world is subject to the Power and Empire of Christ our Redeemer. For He is the Prince of the Kings of the earth: King of Kings and Lord of Lords, so that no man can reign happily who derives not his authority from Him, and directs not all his actions according to His Laws."

47. Courthorpe, *The Genealogy of British Kings*.

At the climax of the ceremony, when the Queen is crowned, everyone present shouts: "God Save the Queen" and then all the other princes, princesses and peers put on their coronets. The Queen is blessed and then enthroned by the Archbishops and others, following which they pay homage to her. The drums and trumpets sound and all shout: "God save Queen Elizabeth, Long live Queen Elizabeth, May the Queen live for ever." The Coronation then instals the British Monarch as a Christian Prince, under the King of King's rule, anointed as the Israelite kings were, in imitation of them, with robes and a crown that invoke the office of the High Priest and regalia that signify that the Monarch is to rule with equity and justice, just as the Israelite kings were to rule, manifesting God's sovereignty in the nations she rules over, with "an everlasting reign."

One of the readings during the service is from Matthew 22:15–22 when Jesus is asked by the Pharisees whether they should pay the imperial tax to Caesar and Jesus responds by asking them whose image is on the coin. When they reply "Caesar's," Jesus tells them to "Give back to Caesar what is Caesar's and to God what is God's." On British coins there are either letters or partial words in Latin surrounding the silhouette of the Queen's head. These are *Dei Gratia Regina* "By the Grace of God, Queen." The other words are *Fidei defensor* "Defender of the Faith." This is not just a nominal title, nor a nominal role. The Queen is a Christian 'Prince' and reigns in the belief that she derives her authority directly from God.

Some might argue that such a grandiose Coronation stands at odds with Jesus' enthronement on the cross and the jewel encrusted crown makes a mockery of Jesus' crown of thorns, but that is to miss the point. The point is, the Queen stands under Christ's authority, the homage that is paid her and the pageantry surrounding the Coronation are all the things that Jesus did not receive on earth, but as his representative, the Queen is demonstrating that this is exactly what he is due, and much more. The homage paid to her is also symbolic of our homage to the King of kings, and a reminder that like Lucy and the others in Narnia, we will also be enthroned. This was the final part of the Narnia experience that night, we all came together, the Lucy and the Edmund group before the four thrones and while the actors prayed for us, we felt a real anointing.

Whatever your opinion of the wider group of Royalty, the Queen plays a huge, often understated and quite often overlooked part in keeping this country Christian. Both recent Royal weddings were conducted as Christian weddings, in Westminster Abbey, with readings from the

Bible, a sermon, prayers and blessings.[48] We should celebrate that, not denigrate it. As Queen Mary said to the young Elizabeth, in *The Crown*: "The Monarchy is a calling from God that is way you are crowned in an Abbey not a government building, why you are anointed, not appointed. It is an archbishop that puts the crown on your head not a minister or public servant which means that you are answerable to God in your duty not the public."

---

48. There's also been a recent prophecy about revival which concerns the Royal princes.

Chapter 7

Our Role in the Kingdom

We started this journey with three problems that we hoped to solve. The first was that although the discourse of kingship runs throughout church dialogue, liturgy and particularly songs we actually seem to know very little about why we use this terminology. Secondly, we noted that the paradigms used to explain Jesus' death and resurrection, that is, the theology of atonement as it stands, seemed disconnected from the Old Testament even though the concept of Messiah, and therefore Jesus' role as Messiah is derived from that source. This also meant that the other titles that are applied to Jesus in the New Testament have been misunderstood, as in fact they are all connected to Kingship too. Finally, we said that because we did not understand kingship, or Jesus' role as King, it left us unsure of our own role in the kingdom.

Having considered how sacral kingship underpins each of the Jewish festivals and how Jesus fulfilled them, as well as identifying the rationale behind Jesus' titles, has, I believe, enabled us to answer the first and second problems. Understanding Jesus' role in terms of sacral kingship opens up a much more expansive understanding of it. This was God the King, come to renew the everlasting covenant, come to renew his Creation—Yahweh, come as promised to his Temple—Melchizedek, the Great High Priest, come to make the Great Atonement that would mend the covenant once and for all—the Servant, "by whose stripes we are healed."

We also noted, that although traditional ways of understanding his death and resurrection as a ransom, a victory or penal substitution *can* be evidenced from the New Testament, understanding his role as King explains this in a *much more integrated* way, one that does cohere with the Old Testament and focuses on renewal and re-Creation. This is not denying the need for his death or the need for justice, nor the recognition of sin and repentance, rather it's about recognizing that Jesus came to renew the cosmos—to bring new life, and new birth. He came, not only to redeem his Creation but to *re-create*—both the world and us, his people, so that with the trees of the field we can clap our hands in joy[1] and enjoy life in all its fullness.[2] He called each one of us to carry on the commission—to bring healing and wholeness—the *shalom* of the Sabbath rest—so that we can dance to the rhythms of the seasons and the cycles of life and so that we can sing the new song that he gave us.

We looked at Jesus in the Jewish festivals because it is here that we get the clearest view of him as King. These are the *moadim*, the appointed times to meet with God. Right from the beginning, God created "lights in the vault of the sky" they were "to separate the day from the night" but they were also to serve as "signs, (*otot*) to mark seasons, (*moadim*) and days and years."[3] Right from the beginning, God gave a structure to our days and our year and a time to celebrate before him. These were written into Creation itself. The signs and the seasons, the appointed feasts were all part of his plan, plan A. It is where he is most accessible and visible and where he is celebrated as King. In the synagogue liturgy, still, at each of the festivals, the prayers contain additional lines proclaiming God as King. Paul said that the festivals "were a shadow of the things that were to come; the reality, however is found in Christ."[4] Jesus fulfilled the festivals as King. What they could only foreshadow, for a limited time, for a chosen people, he turned into reality, for all time, for all people.

We started at *Sukkoth* and journeyed through to Passover searching for our King. We found him on a donkey, we walked with him on the Waters and we met him in the Garden. So we know a little more about him and what he came to do, but what about us, what about the third problem? Who are we in his kingdom? As a result of Jesus' death and

1. Isa 5512: "You shall go out with joy, and be led forth with peace: the mountains and the hills shall break forth before you into singing, and all the trees of the field shall clap their hands."

2. "The thief comes only to steal and kill and destroy. I came that they my have life and have it abundantly." John 10:10.

3. Gen 1:14.

4. Col 2:17.

resurrection, his overcoming of the forces of Chaos and enthronement as King, there is new Creation, a new Temple, a Sabbath rest and, Jubilee—and of course a new song. These are not just conditions that Jesus brought about, it's also who we are in him. We are the new Creation and we are the new Temple. We are called to Sabbath rest in him and we are commissioned to bring in the Jubilee.

The Temple

The Temple and Creation are intricately linked. Each time there is a New Creation, there is a new Temple and a Sabbath rest. In the beginning, God overcame the forces of Chaos, created and on the seventh day rested in his Temple, the cosmos. God created order out of Chaos and created Adam and Eve to sustain the order. However, Adam forsook his work as Priest, and his commission to be fruitful and multiply—to produce offspring who would also see in the spirit. He lost his garments of light and the ability to walk with God in the Garden. The burning sword and the Cherubim guarded the entrance to the Garden, the entrance to the East, where the Tree of Life stood waiting. So God began the process of rescuing his people from the Chaos of their own making, getting his people to see him and walk with him again. He started with Noah rescuing him from the Chaos waters and then called Abram and promised that through him all nations would be blessed, foreshadowing through him how this would be—a beloved son given as a sacrifice. God then chose Israel, rescuing her and leading her through the waters of Chaos to be a royal nation, her festivals and her King sustaining the cosmos, keeping back the Chaos, a Royal Priesthood, interceding for the nations. Israel rose up a new creation and a new temple was built following the same pattern as the first creation, a place where God could Tabernacle in their midst and rest and he commanded Israel to a Sabbath rest. He gave Israel the way, the *halakhah*, so that she could walk with him again. Once in the Promised Land, the man of rest, Solomon built a new Temple for God to rest in, which *also* represented the cosmos. The rituals and the High Priest, as the LORD, keeping back the forces of Chaos, and renewing the covenant, encountering the LORD in the Holy of Holies, between the Cherubim. Even though he showed them the way, his people got lost again and so he came himself, to his Temple as he said he would, to show his people that *he* was the Way. The way back to Eden, the way to live, the way to walk with him and back to the Father who was waiting in the Garden. His body, the new Temple, the meeting place of heaven and earth, the place where God could be encountered. Just before his crucifixion Jesus cleansed the Temple, forcing Chaos out and restoring order, foreshadowing what he would do a few days later on the cross, cleansing the cosmos; cosmos and Temple both cleansed. His death, the final Temple sacrifice that atoned for all sins. The curtain in the Holy of Holies, the earthly Eden where the Cherubim dwelt, torn in two, opening up the way to Eden and the Tree of Life. The rock rolled away, opening up the tomb, the Holy of Holies, where his presence had been, once again between the cherubim.[5] The Temple no longer effective, was eventually destroyed. The way was open and the spirit given, so that people could once again see in the Spirit and walk with God once again in the garden in the cool of the evening. In the new Creation, there will be no Temple, because the Lamb and the Lord *are* its Temple and its light. There will be no more Temple, because there is no more sea.

Until Jesus comes again, we *are* the new Temple, built on the foundation of the apostles and the prophets, with Jesus as the cornerstone.[6] We are filled with his spirit as the Temple was filled with his Glory.[7] As the Temple, we are the meeting place of heaven and earth. The Temple is no longer confined to one place—wherever we are, God is present. We take his presence wherever we go. The great lights in the Temple at *Sukkoth* were a physical manifestation of the spiritual reality that God is light. At *Sukkoth*, Jesus, Yahweh incarnated, King of Israel, High Priest said 'I am the light of the world. Whoever follows me will never walk in darkness, but will have the light of life.'[8] We are a royal priesthood and Jesus says to us:'You are the light of the world.'[9] We are now the light, illuminating God's presence in the world and shining light in the darkness, not just because we have God's spirit dwelling in us but through our actions: "Let your light shine before others, that they may see your good deeds and

5. "Now Mary stood outside the tomb crying. As she wept, she bent over to look into the tomb and saw two angels in white, seated where Jesus' body had been, one at the head and the other at the foot." John 20:11–12

6. "Don't you know that you yourselves are God's Temple and that God's Spirit lives in you?" 1 Cor 3:6.

7. 1 Cor 3:16

8. John 8:12.

9. Matt 5:14

glorify your Father in heaven."[10] The river of life will flow from the throne in the Temple and in the Temple at Sukkoth Jesus said "Whoever believes in me, as scripture has said, rivers of living water will flow from within them." Living water, the holy spirit, flows from within us, watering the dry places, bringing life to those who are thirsty.[11]

We are a Royal Priesthood, wearing his name on our forehead[12] as the High Priest had done. We are the physical manifestation of him, *bet-selem*. We are the Priests, interceding for the nations, co-partnering with him in the re-creation of the world, holding back the forces of Chaos through our prayers and our actions, bringing justice and healing, a holy nation; in the world but set apart: "But you are a chosen people, a Royal Priesthood, a holy nation, God's special possession, that you may declare the praises of him who called you out of darkness into his wonderful light."[13] We are the royal priesthood, carrying out the rituals that sustain the world.[14] We are redeemed sons of Adam and daughters of Eve. We have eaten from the Tree of Life and we can show others the way there, because Jesus is the Way. We know where the living waters flow. We know the way to the throne room; we are seated in the heavenlies.[15] The Priests were also the teachers, and we are commissioned to make disciples of all nations, to take the knowledge of the one true God into world so that "the world will be filled with the knowledge of God."[16]

Sabbath

The Temple and Sabbath are intricately connected, God created his Temple, the cosmos and then rested, *sabat*. In a very real way Temple and cosmos represent each other. The specific Sabbath commandments, the 39 *melachot*,[17] also reflect this understanding because, although it may not

10. Matt 5:16

11. John 7:38.

12. Rev 3:12

13. 1 Pet 2:9

14. "The very essence of ritual derives from the realization that such actions are understood to effect critical changes in relation to the realm of the supra-mundane." Gane, *Cult and Character*, 15

15. Eph 2:6 "And God raised us up with Christ and seated us with Him in the heavenly realms in Christ Jesus."

16. Hab 2:14; Isa 37:20.

17. *Melachah* (*melachot* plural) has a particular *halachic* meaning associated with

be obvious from their content, each of them concerns Temple building.[18] So that on the Sabbath, we are also called to cease from Temple building, from creating. The two reasons given to keep the Sabbath are as a memorial of the Exodus, but also because God instituted it at Creation. Therefore Creation, Sabbath and the Temple are all linked; so too is the Exodus—the recapitulation of Creation. Sabbath is a foretaste of the world to come when there is peace and harmony, when there is no need to work for food, when we can spend time together in unity, with one another and with God; it's a return to Eden. It is an opportunity to bring sacred time into the mundane, where all options that could distract are taken away. No writing, no walking beyond a certain limit, no phones, no television, and no labour; just God and each other—a foretaste of what is to come and a memorial of what was.

The basis of Creation was separation: God separated the waters, light from darkness, clean from unclean animals and Israel to be his chosen people, a holy nation. The Hebrew word translated "holy" derives from a term meaning "separate," that is set apart from common use, from defilement. The Temple was made up of separate areas of increasing holiness: the outer court was for gentiles, the next was the court of Jewish women, the next court of Jewish men, the next the court of priests and finally the Holy of Holies where only the High Priest could enter once a year on the Day of Atonement, where sacred time and sacred place came together. The rituals of the Temple maintained the cosmos, keeping Chaos at bay and separated from the Created order. Sabbath too is a separation of time. That is why at the end of the Sabbath there is a separation ceremony, *havdalah*, when wine is blessed and drunk and spices passed round to "take the fragrance of Sabbath" into the following creative days, accompanied by the *hamavdil*:

> Blessed are You, Lord our God, King of the universe, who distinguishes between the holy and the profane, between light and darkness, between Israel and the nations, between the seventh day and the six days of work. Blessed are you LORD, who distinguishes between the holy and the profane.

Judaism talks about creating "cathedrals in time, rather than cathedrals in space,"[19] and Sabbath is such a time, when nothing else distracts

---

construction of the tabernacle and has the connotation of creative, constructive work.

18. b.Talmud, *Shabbat* 73b.

19. Boteach, *An Intelligent Person's Guide*, 45.

from God and his presence is tangible. The Sabbath is the Holy of Holies of the week. When the High Priest entered into the Holy of Holies into God's presence, he also encountered the angels; God was seated between the Cherubim and surrounded by the Seraphim. Sabbath is a return to the intimacy of creation. For one day each week, we get a glimpse beyond the Cherubim who guard the gate and into Eden. The legend says that at the end of the Sabbath service, two ministering angels follow each person home from the Synagogue and the *Shalom Aleichem* is sung to them: "Peace be upon you ministering angels, angels from above, from the King, who rules over the mightiest Kings—the Holy One blessed be He."[20] The Songs of the Sabbath Sacrifice found at Qumran, also known as the Angelic Liturgy, suggest that the Sabbath services the community there were carrying out, were also expected to bring them into communion with the angels. They believed the Second Temple and its Priesthood were corrupt and used the wrong calendar,[21] therefore, its services were polluted and ineffective. By using the right calendar, the services at Qumran were synchronized with those of the heavenly Temple, consequently, they believed that they *were* worshipping with the angelic Priests in the heavenly Temple. The *Qedushah*, the "Holy, Holy, Holy is the LORD Almighty; the whole earth is full of his glory,"[22] which used to form part of the synagogue liturgy on the Sabbath, and certain festivals are the words Isaiah heard the angels sing in his Holy of Holies experience when he saw the LORD, seated on a throne, high and exalted."[23] John identified Isaiah's vision of the LORD as a vision of Jesus, which coheres with what we have said throughout that Jesus is Yahweh. These are the words we sing, in

---

20. b.Talmud, *Tractate Shabba*t 119b

21. The community at Qumran followed the solar calendar which the same calendar used in Jubilees and 1Enoch. The belief was that the earthly rituals carried out in the Temple were synchronized with the rituals carried out in the heavenly Temple. Consequently, the use of the new lunar calendar following the return from exile meant that this was no longer the case and that the rituals which maintained the cosmos were no longer effective.

22. Isa 6:3.

23. The *serpahim*, meaning the burning or fiery ones, and the highest order of angels. *Seraphim nehashim* (fiery serpents) were sent amongst the Israelites during the Exodus (Num21:6). Satan (Lucifer - light bearer) was also originally a seraph and in Genesis 2, in Eden he was a *nahash* - a serpent). The Bronze Serpent which was lifted up for the Israelites to look at and be cured from the bites of the fiery snakes was mentioned by Jesus as a foreshadowing of his "lifting up."

communion with the angels[24] in our Sabbath service before we go up to the Holy of Holies, to the LORD[25] to receive, as his Priests, the Bread of the Presence.

Both Christianity and Judaism look forward to the eventual Sabbath rest of the world to come, and Judaism experiences a foretaste of that in the weekly Sabbath but what about us? How do Christians experience Sabbath rest now? The Sabbath rest that is spoken of in Hebrews: "There remains, then, a Sabbath-rest for the people of God; for anyone who enters God's rest also rests from their works, just as God did from his."[26] Sabbath rest is distinguished here in Hebrews from the other forms of rest mentioned. It is the only time in the New Testament that *sabbatismos* is used instead of the usual *kaitapausis*. Unlike Judaism we have no rules, that tell us how to keep the Sabbath, which on the face of it might seem to set us free, but in fact it is the Sabbath laws, which place boundaries on what can and cannot be done, that are actually liberating. The infringement on traveling beyond a certain distance, not cooking on the Sabbath, not watching TV or answering the phone, emails or anything else that would otherwise distract you, means that your time is freed up to spend with family, friends and God. Boundaries are a vital part of life, that so often are missing now, parenting boundaries, boundaries on what is permissible on TV, boundaries on spending what we have not yet earned. As Christians, we need to set our own boundaries, to develop our own traditions and to ensure that we have a complete rest, a Sabbath where we can enjoy God's creation with him and with our family.

Even if we don't have *melichot*, to help us know how to spend our weekly Sabbath nonetheless the principles still apply, not just to the day we set aside from all the other creative days to worship in communion with others, but also to our whole lives. Tim Keller writes of the Sabbath as 'Deep Rest' suggesting that the rhythm of work and rest that the Sabbath gives is part of our created nature—a violation of which in either direction either under or over work—"leads to chaos in our life and the world around us."[27] As we have noted throughout these chapters, Chaos is the antithesis of Cosmos—order, but order where Creation can take place however incorporated into Creation, right from the beginning, is

24 According to the Book of Common Prayer, we are worshipping not just with the angels, but "with angels and archangels and all the company of heaven."

25. John 12:41

26. Heb 4:9.

27. Keller, *The Gospel Coalition.*

the need to cease from it, to not just rest, but have a Sabbath rest. Part of God's act of Creation was to set boundaries. He said at the beginning to the Chaos waters 'thus far you can come and no farther.'[28] He set boundaries with the Ten commandments and he set the boundary of Sabbath. There are no longer any natural boundaries, no 9–5 jobs, or shops closed on Sundays or Banks closed on Saturdays, instead there's nothing stopping you working continuously or literally "shopping till you drop." Also, despite all our technology more people than ever are suffering from work related stress. We are ever available, with no rest from communication, mobile phones, emails, social media. No end to TV programs[29] and even if there were there's still Netflix, with its continuous hypnotic rollover to the next episode. There's no pause. No *sabbat*. No rest. Sabbath is much more than "a day off," it's a time to recharge and thereby become more productive, not less. It's a time to take stock, to look at the bigger picture, to simply enjoy being. When God announces who he is to Moses, he says "Tell the Israelites "I am" has sent me to you."[30] When Jesus announces who he is, to the frightened disciples and to the guards come to arrest him, he says "I am." This is the God of being and we are created in his image. On the Sabbath we can simply be.

Just as Israel did, we enter Sabbath rest because we are new Creations, we have risen out of the Chaos of our own lives and risen to new life in Jesus.[31] That Sabbath rest for us is abiding in Jesus, in the Spirit, because what we don't need to work for, in fact, we can't work for, is our salvation. That work has been done. Jesus shouted '*tetelestai*' on the cross just before he died. As Christians, we don't have to work for our salvation but we do expect *good works* as the fruit of our salvation. "By their fruit you will recognize them."[32] Jesus has bought for us our Sabbath rest.

28. Job 38:11.

29. 'Anyone under the age of 40 might find this hard to believe, but even in the 1980s ALL television stopped soon after midnight – but not before playing us the national anthem. After the last program had finished, a BBC announcer with a 'BBC' accent used to wish us all a very good night, remind us to turn our television sets off. . .and, in case you really did forget to turn your TV set off, a few minutes later a loud constant high-pitched warning sound would play for the whole night until the next morning's programming began.'http://smashinglife.co.uk/bbc-closedown-national-anthem/

30. Exod 3:14.

31. "We therefore were buried with Him through baptism into death, in order that, just as Christ was raised from the dead through the glory of the Father, we too may walk in newness of life." Rom 6:4.

32. Matt 7:16.

He's brought us into communion with the Trinity. We are invited into their Sabbath meal, into their dance. An icon of the Trinity[33] depicts them around a table with the glass of wine in front of them representing Christ's sacrifice. The table is open on our side because we are welcomed into the supper, the bride welcomed in by the Son of Man; welcomed into the wedding feast of the lamb, dancing on golden streets. Sabbath isn't just about rest, it is a whole mindset.

Brueggemann talks about Sabbath as resistance—resistance to the same market ideology we have now, that also dominated Egypt and drove Pharaoh to demand more and more.[34] The market ideology that sees those at the top of the pyramid, never satisfied with what they have, driving those below them, more and more harshly to produce goods that never in the end satiate. The working class, just as the Israelites were, forced to do more work in the same amount of time, for the same reward. Sabbath is also a resistance to the pollution and abuse of the land and the depletion of its resources because it's never allowed to rest, because there never is a point from the modern Pharaoh's perspective when "enough is enough."

"It's not accidental that the best graphic portrayal of this arrangement is a pyramid. The supreme construction of Pharaoh's system. Those at the top of the pyramid require huge amounts of cheap labour at a parsimonious 'minimum wage' to make such a life possible."[35] Sabbath stands counter to that and provides an "Exodus" a means for those who practice it to exit from the never ending cycle of production and to step away from being a brick-maker in someone else's empire.[36] Caring about other people, the people who work for you and even your animals is part of the Sabbath rationale, as is caring for strangers. In fact inviting strangers to a Sabbath meal is said to be greater than attending synagogue and greater than welcoming the Divine Presence (the *Shekhinah*).[37]

We all crave intimacy, it's what we were designed for. God said 'Let us make man in *our* image.' God, already in relationship, the Trinity—creates us to be part of that relationship and yet we live in a time

---

33. Andrei Rublev's.
34. Brueggemann, *Sabbath as Resistance, 13.*
35. Brueggemann, *Sabbath as Resistance, 15.*
36. Brueggemann, *Sabbath as Resistance,*15.
37. b.Talmud, *Shabbat*127a

when loneliness is the new epidemic, leading to ill health and premature death.[38] Contrary to what we might think, social media actually exacerbates this problem.[39] People crave community but society is disjointed, families are complicated, people are isolated and there is no meta-narrative to their lives and no boundaries. Living as part of a faith community that celebrates Sabbath goes a long way to providing that. However, that's only if church functions as it should, providing the intimacy that we crave, particularly for those who have either lost or never known it. Ed Shaw, an evangelical Christian argues that intimacy is missing from not just daily lives, but church life. Intimacy, he argues is not just found in a sexual relationship, but is something that we all crave. He believes that the reason the church's stance on homosexuality seems implausible (that is encouraging people not to practice it) is because we don't emphasize the importance of friendship or of being part of a church family in a real way. This lack of intimate friendships is also seen as the root of the current epidemic of pornography addiction among male church members.[40] Why is this relevant to Sabbath? Because Sabbath is about community, about sharing and enjoying God's Creation together. It's about being church together as a family, not just about asking someone back for Sunday lunch but developing real friendships, doing things together, sharing intimate details of our daily walk and knowing that someone cares but also you have someone that understands.

Sabbath affords us the opportunity to realize that there is more to life than work, that we are not brick making slaves but free children of the King, who has rescued us and who invites us to walk with him in his Temple, his Creation in the cool of the evening. We are called to Sabbath rest, to re-create to enter the promised land for a day to enjoy the milk and honey. Six days we create; on the seventh we re-create, that's why we have recreations—these are not just trivial things that we could do without—they are essential to our well-being. We are part of the created order, he made us and placed us in a Garden. It's been demonstrated that we thrive in nature, even green urban spaces can help treat mental illness, break drug dependency and assist with cases of dementia. There's also evidence that acute hospital patients feel better and are discharged earlier

38. A recent Mental Health Foundation study found that 18–34 year olds were likely to feel lonely more often than over 55s.

39. In fact it been demonstrated that more than two hours of social media a day actually doubles the chances of a person experiencing social isolation.

40. Shaw, *The Plausibility Problem*, 79.

when they can visit the hospital garden or even see some greenery from their window. That's why those who take parklands and green spaces away for housing and profit call down a plague on their own houses.

Jubilee

God set the boundaries at Creation. Just one tree. We pushed against the boundary and we fell. He picked us up again and set more boundaries, ten of them and just to be sure, so we wouldn't fall again, we hedged those boundaries with even more, 613 to be precise. Then God came again and set one more boundary and marked it with a cross. The cross is the boundary marker and it has one inscription "love the Lord your God with all your heart all your soul and all your mind, and love your neighbor as yourself." Jesus cleansed the Temple and then cleansed the cosmos. He cleared up our mess and invited us to the dance. He created and he re-created and he anoints us to complete the mission of inviting others to the dance, to the cosmic community, to the wedding feast, to invite the blind and the lame and the deaf, the poor and the oppressed whether physically or spiritually—because his commission is now ours: "The Spirit of the Lord is on me, because he has anointed me to proclaim good news to the poor. He has sent me to proclaim freedom for the prisoners and recovery of sight for the blind, to set the oppressed free, and to proclaim the year of the Lord's favor." This is what Jesus announced at the outset of his ministry that he was the Melchizedek High Priest, come to make the final Day of Atonement sacrifice, mend the covenant and inaugurate the Jubilee. According to Lev 25:8–54 this was a time when:

- everyone was to return to their own property
- all Israelite slaves were to be set free
- all debts between Israelites were to be cancelled
- the land was to be rested.

The conditions of Jubilee have been inaugurated by Jesus but will not be fully realized until his return. His Kingdom is both spiritual and physical and until his return, we are charged with co-partnering with him to fulfill both the physical and spiritual conditions of Jubilee. Jubilee and the Day of Atonement were linked. The Day of Atonement brought the remission of sins—the spiritual effect, Jubilee is about the physical effect—we are freed spiritually and physically. We are commissioned to open people's eyes to the reality of the spiritual world, to extend His invitation to them, to see them renewed by the transformation of the Holy Spirit, and to enter into his promises through repentance and belief in Him. We are also called to make his Kingdom on earth as it is in heaven so that the conditions of Jubilee are put into place:

- no-one is homeless

- no-one is enslaved

- no-one is crushed by debt

- the land is treated with respect

Many Christians are engaged either directly or through charities in addressing these issues, but I think we need to recognize that this isn't just something that we do out of compassion, it's our commission. I think we are in danger, at times, of over-emphasizing the spiritual at the expense of the physical. Here I believe we have much to learn from Jesus' own religion. In Judaism, the physical, that is life here on earth is of utmost importance, even the Sabbath laws are superseded by the preservation of life. Judaism also believes, that by *being* charitable, we *become* charitable, whereas as Christians we tend to emphasize the inward change in us which we hope will lead to an outward change. Nonetheless, there are numerous charities that are carrying out the Jubilee commission, like Foodbank, which feeds the hungry, Christians Against Poverty that help people get out of debt, Shelter that helps the homeless that were all founded by Christians. There are others that seek to release people from slavery, whether physical slavery like the bonded brick-workers of India or addiction.[41] Working to improve the world now, is part of Jesus' Jubilee message. It is also part of his role as King. Right at the beginning in chapter 2 we said that the King's role in the autumnal New Year Festival, was to bring about *mishpat,* justice with all of its connotations. *Mishpat* encompasses the idea of right order, that the world is put to rights; order triumphing again over Chaos. In Judaism *tzedakah* is the word used for charity, but in actual fact means justice:

> By translating the Hebrew word *tzedakah* as 'charity' (the usual translation) one misses the point that the Hebrew word comes from the root meaning justice and righteousness: giving to the

41. One of the most famous being A.A.

needy is a requirement, a matter of doing what is right. "Charity" comes from the Latin *caritas*—love or caring; the idea there,
is that the giving depends on the good will and deep feeling of
the giver, not on the obligation to act with *tzedek*—justice.[42]

I think that both of these ideas are reflected within Christian giving.
Many Christians are stirred by the sense of social justice, just as much as
they are stirred by compassion. These qualities are integral to the Christian faith. In this we have our example in Jesus. No-one can watch '*I,
Daniel Blake*' and not be stirred by a combination of both. It is why I also
believe that Christians should be engaged in politics, even though that
can only rectify so much. What is needed is a change in people's perspective, a Kingdom perspective, which can only come through seeing the
light[43] and encountering the truth.[44] Nevertheless, we should try as much
as we can, to influence things practically too. I think there's a place for
both and perhaps we might find, that working from both the outside and
the inside, we actually get to meet God in the middle. As James said:
"What good is it my brothers if you say you have faith but do not have
works . . . If a brother or sister is poorly clothed and lacking in daily food,
and one of you says to them, 'Go in peace, be warmed and filled,' without
giving them the things need for the body, what good is that?"[45]

We ask God to answer prayers and to do miracles, but we should
also expect to be part of the answer and part of the miracle. He wants us
to partner with him in the miraculous. When the Red Sea was parted,
God sent his *ruach* but he also told Moses to raise his staff and hold out
his hand.[46] In the battle against the Amelekites, when Moses held up his
hands the Israelites were winning the battle, but when he lowered them
the Amelekites were winning.[47] When Jesus carried out his miracles, he
was fully God, but he was also fully man; God and man partnering together in the miraculous. We were created in God's image *betselem*, and
re-created in Christ's image. We are his image bearers and he wants us to
partner with him in the miraculous, to use our hands to bring about his
kingdom here on earth as it is in heaven. He doesn't need us to do it—he

42. Holtz, *Back to the Sources*, 20–22.

43. Jesus said: 'I am the Light of the World, whoever follows me will never walk
in darkness, but have the light of life.' John 8:12.

44. Jesus said: 'I am the way, and the truth and the life.' John 14:6.

45. James 2:14–16.

46. Exod 14:16, 21.

47. Exod 17:11.

is a supernatural God—has all power in heaven and on earth and he still astounds us with his miracles that he does because he loves us. But there's enough food, land, clean water and wealth for us all, we don't need a physical miracle for things to change but a change of heart and attitude and we can be part of *that* miracle, of changing hearts and minds, helping others to gain a Kingdom perspective, to bring them into the cosmic community, to lead them out of chaos into order so together we can bring order to the world.

The final Jubilee condition concerns the land. Christians have had an ambivalent attitude towards it; some claiming that as there will be a new heaven and a new earth, we are not obliged to look after this one. Thankfully that's not the dominant position any more. It's been recognized that in fact, we should be at the forefront of looking after the planet as we were given the job of stewarding God's good Creation. "From a Scriptural perspective, Christians should have been leading the environmental agenda. The very existence of the universe is the result of God's creative activity and its ultimate destiny redeemed by Christ's sacrifice on the cross is to be renewed along with all believers."[48]

New Creation

We all appreciate a new beginning. A debt wiped clean, a wrong forgiven, a new start. In Christ we are a new creation. We have a new beginning, not just once when we ask Jesus into our lives, but every day: "his mercies are new every morning."[49] That's the message Jesus was conveying when washing the disciples feet. Peter refused at first until Jesus said "unless I wash you, you have no part with me," to which he responded:"Then Lord, not just my feet but my hands and my head as well." Jesus replied "Those who have had a bath need only to wash their feet; their whole body is clean. And you are clean though not every one of you." We have been washed in the blood and so are clean but throughout the day there are things that will cling to us that need "washing off" through prayer and repentance.

We are new creations, but we are also daily renewed. We are new in the sense of renewed, it's still us but renewed. Just as the new covenant

---

48. White, Bob Professor of Geophysics at Cambridge University, *http://cis.org. uk/upload/Resources/Environment/Bob_White_IDEA.pdf*

49. Lam 3:22–23.

was the old covenant renewed, not done away with. All the essence of the old, is still there, just as Jesus body was renewed, his resurrection body was still him, still with the holes of the nails in his hand and the sword in his side but it was him, transformed. That's why what we do on earth matters, even the physical earth and physically with people is important. The renewal of the earth doesn't mean this earth doesn't matter. This is God's creation that he said "is good." Just as we are his creations, but we are renewed in him, in the transforming power of the holy spirit. We matter and the earth matters and what we do matters. It will be refined and the gold will become visible.[50] "By the grace God has given me, I laid a foundation as a wise builder and someone else is building on it. But each one should build with care. For no one can lay any foundation other than the one already laid which is Jesus Christ. If anyone builds on this foundation using gold, silver, costly stones, wood, hay or straw, their work will be shown for what it is, because the day will bring it to light. It will be revealed with fire, and the fire will test the quality of each person's work."[51]

At creation the morning stars sang; the first song.[52] When the waters receded and his creation stepped out again into his Temple God sang a second new song.[53] When they rose up out of the waters, a new creation, Israel sang a third new song.[54] When the Anointed was enthroned at the New Year Festival and the earth was recreated Israel sang a fourth new song.[55] When they returned from exile, a new Exodus,[56] Israel sang a fifth new song.[57] When Jesus, *the* Anointed, Son of God and King was resurrected, the first fruits of the new creation the church sang a sixth new song.[58] When we become betrothed to the Bridegroom as a new creation, we sing the seventh song, the song of the sabbath rest, our new song.[59]

50. Zech 13:9, Job 23:10, 1 Pet 1:7.

51. 1 Cor 3:10–13.

52. Job 38:4–7.

53. Gen 8:22.

54. Exod 15:1–18.

55. Ps 96:1.

56. Isa 43:16–21. God reminds Israel how he saved her through the Exodus but he says 'Forget the former things, do not dwell on the past. See I am doing a new thing!'

57. Isa 42:10.

58. Phil 2:6–11 Considered an early christian hymn.

59. "Let those who have ears, hear." You need to listen to the song he has for you. He is your song but only you can sing it the way he intended it to be sung by you.

We each have a new song to sing because each of us are new creations. He rescued us from our own Chaos waters, and now he calls us
out onto the water, so that we can be part of the miracle, so that we can
realize, by trusting in him, we can overcome the waters too, that we won't
sink. He has mastery over the waters because he is the Son of David,
whose 'hand is over the sea and his right hand over the rivers'[60] because
he is the Son of God, because he is the Name (above all names), because
he is Yahweh, who overcame the Chaos waters and created. We are his
new creation and we sing the seventh new song, a song of waiting, a song
of sabbath rest, a seventh song for the seventh day so that others can hear
it and join in the song.

When the Bridegroom comes to take us to the wedding feast, the
earth and the heavens will be new and we will sing together a new song;
the eighth song for the eighth day, the song of the Lamb:

> And they sang a new song to the Lion of the Tribe of Judah, the
> Root of David, the Lamb looking as if it had been slain, saying:
> "You are worthy to take the scroll and to open its seals, because
> you were slain, and with your blood you purchased for God per-
> sons from every tribe and language and people and nation. You
> have made them to be a kingdom and priests to serve our God,
> and they will reign on the earth.[61]

> I, Jesus, have sent my angel to give you this testimony for the
> churches. I am the Root and the Offspring of David, and the
> bright Morning Star. The Spirit and the bride say, "Come!" And
> let the one who hears say, "Come!" Let the one who is thirsty
> come; and let the one who wishes take the free gift of the water
> of life.[62]

> Whoever has ears to hear, let them hear.[63]

---

60. Ps 89:25.
61. Rev 5:9-10.
62. Rev 22:16–17.
63. Mark 4:9

Bibliography

Allison, Dale Jr. *The New Moses*. Edinburgh: T & T Clark, 1993

Barker, Margaret. *Adam the High Priest in the Paradise Temple*. http://www.templestudiesgroup.com/Papers/Barker

———. *Creation Theology*.http://www.margaretbarker.com/Papers/CreationTheology.pdf.

———. *The Everlasting Covenant between God and Every Living Creature*, Dublin, 2014.

———. *Great High Priest: The Temple Roots of Christian Theology*. London: T & T Clark, 2003

———. *The Revelation of Jesus Christ*. Edinburgh: T & T Clark, 2000.

———. *Text and Context. margaretbarker.com*. 2002.

———. *What Did King Josiah Reform*, (May 2003). http://www.thinlyveiled.com/barker/josiahsreform.htm

Batto, Bernard, F. *Slaying the Dragon: Mythmaking in the Biblical Tradition*, Louisville: Westminster/John Knox, 1992.

Beale, Gregory K. *Temple and the Church's Mission*. Downers Grove: InterVarsity, 2004.

Benoit, P. *Jesus and the Jewish Gospel*. London: Darton, Longman & Todd, 1973.

Boteach, Shmuley. *An Intelligent Person's Guide to Judaism*. London: Duckworth Publishers, 2006.

Boyarin, Daniel. *The Jewish Gospels*. New York: The New Press, 2012.

Brueggemann, Walter. *Sabbath as Resistance*. Louisville: Westminster John Knox Press, 2014.

Brunson, Andrew C. *Psalm 118 in the Gospel of John: An Intertextual Study on the New Exodus*. Tubingen: Mohr Siebeck, 2003.

A Clerk of Oxford. "C S Lewis: The Medievalist" 22 (November 2013). https://aclerkofoxford.blogspot.com/2013/11/c-s-lewis-medie.

———.A Little History of Lammas, 1(August 2017) https://aclerkofoxford.blogspot.com/2017/08/a-little-history-of-lammas.html

Collins, Adela Yarbro and J. J. *King and Messiah as Son of God*. Grand Rapids: Eerdmans, 2008.

Courthope, William. *The Genealogy of British Kings*. British Library, MS43968.

Davies, W. D. *Torah in the Messianic Age/Age to Come*. Philadelphia: Society of Biblical Literature, 1952.

Day, John. *Psalms*. London: T & T Clark, 2003.

———. *Yahweh and the Gods and Goddesses of Canaan*. London: Sheffield Academic, 2002.

The Doctrine Commision of the Church of England, *The Mystery of Salvation, the Story of God's Gift. A Report*. Caerphilly: Moorhouse Group, 1996.

Eaton, John. *The Psalms*. London: T & T Clark, International, 2005.

Eisler, Robert 'Das Letzte Abendmahl' (The Last Supper), Zeitschrift fur die neutestamentliche Wissenschaft (ZNW), Vol 24 (1925).

Emerton, John. *Studies in the Pentateuch*. Leiden: Brill, 1990.

Engnell, Ivan, *Studies in Divine Kingship in the Ancient Near East*, 2d ed. Oxford: Blackwell, 1967.

Fletcher-Louis, Crispin. *Further Reflections on a Divine and Angelic Humanity in the Dead Sea Scrolls*. ttps://studylib.net/doc/7382742/further-reflections-on-a-divine-and-angelic-humanity-in-the-dead-sea-scrolls.

———. *Jesus and the High Priest*, Marquette.edu.

Foster, Russell and Kreitzman, Leon. *Circadian Rhythms: a very Short Introduction*. Oxford: Oxford University, 2017.

Frankfort, Henri. *Kingship and the Gods*. London: University of Chicago Press, 1978.

Gane, Roy, E. *Cult and Character: Purification Offerings, Day of Atonement and Theodicy*. Winona Lane: Eisenbrauns, 2005.

Grabbe, Lester L. *Priests, Prophets, Diviners, Sages*. Valley Forge: Trinity International, 1995.

Greig, Peter. *Dirty Glory*. Colorado Springs: NavPress, 2016.

Hagner, Donald. *The Jewish Reclamation of Jesus*. Grand Rapids: Zondervan, 1993.

Hartley, John E. *Leviticus*. Dallas: Word, 1992. Thomas Nelson

Heisler, Michael S. *The Unseen Realm: Recovering the Supernatural Worldview of the Bible*. Bellingham: Lexham, 2015.

Hick, John, (ed.). *The Myth of God Incarnate*. London: SCM, 1977.

Hill, Christopher. *Holidays and Holy Nights: Celebrating Twelve Seasonal Festivals*. Wheaton: Theosophical Publishing House, 2003.

Holtz, Barry W. *Back to the Sources: Reading the Jewish Classic Texts*. New York: Simon and Schuster, 1984.

Idel, Moshe. *Messianic Mystics*. London: Yale University Press, 1998.

Jaubert, A. *The Date of the Last Supper*. New York: Alba, 1964.

Keegstra, Jacob. *God's Prophetic Feasts*. translated by Hannie Tijman Jerusalem: Tsur Tsina, 2012.

Keller, Tim, https://www.thegospelcoalition.org/article/the-power-of-deep-rest/ 25 (November 2012).

Kovacs, Charles. *The Spiritual Background to Christian Festivals*. Edinburgh: Floris Books, 2007.

Kraus, Hans Joachim. *Worship in Israel: A Cultic History of the Old Testament*. Translated by Geoffrey Buswell, Oxford: Blackwell, 1966.

Kumer, Dinka, "*What is Taschlich?*:chabad.org.

Levey, Samson H. *The Messiah: An Aramaic Interpretation*. New York: Hebrew Union College, Jewish Institute of Religion, 1974.

Lewis, C. S. *God in the Dock: Essays on Theology and Ethics*. Grand Rapids :Eerdmans, 1970.

Longman II, Tremper. "The Messiah: Exploration in the Law and Writings" in Porter, ed., *The Messiah in the Old and New Testament*. Grand Rapids: Eerdmans, 2007.

Maccoby, Hyam. *The Mythmaker: Paul and the Invention of Christianity*. London: Weidenfield and Nicholson, 1986.

McGrath, Alister E. *Christian Theology: an Introduction*. Chichester: John Wiley & Sons, 2017.

McKnight, S. *The King Jesus Gospel*. Grand Rapids: Zondervan, 2011.

Morrow, Jeff. *Creation as Temple-Building and Work as Liturgy in Genesis 1–3*. http://ww.ocabs.org/journal/index.php/iocabs/article/viewFile/43/18.

Moses, A. D. A. *Matthew's Transfiguration Story and Jewish-Christian Controversy*. London: Sheffield Academic, 1996.

Neusner, Jacob. *The Way of Torah: An introduction to Judaism*. Belmont: Dickenson, 1970.

O'Carragain, Eamonn. *Ritual and the Rood: Liturgical Images of the Old English Poems of the Dream of the Rood Tradition*. London: The British Library, 2005.

Patai, Raphael. *Man and Temple in Ancient Jewish Myth and Ritual*. Edinburgh: Thomas Nelson & Sons, 1947.

Pitre, Brant. *Jesus and the Jewish Roots of the Last Supper*. New York: Doubleday, 2011.

————. Jesus, the New Temple and the New Priesthood: static1.squarespace.com.

Seyoon, Kim. *The Son of Man as the Son of God*. Eugene: Wipf and Stock, 2011.

Shakespeare, Tom. 'A Point of View: Solstice and the lack of symbolism in Britain'. 21.6.2013. https://www.bbc.co.uk/news/magazine-23000963

Shaw, Ed. *The Plausibility Problem, the Church and Same-Sex Attraction*. Nottingham: InterVarsity Press, 2015.

Stolper, Pinchas. *Living Beyond Time: The Mystery and Meaning of the Jewish Festivals*. Brooklyn: Mesorah, 2003.

Sweet, Daniel. *The 10 Biggest Issues Christian Americans are Facing Today*, http://www.beliefnet.com/faiths/Christianity/galleries/the-10-

Vermes, Geza. *Jesus the Jew: An Historian's Reading of the New Testament*. London: Collins, 1973.

Walton, John, *Creation in Genesis 1:1–2, 3 and the Ancient Near East*, Calvin Theological Journal. http://www.michaelsheiser.com/TheNakedBible/Creation.

Walton, John H. *The Lost World of Genesis One*. Downers Grove: InterVarsity, 2009.

Weiser, Arthur. *The Psalms*, London: SCM, 1965.

https://www.westminster-abbey.org/media/7143/Coronation-service-guide-reading-list.pdf.

Wright, Tom. *Simply Jesus*. London: SPCK, 2011.

Wyatt, Nicholas, "There's Such Divinity doth Hedge a King": *Selected Essays of Nicholas Wyatt on Royal Ideology in Ugaritic and Old Testament Literature*. Aldershot: SOTSMS, 2005.

Printed in Great Britain
by Amazon

54434966R00119